# FOUNDATIONS OF EURASIANISM

## Volume I

Translated and Edited by
Jafe Arnold and John Stachelski

With an Introduction by Leonid Savin

2020

# PRAV Publishing
www.pravpublishing.com
pravpublishing@protonmail.com

*Cover image*: "The Duel of Peresvet and Chelubey"
by Viktor Vasnetsov, 1914.

978-1952671-03-6 (Paperback)
978-1-952671-04-3 (Hardcover)
978-1952671-05-0 (Ebook)

# TABLE OF CONTENTS

# PREFACE: TRANSLATING EURASIANISM

## Jafe Arnold & John Stachelski

The publication of a collection of Eurasianist texts in the English language is a momentous and overdue development. Exactly one century has passed since Prince Nikolai Trubetzkoy (1890-1938) published his pamphlet *Europe and Mankind*, which was followed a year later by the unveiling of the collective Eurasianist manifesto *Exodus to the East: Premonitions and Fulfillments - The Affirmation of the Eurasians*, texts that would prove both foundational and auspicious.[1] In the uneasy aftermath of the First World War and amidst the chaos following the Russian revolution, the authors of this volume declared themselves "Eurasians" and outlined a cathartic new perspective on the history and identity of Russia and the dynamics of civilizations in general, giving birth to a movement and school of thought which would be christened "Eurasianism." In the run up to this centennial anniversary, the first two decades of the 21st century have seen arguably more attention, discussion, and literature devoted to Eurasianism in its classical and contemporary forms than ever before, both in Russia and the West.

Formerly neglected as an idiosyncratic experiment peculiar to a handful of Russian émigré-intellectuals of the fleeting interwar period and consigned to the domain of specialist historiography, Eurasianism and its central concept "Eurasia" have since become common references in a number of fields and discourses

---

1  Petr Savitsky, P. Suvchinsky, Prince N.S. Trubetzkoy, Georgy Florovsky, *Iskhod k Vostoku. Predchuvstviia i sversheniia. Utverzhdenie evraziitsev* (Sofia: Bulgarian-Russian Publishing House, 1921); N.S. Trubetzkoy, *Evropa i chelovechestvo* (Sofia: Bulgarian-Russian Publishing House, 1920).

concerned with the present situation in and around the Russian Federation. In 2008, the director of the Center for Russian and East European Studies at the University of Kansas, Maria Carlson, anticipatorily wrote in her review of the first English-language monograph on Eurasianism that understanding this current is imperative for "intellectual historians, policymakers, cultural scholars, Russia Watchers, or for that matter, anyone who uneasily senses that something is moving in the deep currents beneath the surface of contemporary Russia, but is not sure of what it is."[2] Another reviewer echoed this impression in the *Journal of Slavic Military Studies*, submitting that the study of Eurasianism promises to provide "deeper understanding of the forces shaping Russia's identity and the unfolding of circumstances for the entire Eurasian region."[3] The monograph under review itself, *Russian Eurasianism: An Ideology of Empire*, by the leading French-American scholar of Eurasianism Marlène Laruelle, affirmed that Eurasianism "is not a marginal phenomenon in any sense. Far from it," and suggested that the spectrum of Eurasianist ideas is on an historic ascent in the context of a greater global resurgence of concerns with fundamental cultural identity.[4] According to Laruelle, although the historical Eurasianist movement proper remains little known to this day, core Eurasianist ideas have enjoyed remarkable diffusion: "the idea of 'Eurasia,'" Laruelle writes, "has undergone a profound transformation. It has grown beyond the purely intellectual circles to which it had been confined... entering a larger public space... it is now being used as a catchall vision of Russia."[5] Of symbolic import, Laruelle cited a 2001 poll of the Russian Public Opinion Research Center,

---

2    Maria Carlson, "Russian Eurasianism: An Ideology of Empire by Marlène Laruelle," *The Russian Review* 68:3 (2009): pp. 561-562.

3    Sharyl N. Cross, "Russian Eurasianism, An Ideology of Empire by Marlene Laruelle," *Journal of Slavic Military Studies* 22 (2009): pp. 712-715.

4    Marlène Laruelle, *Russian Eurasianism: An Ideology of Empire* (Washington, D.C./Baltimore: Woodrow Wilson Center Press/John Hopkins University Press, 2008), pp. 9-10.

5    Ibid, pp. 1-2.

71% of whose respondents saw Russia's "civilizational path" as
"Euro-Asian."[6] Subsequently, in 2017, an anthology of studies
supported by Södertörn University's Foundation for Baltic and
East European Research, entitled *The Politics of Eurasianism:
Identity, Popular Culture, and Russia's Foreign Policy*, established
that "Eurasianism today enjoys a resonance and level of
popular engagement that is unmatched in its long history,"
and proposed "to map Eurasianism's myriad intellectual,
cultural and geopolitical ramifications, underscoring its
extraordinary political pull, its great adaptability and its
surprising geographical mobility."[7] Most significantly, the
volume's editors suggested that "the vitality and resilience of
Eurasianist thinking tells us that it has a future and that it
will continue providing a key to understanding the ideological,
cultural, national and territorial development of the post-Soviet
world. Elsewhere, in many parts of Europe, its presence is and
will continue to be felt not only by strategists and geopoliticians
but on the street..."[8]

As is the norm for such ambitious ideational projects as
the one initiated by the interwar Eurasianists, heightened
Western attention to the history and current relevance of
Eurasianism underscored by Laruelle and other scholars' work
has been paralleled by more than its fair share of controversy
and sensationalism, especially aggravated by present tensions
in international relations. In 2014, the American editorial
magazine *National Review* warned of a "Eurasianist threat."[9]
The same year, the philosopher and political figure whom
Laruelle identified as the "principal theoretician of Neo-

6   Ibid, p. 9; *"Rossiia: zapadnyi put' razvitiia dlia 'evroaziatskoi' tsivilizatsii - Ekspress-opros 2-5 noiabria"* [Russia: A Western path of development for 'Euro-Asian' civilization - Express Poll, 2-5 November], Polit.ru (15/11/2001) [https://polit.ru/article/2001/11/15/477387/].

7   Mark Bassin and Gonzalo Pozo (eds.), *The Politics of Eurasianism: Identity, Popular Culture, and Russia's Foreign Policy* (London: Rowman & Littlefield International, 2017), pp. 2, 3.

8   Ibid.

9   Robert Zubrin, "The Eurasianist Threat," *National Review* (4/3/2014) [https://www.nationalreview.com/2014/03/eurasianist-threat-robert-zubrin/].

Eurasianism"[10], Alexander Dugin (1962-), was deemed by the high-profile American journal *Foreign Policy* to be one of the "leading global thinkers and agitators."[11] Dugin was placed under sanctions by the United States and Canada in connection to the conflict in Ukraine, resulting in the removal of Dugin's books from the world's largest online retailer, Amazon, thereby frustrating access to Eurasianist thought in one of its most relevant contemporary trajectories. In 2016, the year of the establishment of the Eurasian Economic Union, which many observers saw as a fruition of the anticipations of the classical Eurasianists and a confirmation of the weight carried by contemporary Eurasianist advocacies, Yale University Press published *Financial Times* correspondent Charles Clover's book *Black Wind, White Snow: The Rise of Russia's New Nationalism*, which spotlighted Eurasianism as having evolved "from somewhat tendentious scholarship, to popular history, to a political platform, and more recently to become the officially sanctioned national idea of Russia, articulated by its head of state," thus embodying "a conquest of reality itself."[12] In the dramatic conclusion of his 'exposé', Clover declaratively warned: "Eurasianism is a forgery that has superseded the original - not because it is a good forgery, but because it is so audaciously false that it undermines the true. Eurasianism is a testament to the audacity of the 'scribblers'..."[13]

Moreover, amidst skyrocketing American and European discourses on the current relevance of "populist nationalisms," "far-rights" and even "neo-fascisms," Eurasianism has been fashionably branded with any or all of these appellations - for instance, in *Stanford Politics'* sensational headline "Eurasianism

10  Marlene Laruelle, "Aleksandr Dugin: A Russian Version of the European Radical Right?," *Kennan Institute Occasional Papers Series* #294 (Washington, D.C.: Woodrow Wilson International Center for Scholars, 2006), p. 6.

11  "A World Disrupted: The Leading Global Thinkers of 2014," *Foreign Policy* (2014) [http:// globalthinkers.foreignpolicy.com/#agitators/detail/dugin].

12  Charles Clover, *Black Wind, White Snow: The Rise of Russia's New Nationalism* (New Haven: Yale University Press, 2016), p. 331.

13  Ibid, p. 332

is the New Fascism."[14] In scholarly literature, as well, the seminal 2015 anthology *Between Europe and Asia: The Origins, Theories, and Legacies of Russian Eurasianism* advertised revealing that "Eurasianism was akin to many fascist movements in interwar Europe," even though the volume's essays did not actually engage in any such deliberation.[15] Additional volumes such as *Eurasianism and the European Far Right: Reshaping the Europe-Russia Relationship* and the more recent *Entangled Far Rights: A Russian-European Intellectual Romance in the Twentieth Century* have further cemented Western scholars' distinctly political perception of Eurasianism.[16]

Dmitry Shlapentokh opened the 2007 volume *Russia Between East and West: Scholarly Debates on Eurasianism* with the observation that Eurasianism has only slowly and barely attracted serious attention from American scholars because: "Eurasianism is deeply 'politically incorrect.' It does not fit well in any of the paradigms espoused by the political and intellectual elites prevailing in the USA… Indeed, the major ideas of Eurasianism are in sharp contrast to the basic paradigm shared by most American specialists in Russian studies, regardless of their political affiliation."[17] Amidst the prevailing political crises in the United States and much of the European Union, where anything Russian or from Russia has, once again and to an extent unparalleled since the height of the Cold War, come to be subjected to the most glaringly

---

14  John Rice-Cameron, "Eurasianism is the New Fascism: Understanding and Confronting Russia," *Stanford Politics* (2/2/2017) [https://stanfordpolitics.org/2017/02/02/eurasianism-new-fascism/].

15  Mark Bassin, Sergey Glebov, and Marlene Laruelle (eds.), *Between Europe and Asia: The Origins, Theories, and Legacies of Russian Eurasianism* (Pittsburgh: University of Pittsburgh Press, 2015).

16  Marlene Laruelle (ed.), *Entangled Far Rights: A Russian-European Intellectual Romance in the Twentieth Century* (Pittsburgh: University of Pittsburgh Press, 2018); Ibidem (ed.), *Eurasianism and the European Far Right: Reshaping the Europe-Russia Relationship* (Maryland: Lexington Books/Rowman and Littlefield Publishing Group, 2015).

17  Dmitry Shlapentokh (ed.), *Russia between East and West: Scholarly Debates on Eurasianism* (Leiden: Brill, 2007), pp. 1, 3.

derogative caricaturization, mistreatment, and suspicion, it remains difficult to imagine any empathetic receptivity to Eurasianist perspectives.

All the same, treatments of Eurasianism in Western scholarly literature have begun to appear which emphasize the significance of this current in broader terms, with far more nuance, and sometimes even with appreciation. The emergence and development of classical Eurasianist thought would receive full monographic treatment in Sergey Glebov's 2017 *From Empire to Eurasia: Politics, Scholarship, and Ideology in Russian Eurasianism*, which posited: "A history of Eurasianism, thus, is not a history of Russian nationalism or modernism, of geopolitics or structuralism, but of all these contexts that came to shape the movement in various, often contradictory ways."[18] Glebov offered compelling evidence that although "Eurasianism seemed a fleeting moment in Russian intellectual history"[19], its ideological and cultural influence has extended far further and broader than this initial context and the first attempted movement itself. The intricacies and complexities of the classical Eurasianist current chronicled by Glebov have even come to be recognized by otherwise adamant critics and self-styled opponents of Eurasianism. Andreas Umland, for instance, admits that classical Eurasianist thought "represented a complex cultural-theoretical construct developed by some of the most remarkable Russian émigré scholars... [b]ased on various academic approaches and significant empirical research."[20]

Another recent treatment of Eurasianism, representing an exception to the above-mentioned trend of associating this current with modern right-wing political nomenclatures, has

18  Sergey Glebov, *From Empire to Eurasia: Politics, Scholarship, and Ideology in Russian Eurasianism, 1920s-1930s* (DeKalb; Northern Illinois University Press, 2017), p. 6.

19  Ibid, p. 187.

20  Andreas Umland, "Why Aleksandr Dugin's 'Neo-Eurasianism' is not Eurasianist," *New Eastern Europe* [8/6/2018].

emerged in Nikolay Smirnov's thesis that classical Eurasianism should be considered "one of the first experiments in postcolonialism, as a forerunner of postcolonial theory."[21] This approach, Smirnov elaborates, explains this ideational legacy's heterogeneity and its "permeation of politics" in contemporary Russia, as well as highlights the significance of the "left-wing Eurasianism" which emerged in the late 1920s and early 1930s. Smirnov draws attention to how "left-wing Eurasianism sought to make its mark more emphatically in art than in theory and politics alone," thus indicating the broader cultural context for tracing the "Eurasianist optic." As potentially rich as further projects aimed at recovering a certain branch of the movement's "left"-orientation and anti-colonial lineage might be, the established tendency to categorically associate ideas with one expansively defined side of an immutable political binary more often than not leaves Eurasianism pigeonholed, artificially "detached" from the broader fields to which the Eurasianists' corpus was by and large devoted. Such an approach also disregards the fact that different Eurasianists put forth differing views on political philosophy, the state, and the desirability of "politicizing" their movement, divergences which proved fateful for the historical Eurasian movement. As the complexities and scope of Eurasianist thought continue to be brought to light, it becomes increasingly difficult to dismiss the Eurasianist framework as narrowly "identitarian" by virtue of its authors' attention to the question of national self-identity, a discourse now prone to anachronistic association with "far-right" ideas, or as singularly "political" (and, moreover, politically singular) in trajectory. The Eurasianists themselves saw their perspectives and discourse as a broader theoretical-cultural framework irreducible to ephemeral political phenomena, as is encapsulated in the very designation of *evraziistvo* ("Eurasianity," "Eurasianness"), which underscored an anathema to programizing an "-ism."

---

21  Nikolay Smirnov, "Left-Wing Eurasianism and Postcolonial Theory," *E-Flux Journal* 97 (2019).

The more serious and in depth an examination of the current goes, the clearer it becomes that the interdisciplinarity and complex diversity of Eurasianist thought ultimately refuses such categorical verdicts, wholesale "deconstructions," and simplistic "exorcisms" of historicist contextualization. Avoiding the pitfalls of political projection is likely best accomplished by taking the movement's idiosyncratic efforts at superseding the modern political binary seriously, and examining Eurasianism on its own terms as an attempt at elaborating a broader cultural-theoretical framework. As the editors of *The Politics of Eurasianism: Identity, Popular Culture, and Russia's Foreign Policy* remind us of the current experience of Eurasianist engagements: "Eurasianism today must be taken as much more than primarily a (Russian) nationalist or conservative type of ideology, or as a more or less consistent set of views informing (Russian) foreign policy – even if these dimensions are essential to it."[22] Working toward this broader understanding requires tracing the profound and vast influence Eurasianism and the Eurasianists had on numerous civilizational vectors, ranging from art and aesthetics to literature and linguistics. While there is still much work that needs to be done illuminating the details of these eventful intersections, it bears mentioning that figures as definitional of Russian art and as diverse as the composers Prokofiev and Stravinsky, the poets Tsvetaeva and Esenin, and the writer Bunin (to name just a few) knew and worked in tandem with the Eurasianists, including on *tamizdat'* publications predominately dedicated to literature, such as the seminal *Versty*. Ultimately, examining the different fields which the Eurasianists engaged and contributed to, and the overall outlook on culture which they presented in so doing, promises to be a more fruitful and illuminating path. Most critically of all, such a broader understanding is contingent upon paying attention to what the Eurasianists themselves said in their own words and times.

---

22  Bassin and Pozo, T*he Politics of Eurasianism: Identity, Popular Culture, and Russia's Foreign Policy*, p. 9.

Paradoxically - or perhaps, as a growing number of critical voices contend, altogether expectedly - translations of the original Eurasianists' works have not followed scholarly and popular emphasis on the urgent relevance of understanding this current's past and present significance. With the exception of the University of Michigan's now rare 1991 volume of selected texts by Trubetzkoy[23], Alexander Dugin's English-language book *Eurasian Mission: An Introduction to Neo-Eurasianism*[24], and the individual translations published online by Eurasianist Internet Archive[25], the Eurasianist corpus has not been made widely accessible in English, until now.

As the quantity of Western scholarly and popular literature addressing (and often passing serious judgements on) Eurasianism continues to grow, and as the influence of Eurasianism itself continues to spread, the need for an accessible basis of translations of Eurasianist works will prove vital. Here it would be appropriate to quote the Russian scholar Rustem Vakhitov's remarks - arguably even more applicable in the Western context than their intended Russian one - in his preface to the compilation of the online *Library of Eurasianist Primary Sources*:

> Contemporary scholars possess a far from complete, one-sided view of Eurasianism. Although the majority of contemporary scholarly works on Eurasianism argue that the Eurasianism of the 1920s-'30s is well-studied, it is nonetheless obvious that without the presence of a more or less complete collection of Eurasianist works, it is hardly possible to speak of any final assessments of Eurasianism (there are, nevertheless, many such assessments, practically all of which, alas, are imperatively insensitive, and many of which are altogether odious). In all actuality, the serious scholarly study of Eurasianism, which must necessarily be based on a solid textuological analysis, still lies ahead.[26]

---

23  N.S. Trubetzkoy, *The Legacy of Genghis Khan and Other Essays on Russia's Identity* (Ann Arbor: Michigan Slavic Publications, 1991).

24  Alexander Dugin, *Eurasian Mission: An Introduction to Neo-Eurasianism* (London: Arktos, 2014).

25  https://eurasianist-archive.com/

26  Rustem Vakhitov, "Trudy klassikov evraziistva i situatsiia s ikh republikatsiey" [The works of the classics of Eurasianism and the situation with their republication], *Biblioteka pervoistochnikov evraziitsev: 20-30-e gody* [*Library of Eurasianist Primary Sources*], Nevmenandr.net [http://nevmenandr.net/eurasia/situacia.php].

It is in light of the above considerations that we present readers and researchers with *Foundations of Eurasianism - Volume I*. This tome is the first installment of the *Foundations of Eurasianism* series, envisioned as a set of anthologies of original English translations of the works of prominent classical and neo-Eurasianists.

The *Foundations of Eurasianism* series is planned to proceed chronologically, covering the development of Eurasianist thought from its origins up to its contemporary representations. This inaugural volume opens with excerpts from Nikolai Trubetzkoy's *Europe and Mankind*, followed by Savitsky's critical response to the latter, "Europe and Eurasia," both of which are widely considered to be the first proper Eurasianist works. In turn, the greater part of this volume consists of all but three of the texts which composed the Eurasianists' 1921 founding volume *Exodus to the East*. Given the prevailing absence of introductory Eurasianist works in translation, we have resolved to feature three slightly later texts which provide arguably more extensive insight into the early conceptualization of classical Eurasianism as articulated by its two leading figures, Trubetzkoy and Savitsky. Thus, the three *Exodus to the East* contributions "The Era of Faith" by Petr Suvchinsky, "The Cunning of Reason" by Georges Florovsky, and "The Heights and Depths of Russian Culture (The Ethnic Basis of Russian Culture)" by Trubetzkoy will feature in volume two, yielding place here to the major programmatic articles "Eurasianism" and "The Geographical and Geopolitical Foundations of Eurasianism" by Savitsky from 1925 and 1934, and Trubetzkoy's "Pan-Eurasian Nationalism" from 1927. Taken together, it is our hope that *Foundations of Eurasianism - Volume I* can stand as an introduction to Eurasianist thought in its original, most seminal formulations.

The texts featured in this volume were translated from precisely those sources which have figured as pivotal in the republication and dissemination of Eurasianist works in the Russian-speaking world. Our selected excerpts from Trubetzkoy's *Europe and Mankind* were drawn from the 1999 volume of selected works by Trubetzkoy, *Nasledie Chingiskhana* ("*The Legacy of Genghis Khan*"), produced by the Moscow-based publishing house Agraf, which in the late 1990s pioneered the republication of major Eurasianist works. Among the latter figured a collection of works by Petr Savitsky, entitled *Kontinent Evraziia* ("*Continent Eurasia*"), on which our translation of Savitsky's "Europe and Eurasia" was based.[27] Both of these texts have been made publicly available by the online *Library of Eurasianist Primary Sources* (*Biblioteka pervoistochnikov evraziitsev*), curated by the above-quoted Rustem Vakhitov and hosted by the online Nevmenandr resource of the philologist Boris Orekhov, which has also republished the texts of *Exodus to the East* that were used for the translations of this volume. Alongside the latter resource, for the *Exodus to the East* texts and the later works by Savitsky and Trubetzkoy, we also consulted the hitherto largest Russian anthology of classical and neo-Eurasianist works, *Osnovy evraziistva* ("*Foundations of Eurasianism*") published in 2002 under the editorship of Alexander Dugin.[28] All of our translations are uniquely original to this volume - the versions of some of the present texts which previously appeared online at Eurasianist Internet Archive were considerably reedited and, in some instances, retranslated for this collection. Only after the completion of the manuscript of *Foundations of Eurasianism - Volume I* and during the final editing process did it come to our attention that the Californian publisher Charles Schlacks Jr. released an English edition of *Exodus to the East* in 1996, consisting of original translations by Ilya Vinkovetsky and the versions of Trubetzkoy's contributions from the

---

27  P.N. Savitsky, *Kontinent Evraziia* [*Continent Eurasia*] (Moscow: Agraf, 1997); N.S. Trubetzkoy, *Nasledie Chingiskhana* [*The Legacy of Genghis Khan*] (Moscow: Agraf, 1999).

28  Aleksandr Dugin, *Osnovy evraziistva* [*Foundations of Eurasianism*] (Moscow: Arktogeia, 2002).

above-cited 1991 Michigan Slavic Publications volume.[29] Our translations differ from the long-since out of print 1996 volume considerably in terms of style: whereas Vinkovetsky's translations strove to be first and foremost literal, we have aimed above all for preserving the Eurasianists' Russian prose (and at times poetry) with due adjustment for English syntax. We have also paid particular attention to avoiding the lapsing of important terms into colloquially similar but conceptually incorrect associations: for instance, we have kept the term *narod* as "people" instead of rendering such as the modern Western term "nation" which the Eurasianists hardly would have accepted as a translation of their notions. Moreover, whereas the Charles Schlacks edition was produced in limited run for Slavicist scholars, our volume has been created with an eye towards greater public accessibility and dissemination.

Unique to *Foundations of Eurasianism - Volume I* is the introduction, "The Genesis of the Eurasian Theory," by Dr. Leonid Savin, the founding editor-in-chief of the *Journal of Eurasian Affairs* and *Geopolitica.ru*, the director of the Russian Foundation for Monitoring and Forecasting Development for Cultural-Territorial Spaces, and the administrative head of the International Eurasian Movement. Savin's introduction provides an overview of the main preoccupations of the original Eurasian movement and authors, touches on some of the nuances of their respective profiles and ideas, and in so doing allots considerable space to the presentation of the Eurasianists in their own words for English-language readers. In addition, Savin ventures to briefly present two of the most influential neo-Eurasianist thinkers and to highlight the prospects of Eurasianism today.

With *Foundations of Eurasianism - Volume I* and the *Foundations of Eurasianism* series as a whole, we have undertaken to grant the English-speaking world unprecedented access to one of the most original, complex, controversial, and relevant schools of

---

29  Petr Savitskii, P. Suvchinskii, Prince N.S. Trubetskoi, Georgii Florovskii, *Exodus to the East: Forebodings and Events* (translated and edited by Ilya Vinkovetsky and Charles Schlacks, Jr.; Idyllwild, California: Charles Schlacks, Jr. Publisher, 1996).

Russian thought whose perspectives, born out of existential concern for the history and future of the cultures inhabiting one-sixth of the Earth's land surface, might be found to have much to say and to be understood for the many other cultures and expanses in the current history of civilizations and ideas. Translating Eurasianism is, without a doubt, a transitional role and endeavor, and one fraught with all the potential controversies and misunderstandings which besiege any attempt at opening the window of one structure of culture, impressions and ideas onto others. Nevertheless, it is with immense pleasure, serious expectations, and daring intuition that we present the foundations of Eurasianism in English translation for the sake of the ever-possible polylogue of civilizations to which the "Eurasians" who announced themselves in 1921 unhesitantly sought to present their own unique perspectives during those most turbulent times of the past century.

# INTRODUCTION:
# THE GENESIS OF THE
# EURASIAN THEORY

## Leonid Savin

Eurasianism is commonly described as a socio-political movement within the Russian emigration in Europe in the 1920s-30s. Eurasianism is also understood by some to have been an ideological-philosophical current typified by its critique of Western European culture and insistence on reconsidering the role of the Golden Horde and nomadic peoples in the history of Russian statehood. A third definition holds that Eurasianism is a current of Russian historical thought which emphasizes the diverse uniqueness of Russia arising out of its simultaneous position within both Europe and Asia which, taken together, constitute the largest continent on Earth: Eurasia. One of the leaders of the interwar Eurasian movement[30], Petr Savitsky (1895-1968), stated: "The Eurasianists have proposed a new geographical and historical understanding of Russia, as well as that whole world which they call Russian or 'Eurasian.'"[31]

Eurasianism sharply distinguished itself from other currents among the White emigration by its scholarly approach, which might be defined as interdisciplinary by virtue of the breadth of its views on culture, politics, history, ethnography,

---

30  It should be noted that in Russian the term *evraziistvo* is not an "-ism," but rather is more approximate to "Eurasianness" or "Eurasianity." Moreover, the name *evraziitsy* does not harbor any distinction between the possible English variations of "Eurasians" and "Eurasianists." The founding thinkers of this current, opposed as many of them were to attempts at strict ideologization or doctrinalization, would have likely referred to themselves and their movement in the sense of the former.

31  P.N. Savitsky, *Kontinent Evraziia* [*Continent Eurasia*] (Moscow: Agraf, 1997), p. 81. See Petr Savitsky, "Eurasianism," in this volume.

linguistics, religion, poetry, and music, all fields which were considered in the Eurasianists' works. Eurasianism was recognized for its contributions to these fields, in many of which its leading thinkers were professional scholars, as well as its patriotic platform. With regard to the latter, despite the Eurasianists' criticism of Bolshevism over the entire course of their activities and works, they did not engage in derogatory attacks on the Soviet government and its representatives, instead directing their critiques essentially on the level of its ideological-philosophical platform, as they saw Bolshevism as bearing an anti-spiritual and pronounced materialist character. The Eurasianists nevertheless positioned themselves not only as theoreticians, but also aspired to political practice, founding cells of their movement in various European cities and establishing ties with other emigre organizations. In addition, Eurasianism has been associated with the birth of Russian geopolitical thought, following the criteria of the organicist school. Again in the words of Savitsky: "Eurasianism is not only a system of historiosophical or theoretical assessments. It strives to combine thought and deed and to ultimately lead to the affirmation of a certain methodology of action alongside this system of theoretical views."[32]

Several stages in the history of the Eurasian movement can be noted. The years 1920-1923 saw the Eurasianists' formative organization. The distinct theses which they put forth on the unique identity of Russia-Eurasia, their critique of Western culture and analysis of its decline (a point which resonated with the works of many European thinkers, from Nietzsche to Spengler), and their recognition of a need to "pivot to the East" attracted broad social resonance and drew diverse sections of the Russian emigration to Eurasianism, as well as the attention of the intelligence departments of Soviet Russia, which saw in Eurasianism a certain threat to the ideas of Bolshevism and Communism.

32  Savitsky, *Kontinent Evraziia*, p. 93. See: Petr Savitsky, "Eurasianism," in this volume.

The period from 1924 to 1929 is associated with the emergence of the "left-wing" faction within the Eurasian movement. During this time, the attention paid in the Eurasianists' programmatic works shifted from religious and cultural questions to political economic ones, such as to assessing the USSR's New Economic Policy and the possibility of further transformations, including the transformation of Soviet ideology. Attempts were also undertaken to streamline Eurasianist ideology with the aim of expanding their target audience. In the newspaper *Eurasia* (*Evraziia*), launched in 1928 and including in its editorial board Petr Suvchinsky (1892-1985), Lev Karsavin (1882-1952), and Sergey Efron (1893-1941), various sympathies were expressed for the Soviet model. This led to a split within the Eurasian movement and to its being discredited in the eyes of many among the Russian emigration.

The final stage of 1930-1939 is characterized by the inertia of previous activities and attempts at summating conclusions and results. Following the death of Nikolai Trubetzkoy (1890-1938), the movement ceased to exist as a political-philosophical organization. Individual figures, first and foremost Petr Savitsky, would continue their intellectual activities which after some time would become the source of inspiration for the Soviet-era scholar Lev Gumilev (1912-1992), who further interpreted many of Savitsky's ideas.

While Eurasianism is considered to have been an independent ideological-philosophical current with political overtones, the unambiguous conclusion can be drawn from the works of the Eurasianists themselves as well as contemporary studies on the current that the Eurasianists' ideological forerunners were the Slavophiles and the Pochvenniki.[33] Before

---

33   See: A.I. Fedorov, "*Istoki evraziiskoi ideologii v russkom slavianofil'stve*" [*The origins of Eurasian ideology in Russian Slavophilia*], *Vestnik Tambovskogo Universiteta* (*Tambov University Bulletin*) 7:87 (2010); A.V. Sobolev, "*Evraziistvo v kontektse pochvennicheskoi traditsii*" [*Eurasianism in the context of the Pochvennik tradition*], *Vestnik Russkoi khristianskoi gumanitarnoi akademii* [*Bulletin of the Russian Christian Humanitarian Academy*] 8:2 (2007). The name of the Pochvennichestvo movement is derived from the word *pochva*, or "soil," and has thus figured in English as the "native soil," "return to native soil," or simply "nativist" movement.

the Eurasianists, the Slavophiles had already spoken of a special path of development of Rus/Russia, of the importance of Orthodox Christianity in Russian history and culture as an antipode of Catholicism and Protestantism, and of the existence of a unique Russian civilization with its own characteristics and markers. The Pochvenniki were spiritually close to the Slavophile movement, their main representative being none other than the philosopher and author Fyodor Dostoevsky (1821-1881) as well as such figures as Apollon Grigoryev (1822-1864) and Nikolai Strakhov (1828-1896). The Pochvenniki criticized liberal cosmopolitanism and Westernism and insisted on the need for the intelligentsia and certain other estates of society to merge with the popular masses on a religio-ethical basis. Thus, the Eurasianists had a logical basis for their activities, but the intellectual conceptualization and realization of their movement unfolded under new conditions outside of Russia, which inevitably compelled them to employ somewhat different lines of argumentation.

The first author to employ the concept of "Eurasia" was the geologist Eduard Suess (1831-1914), who, in his fundamental work of 1885-1901 *The Face of the Earth*, pointed to the pure conventionality of drawing a border between Europe and Asia.[34] A definite role in the development of the idea of Eurasia was also played by the ethnographer and Slavicist Vladimir Lamansky (1833-1914), who, in his 1892 book, *The Three Worlds of the Asian-European Continent*, illustrated the uniqueness of Russia in the context of civilizational development on the "Eurasian continent."

The beginning of the Euraisian movement proper is commonly dated to 1920, when Nikolai Trubetzkoy published the book *Europe and Mankind*. The latter did not speak of Eurasia directly, but rather repeated the leitmotifs of Nikolai Danilevsky's (1822-1885) renowned 1869 work *Russia and*

---

34  Leonid Savin, "*Formirovanie evraziiskogo geopoliticheskogo konteksta*" [*The Formation of the Eurasian geopolitical context*], *Kazakhstan v global'nykh protsessakh* [*Kazakhstan in Global Processes*] 2 (2012), p. 36.

*Europe: A View on the Cultural and Political Relations of the Slavic and Germano-Romanic Worlds* on the principally different points of view of these two regions' peoples on the surrounding world. Trubetzkoy counted various Asian peoples alongside Russians and contrasted them together to the peoples of the "Romano-Germanic" world. In Petr Savitsky's review of *Europe and Mankind* written in January 1921 and published under the title "Europe and Eurasia" in the journal *Russian Thought*[35], "Eurasia" figured as a spiritual and geopolitical category. Noteworthy in these first discourses of Eurasianism was the allusion to a connection between "Eurasia" and mankind in contrast to Europe as Romano-Germanic civilization which, being on the periphery of geographical Eurasia, had established the principles of inequality between peoples, political hegemony, and cultural racism. Savitsky stated: "Instead of the usual two on the mainland of the 'Old World', we distinguish three continents: Europe, Eurasia, and Asia... The borders of 'Eurasia' cannot be determined as indisputable according to any one standard."[36] Further, Savitsky proposed to identify Eurasia with Russia, thus imparting the notion of "Eurasia" with the compressed cultural-historical characteristics of the Russian world as including elements of both Europe and Asia but being, by analogy with geographical nature, neither European nor Asian.

These works were followed by the publication of the collection of articles *Exodus to the East: Premonitions and Fulfillments - The Affirmation of The Eurasians* in Sofia in 1921, after which began the periodical production of printed materials and texts which were carefully selected by topic and edited. Russian scholars have pointed to the fact that:

> [The Eurasianists'] works attracted attention by virtue of their non-traditional analyses of traditional Russian problems. Unlike the Slavophiles, Danilevsky, Leontiev, and others who pinned their hopes on the autocratic state, the Eurasianists proceeded from

---

35 *Russkaia mysl'* 1-2 (Sofia: 1921). See the translation presented in this volume.

36 Savitsky, *Kontinent Evraziia*, p. 154.

the recognition that the old Russia had collapsed and become the property of history. In their opinion, the First World War and the Russian Revolution opened up a qualitatively new era in the country's history characterized not only by the collapse of Russia, but also by an all-encompassing crisis of the West which, having completely exhausted its potential, had begun to decompose.[37]

Also noteworthy was the Eurasianists' presumption of an impending decline of Communist ideology and a return to the traditional worldview of the peoples of Russia. For instance, the Eurasianist resolution from November 1936 read:

> The USSR's growing need to reconcile the revolution with tradition is favorable for the establishment of Eurasianist views on Soviet soil. In the field of historical views, steps toward this reconciliation have already been taken. Eurasianism, which has long since set such reconciliation as its goal, is fully conscious of the significance of these steps… The Eurasian idea, as a position on the uniqueness of the 'special world' of Russia/the USSR is, in the totality of its traditions and tasks, capable of fertilizing all branches of cultural work and imparting such with new life. Neither superficial "Europeanism" nor all-out Communism are capable of fulfilling this role. Only Eurasianism, as a new, unprecedented understanding of the whole surrounding world and Russia-Eurasia's role therein can contribute to the establishment of the unique, fully-fledged art and science of the Eurasian peoples.[38]

In order to better understand the Eurasian movement in its classical period, and in light of the hitherto absence of English-language translations of relevant works, we propose an overview of some of the major Eurasianists and their key concepts as presented in the words of their own publications.

Nikolai Trubetzkoy, a philologist and linguist by profession, initially emigrated to Bulgaria, acquiring a position at the Historical-Philological Faculty of Sofia University, largely thanks to which the first Eurasianist volume was published

---

37  K.S. Gadzhiev, *"Vklad evraziistva v razrabotku geopoliticheskikh idei"* [*The contribution of Eurasianism to the development of geopolitical ideas*] in *Geopolitika: Uchebnik* [*Geopolitics: A Textbook*] (Moscow: Iurait, 2014).

38  Resolution 4-6.IX, *Evraziiskaia khronika* [*Eurasian Chronicle*] 7 (Berlin: 1937), p. 5-9.

out of Sofia. Trubetzkoy left in 1922 to live in Vienna, where he would head the Department of Slavonic Studies at the University of Vienna and regularly visit Paris and Prague, where Eurasianist cells operated. Trubetzkoy's *Europe and Mankind*, as the first programmatic Eurasianist publication, contributed to the unification of many different personalities into a single ideological trend.[39] In the latter work, Trubetzkoy argued that the "exceptionalism of European civilization" harbors at once two phenomena: chauvinism and cosmopolitanism. Trubetzkoy justly observed that in Europe "civilization" was understood exclusively to be the culture developed by the Romanic and Germanic peoples, and therefore the latter were recognized to be "civilized peoples" behind which trail those others who have voluntarily accepted and submitted to their specific definition of culture and civilization. At the same time, Trubetzkoy noted, Europeans do not recognize other cultures as equals. This observation resonated with the recent conclusions of the Russian ethnographer Nikolai Miklouho-Maclay (1846-1888) who engaged in field studies in the Pacific region and argued against European scholars that all peoples are equal and any conclusions on superiority or inferiority cannot and should not be drawn in terms of racial differences. Trubetzkoy in turn pointed out that no scientific data supports the notion of the superiority of Romano-Germanic civilization, and that all accounts pertaining to the supposed "evolutionary ladder" of cultures are based either on prejudices or misinterpretations tied to an egocentric psychology. Trubetzkoy cited as an example the fact of the destruction of the great cultures of antiquity by "barbarians." Since European science recognized a victorious people to be superior, the dilemma thus arises: were the historical nomadic barbarian peoples more developed than the highly-developed settled cultures? If yes, then the Romano-Germanic peoples cannot be held to be more perfect. If no, then the victories of European peoples over others since the beginning of the era of

---

39  N.S. Trubetzkoy, *Evropa i chelovechestvo* [*Europe and Mankind*] (Sofia: Rossiiskoe-Bolgarskoe knigoizdatel'stvo [Russian-Bulgarian Book Publishing House] , 1921).

colonial conquests cannot be considered standards of higher development and perfection. Further, Trubetzkoy analyzed the process of the Europeanization of different peoples and concluded that this process bears a decisively negative character which hinders the authentic development of peoples and renders them more dependent on Europeans. Overall, in *Europe and Mankind*, Trubetzkoy laid the foundations for what can be seen as one of the most significant aspects of the Eurasianist legacy, namely, their pioneering of a systematic analysis and critique of Eurocentrism and the racist approaches endemic to colonialism. Trubetzkoy's critique anticipated the political and intellectual processes of decolonization and presented a first attempt at calling into critique the notion of "universal human values" as defined exclusively from the position and for the benefit of one political-cultural hegemon.

Trubetzkoy proclaimed a "new principle of the equivalence and qualitative incommensurability of all of the globes' cultures and peoples" and insisted that "there are neither higher nor lower [cultures and peoples]; there are only similar and different ones."[40] Most importantly, in arguing that "European civilization is no higher than any other"[41], Trubetzkoy pointed to the existence of other civilizations and thereby laid the foundations for intercivilizational polylogue. At the same time, a red thread running throughout *Europe and Mankind* was, as reflected in the very title of Trubtezkoy's work, the principle of an opposition between the Romano-Germanic civilization's pretensions and all other peoples of the world. Trubetzkoy himself believed his book to be a rejection of European egocentrism and, as follows, a "revolution in the consciousness of peoples" which should lead to an original, true nationalism for every people. As a result, peoples would organically merge into several large cultures and "every people will belong to such a culture not by chance, but because it is in harmony with their

---

40  N.S. Trubetzkoy, *Istoriia. Kul'tura. Iazyk.* [*History, Culture, Language*] (Moscow: Progress, 1995), p. 81

41  Ibid, p. 98

inner essence and this inner essence finds its fullest and most vivid expression in culture."[42]

The subject of nationalism was further developed by Trubetzkoy in his article "On True and False Nationalism," which was originally intended to be the second part of *Europe and Mankind*, but would instead be published in 1921 as part of the Eurasianists' founding anthology *Exodus to the East*.[43] This work was a logical continuation of Trubetzkoy's critique of Eurocentrism and his emphasis on other peoples' need for self-knowledge. Trubetzkoy identified several false versions of nationalism. The first type is when the original identity of a culture is not assigned any significance in comparison to the priority of merely acquiring state independence. Insofar as such state independence would, in Trubetzkoy's opinion, be senseless and some national movements would sacrifice their original culture for such (often by imitating European forms), this type of nationalism was seen not only as false, but as harmful and driven by petty vanity. Another type of false nationalism is, in Trubetzkoy's terms, that of "militant chauvinism," which denies the equivalence of other peoples and cultures. The third type of false nationalism proceeds from a cultural conservatism which equates unique, original national identity with various historical artifacts and previously established values. This type leads to cultural stagnation insofar as it denies the possibility of changes in the national psyche. All three of these types of false nationalism could, in Trubetzkoy's opinion, be combined with one another to yield mixed types. True nationalism, on the other hand, is built on self-knowledge. Trubetzkoy observed that only false forms of nationalism, such as Slavophilia, had hitherto emerged in Russia, and therefore a true Russian nationalism still stood to be created.

In his article "Pan-Eurasian Nationalism" published in the journal *The Eurasian Chronicle* (*Evraziiskaia khronika*) in 1927,

---

42 Roman Jacobson et al. (eds.), *N.S. Trubetzkoy's Letters and Notes* (The Hague/ Paris: Mouton, 1975), p. 16.

43 See the translation presented in this volume.

Trubetzkoy attempted to outline criteria for defining a Eurasian nationalism. Firstly, Trubetzkoy critiqued the political national rights proscribed in the USSR, remarking that the erasure of class contradictions and the development of scripts for national languages contributed to "the development of nationalism with a separatist slant among each of the peoples of the USSR."[44] Secondly, Trubetzkoy proposed to call "national substrata" the sum of peoples living on the territory of the USSR, which Trubetzkoy deemed a special multiethnic "nation" with its own nationalism. Thirdly, Trubetzkoy repeated the thesis of the commonality of historical destinies in contrast to narrow ethnic, linguistic, and religious kinships. Fourthly, he once again called for self-knowledge, insofar as without re-education it would be difficult to create a unified multiethnic Eurasian nation. Fifthly, Trubetzkoy posited that the Russian people should stand at the head of this movement, since before the revolution the Russian people were the de facto masters of the whole territory of Russia-Eurasia now confronted with the task of setting an example for the others. It is worth noting that the term "nation" which Trubetzkoy employed here is not entirely correct in this context, as it introduces a certain confusion of notions. Lev Gumilev would later attempt to correct this inaccuracy by proposing the term "super-ethnos."

It is also necessary to take note of Trubetzkoy's article "On the Ruling Idea of the Ideocratic State" published in *Eurasian Chronicle* in 1935. Although the latter was a fairly late work and the thesis of ideocracy had already been put forth by Nikolai Alekseev, Trubetzkoy proposed to examine the importance of ideas in the context of the political struggle that was then unfolding in the European space, namely, the clash between Fascism, National Socialism, Socialism, Marxism, and Liberalism. Positing that neither the good of a certain class, a certain people, nor any abstract "humanity" could serve as substance for the ruling idea of an ideocratic state, Trubetzkoy

---

44  Trubetzkoy, *Istoriia. Kul'tura. Iazyk*, p. 422. See: Nikolai Trubetzkoy, "Pan-Eurasian Nationalism" in this volume.

proposed an intermediate model between a given people and humanity, that of a "special world," a totality of peoples "populating an economically self-sufficient (autarkic) place-development and related to one another not by race but by commonality of historical fate and joint work on the creation of the state-culture." Thus, Trubetzkoy argued, "the ruling idea of an authentic ideocratic state can only be the good of the totality of peoples inhabiting this autarkic special world."[45]

While Trubetzkoy did not devote as much attention to Orthodox Christianity as other authors, there are grounds to believe that Orthodoxy was one of the Eurasianists' fundamental imperatives. This can be seen in a letter to Petr Suvchinsky dated 26 February 1924, in which Trubetzkoy spoke of the need to formulate realistically attainable and wholly concrete practical goals for society as one element of the Eurasianist program. In the external field, Trubetzkoy proposed: (1) actively defending Orthodoxy against the machinations of the Latin creed, and (2) actively rebuffing Catholic and Uniate preaching. And in the internal field: (1) disseminating Orthodox theological knowledge among the religious intelligentsia; (2) drawing the religious intelligentsia toward strict adherence to church rites and indoctrinating an authentically ecclesiastical approach to rites free from both vulgar superstition and Protestant frivolity.[46]

In fact, church circles in emigration showed constant interest in the activities of the Eurasianists. Particularly noteworthy are such hierarchs as Metropolitan Evlogy (Georgievsky, 1868-1946), Metropolitan Platon (Rozhdestvensky, 1866-1934), and Metropolitan Antony (Khrapovitsky, 1863-1936) who were attracted by the Eurasianists' defensive and anti-ecumenist position. Telling in this regard was the Eurasianists' dislike for the tendency among church circles toward autocephaly, and

---

45  Trubetzkoy, *Istoriia. Kul'tura. Iazyk*, p. 441.

46  N.S. Trubetzkoy, "Pis'ma k P.P. Suvchinskomu 1921-1928" [*Letters to P.P. Suvchinsky, 1921-1928*] (Moscow: *Russkii put'* [Russian Way], *Russkoe zarubezh'e* [Russian Abroad], 2008), p. 81-82.

Evlogy's recognition of the existence of the church in Russia and advocating for the preservation of ties with it. In addition, their call for rapprochement with the Old Believers suggests that the Eurasianists well understood the prehistory of the conflicting currents within Orthodoxy as well as recognized the importance of recreating the cultural codes that had been lost by the masses but preserved among the Old Believers.

Alongside Trubetzkoy, the role of founding father of Eurasianism was held by Petr Nikolaevich Savitsky, who became the de facto leader of the Eurasian movement. Savitsky was a geographer and economist by education, which meant that the idea of (re)organizing space was close to him, and as an author Savitsky was already well-known in the Russian Empire. Savitsky would be responsible for the work of the Eurasian branch in Prague, which was supported by the Russian Action organization established on the initiative of the government of Tomáš Masaryk for the preparation of new intellectual cadres to replace the Bolsheviks following what was thought would be the imminent defeat of Communism in Russia. Savitsky formulated the majority of Eurasianism's most prominent concepts and would continue to advocate these ideas until the end of his life, including as an informal mentor to Lev Gumilev.

Savitsky asserted the foundational worldview of Eurasianism to be Orthodoxy, but defined Eurasianist ideology as an organic system of ideas.[47] Like the first German-speaking scholars of the psychology of peoples (*Völkerpsychologie*) Savitsky discerned a specific Eurasian worldview differing from the world-outlook of European peoples. In Savitsky's opinion, the natural conditions of lowland Eurasia, its soils, and special steppe zone defined the socio-economic processes of both its nomadic and sedentary traditions and cultures, directly influencing the Eurasian psychological mode. The main features of this "Eurasian mentality" were seen as consciousness of the organicity of socio-

---

47  See the collective manifesto *Evraziistvo: opyt sistematicheskogo izlozheniia* [*Eurasianism: The Experience of Systematic Presentation*] (Paris: Eurasian Book Publishing House, 1926), republished in Savitsky, *Kontinent Evraziia*. The collective manifesto was to a significant extent written by Savitsky.

political life and its connection with nature, "continental" scope, "Russian breadth," and boundless national self-consciousness. Savitsky remarked that "Eurasian traditionalism is an altogether unique, special type."[48]

It is also important to note that Savitsky's practice of writing "Russia-Eurasia" with a hyphen was intended to not only emphasize the presence in Russia of numerous ethnic groups, but also to point to the very original identity of the Russian people. In his article "Eurasianism as an Historical Idea," Savitsky wrote: "The Eurasianists feel the Russian world to be a special one in geographic, linguistic, historical, economic, and many other senses."[49]

The conceptualization of "Eurasia" itself was lent the following characteristics across various publications. In his "The Eurasian-Russian Cultural World," Savitsky articulated:

> It is the geographical wholeness and distinctness of Russian-Eurasian culture that links it to being called "Eurasian," and it is with such that this term, having long been established in science and denoting Europe and Asia as one landmass, acquires more narrow and precise meaning … [T]he borders of Eurasia coincide with the borders of the Russian Empire, the "naturalness" of which has been evidenced in recent time by the fact that they have been more or less restored despite the terrible jolts of war and revolution. Representing a particular part of the world, a special continent, Eurasia is characterized as a certain closed and typical whole both from the point of view of climate and from the point of view of other geographical conditions… Eurasia is excluded from the active participation in the oceanic economy that is characteristic for Europe. The natural riches of Eurasia and their distribution open up for it the path to economic self-sufficiency and render it a kind of continent-ocean.[50]

Savitsky highlighted three geographical zones on the continent of Eurasia: (1) the middle continent or Eurasia proper, (2) the peripheral Asian world (including China,

---

48   Ibid, p. 42.

49   Ibid, p. 98.

50   Savitsky, *Kontinent Evraziia*, p. 41.

India, and Iran), and (3) the peripheral European world bordering Eurasia roughly along the line of the Neman, Western Bug, and San rivers and the Danube Delta. In his "Europe and Eurasia," Savitsky wrote: "Instead of the usual two on the mainland of the "Old World," we distinguish three continents: Europe, Eurasia, and Asia... The borders of "Eurasia" cannot be determined as indisputable according to any one standard, just as such a border cannot be established with respect to the habitual division between Europe and Asia."[51] In his geo-economic and worldview constructions, Petr Savitsky employed the expression "zero isotherm of January," meaning the zone in which the average January temperature is equal to 0 degrees Celsius, which Savitsky took to demarcate the conditional border between Eurasia and Europe.

Further, in his article "Eurasianism (The Experience of Systematic Presentation)," Savitsky put forth an unusual formulation whose connotations can also be noted among other Eurasianists, namely, that "Eurasia-Russia is a developing, unique culture-personality."[52] This idea was recapitulated in more detail in his article "Eurasianism as an Historical Idea" and formulated as a relativistic approach to other peoples. Savitsky wrote: "The Eurasianists perceive Russia-Eurasia as a 'symphonic personality.' They affirm the continuity of its existence... Affirming the individual nature of Eurasian culture, the Eurasianists value and honor this quality in other surrounding cultures as well. Even in a purely formal sense, for them it is unacceptable for their decision to be imposed on other cultures."[53] Savitsky also defined Russia-Eurasia as a "differentiated and integral 'place-development'," a "geographic individual" that is at once geographical, ethnic, economic, and historical as a "landscape."[54]

---

51  Ibid, p. 154.

52  Ibid, p. 43.

53  Ibid, p. 101.

54  Ibid, pp. 282-283.

**34**

"Place-development" or "topogenesis" (*mestorazvitie*) for Savitsky embodied the merging of a socio-historical environment and its territory into a unified whole. For Eurasia, the unifying factor is the steppe, thanks to which historical peoples could enjoy mobility and move from the expanses of Siberia to the Balkan Peninsula. Savitsky also recognized the possibility of drawing an equal sign between "place-development" and the notion of "culturo historical type" of Nikolai Danilevsky, who counted ten unique civilizations with their own peculiarities of spiritual nature and external conditions of life. According to Savitsky, "the concept of 'place-development' is compatible with the recognition of the multiplicity of forms of human history and life and the discernment of an original, unique spiritual as well as geographical element of life irreducible to any one other."[55]

With regard to the political organization of space, in his article "Geopolitical Notes on Russian History" Savitsky articulated: "it is as if Eurasia as a geographical world was 'pre-created' to form a single state."[56] The first impulse to Eurasian cultural unity, in his opinion, was imparted by the establishment of the Empire of Genghis Khan: "The Mongols formulated the historic task of Eurasia, laying the foundation for its political unity and the basis of its political system."[57] Savitsky also proposed as a form for the organization of governance for Russia-Eurasia the above-mentioned ideocracy, introduced by Trubetzkoy, which implied that the state ought to be built on a spiritual basis and all of its parts and classes should follow a ruling idea.

In Savitsky's works, one can also note a clear tendency toward substantiating land-based power. For instance, in his article "Continent-Ocean: Russia and the World Market," he wrote: "It is not in copying the 'oceanic' policy of others, which is in many respects inapplicable for Russia, but in the consciousness

---

55  Savitsky, *Kontinent Evraziia*, p. 292.

56  Ibid, p. 322.

57  Ibid, p. 45.

of 'continentality' and adaptation to it, that Russia's economic future lies."[58] Nevertheless, Savitsky did not deny the possibility of Russia gaining access to the warm seas, particularly through Iran. In terms of economics, Savitsky advocated a convergence of both the state and private sector, believing that only in such a case could the operations of the state be feasible, flexible, and successful. At the same time the Soviet Union's Five Year Plans were in full swing, Savitsky proclaimed: "The Eurasianists are ardent supporters of the element of planning."[59] Savitsky also introduced new concepts in his articles on economic matters. For instance, in his article "The Master and the Economy" he put forth the new term *khoziainoderzhavie*, which might be translated as "masterocracy." Contrasting what he called the *khoziain-obshchestvo*, or "master-society" which he saw manifest in socialism, and the *khoziain-lichnost'*, i.e. "master-personhood" or "master-personality," Savitsky suggested that "the system of masterocracy (*khoziainoderzhavie*) as a public (sovereign) 'conciliar' foundation, provides for the personal-creative element in the economy."[60]

As for his historic-political views related to his critique of Europe, Savitsky's views were largely similar to those of Trubetzkoy. In his critique of Western European models of society, Savitsky expressed: "They have replaced organic unity with the abstract concept of the sum of individual atoms."[61] Savitsky also took note of what he saw as "the origins of Russian atheism in the ideas of the European 'Enlightenment', the introduction of socialist ideas into Russia from the West, the link between Russian Communist 'methods' and the ideas of the French Syndicalists, as well as the significance and "cult" of Marx in Communist Russia."[62]

---

58  Ibid, p. 418. See: Petr Savitsky, "Continent-Ocean: Russia and the World Market" in this volume.

59  Ibid, p. 104.

60  Ibid, p. 246.

61  Savitsky, *Kontinent Evraziia*, p. 61.

62  Ibid, p. 90.

At times, Savitsky's pronouncements could sound paradoxical, for example, when he proclaimed that "Eurasianists are essentially and at once advocates of religious principles as well as consistent empiricists."[63] In his "Eurasianism as an Historical Idea," Savitsky explained this approach thusly: "Eurasianists are not afraid of contradictions... Eurasianists live in oppositions. In their system they combine tradition and revolution."[64]

Another important yet relatively understudied author of the Eurasian group from the very beginning was the scholar of law Nikolai Alekseev (1879-1964). In his work "The Spiritual Preconditions of Eurasian Culture," Alekseev emphasized the global scale of Eurasianist ideology:

> Eurasianism wants to overcome the West not from without, but from within, the very spirit of the West which has since become the Eurasian man's proper own... Proceeding from this, the task of Eurasianism becomes not only national, but universal: the Russian people must overcome the Western within themselves and through themselves overcome Western man, who has spread his culture across the whole world. This universality sharply distinguishes Eurasianism from fascism, national socialism, and other currents which are nationalist doctrines that do not set themselves any universal goals.[65]

Also of interest was Alekseev's approach to European critics of Western culture, particularly Oswald Spengler (1880-1936) and Leo Frobenius (1873-1938), whom he mentioned and cited repeatedly across his publications. Alekseev remarked that attempts at contrasting different types of cultures "move along the line of purely spatial definitions" which, Alekseev argued, "testifies to the fact that they have been created by Western man, who himself is immersed in the contemplation of space and understands his whole culture to be the mastery of space and everything enclosed within space."[66] Alekseev did not distinguish a "non-Western" culture as an opposite to Western culture in

---

63  Ibid, p. 93.

64  Ibid, p. 98.

65  N.N. Alekseev, *Russkii narod i gosudarstvo* [*The Russian People and the State*] (Moscow: Agraf, 1998), p. 144.

66  Ibid, p. 148.

its various forms and manifestations, but instead proposed to reconcile metaphysical antitheses which, he believed, was the historic task of Eurasianism. Reconciling the "sleeping East" and the "energetic West," facilitating the convergence of science and religion, paying attention to "motionless activity," and accepting worldly affairs such as social, economic, and political construction while aiming to "sanctify and conceptualize such with striving for the otherworldly" - such were the terms with which Alekseev pointed to the need for a profound synthesis that could constitute the prerequisite condition for the development of a future Eurasian system.

Alekseev was known best of all as an outstanding scholar of law who was well versed in both historical materials and the latest trends in European science. In his article "Russian Westernism," Alekseev noted:

> All Russian Westernizers are, without exception, equally alike in their misunderstanding of the practical tasks which stood before the Russian state as a fully unique and special geographic, economic, and cultural whole. All of them were convinced that for Russia to succeed it was enough to take foreign institutions with all the purely immanent goals peculiar to them from abroad, transplant them onto Russian soil, and implement the aims intrinsic to them in the manner in which they were applied in their original source.[67]

In his "Duty and Law," Alekseev in turn advocated "the inner, organic combination of rights and duties."[68] In his article "The Russian People and the State," he argued that the future belongs to an Orthodox rule of law that will be capable of combining hard power (the element of dictatorship) with popular rule (the element of freemen) in the service of social truth.[69] Alekseev refined this view in his article "The Eurasians and the State": "We aim to consciously register in the political being of our state that which Western

---

67 Alekseev, *Russkii narod i gosudarstvo*, p. 140.

68 Ibid, p. 158.

69 Ibid, p. 116.

democracies intentionally conceal: the guiding idea of the state as a whole, its foundational vocation, its aim. In this sense, our state could be called an ideocracy or, in other terms, a state of stabilized public opinion."[70] Alekseev did not reject the idea of voting, which would be important for the determination of the dynamics of public life; however, insofar as the people is a totality of historical generations, voting is not ascribed decisive significance. Alekseev also emphasized that political parties should be replaced by real social strata, although there would be no ban on parties. Ultimately, Alekseev theorized what he termed the "guarantee-state," or a state that "guarantees" because it ensures the realization of constant goals and objectives.[71] This is a state with a positive mission, contrasting the "relativist state" which does not set before itself positive goals. This expression is reminiscent of John Stuart Mill's (1806-1873) distinction between positive and negative freedom. Mills associated liberalism with negative freedom or "freedom from" insofar as he could not determine clear criteria for positive freedom. Alekseev referred to the relativist state as liberalism with the function of the "night watchman" and treated formal democracy as a system in which matters are resolved by the distribution of votes and party majorities. At the same time, Alekseev warned against confusing the "guarantee state" with a "doctrinal state" in which the state follows a definite philosophical and (or) religious world outlook which is indoctrinated into citizens by all available means. "The guarantee-ideocratic state," Alekseev wrote, "differs from the doctrinal state in that it insures the implementation in life of various positive social principles, a certain stabilized socio-political program which can count on general recognition by people of altogether different philosophical, scientific, and religious convictions."[72] In this case, the confession of any

---

70   Ibid, p. 182.

71   Ibid, p. 372.

72   Alekseev, *Russkii narod i gosudarstvo*, p. 373.

world outlook should remain the personal matter of citizens. Thus, Alekseev's ideocratic and guarantee-state combined the possibility for the wide discussion and deliberation of a constructive socio-political program of action with freedom of conscience for all groups of citizens. The popular masses, according to Alekseev, should "defend the state and encourage it to serve the common good."[73]

It is further interesting to note that Alekseev's opinion on the establishment of alliances came close to the ideas of Carl Schmitt (1888-1985) and Karl Haushofer (1869-1946) regarding "*Grossraumen*" or "Great Spaces." Alekseev held that "the era of sovereign nation-states must be considered variable in the sense that these states will believe themselves to be compelled to resort to larger political units."[74] In effect, Alekseev demonstrated the coincidence between many of the views of Western-European geopoliticians and the Eurasianists, from which the conclusion was drawn that there has been a parallel process of coming to consciousness of unique cultural identities and forms. Alekseev positively viewed the idea of creating interstate associations that had already begun to be discussed in Europe at the time.

At the same time, Alekseev critiqued the concept of nation-states, arguing that history has largely known multi-tribal and multinational states, and that the "state-world" or Imperium is multinational. The modern British and French states were not national insofar as they possessed colonies inhabited by peoples different from the population of the metropolises. Alekseev thus posed the question: "Is there no 'people' there? Or should they not be called a 'people' only because they often have not yet acquired political and even civil rights?" Alekseev answered this rhetorical question with the remark that only the representatives of one people wield real power in such states.[75] In his analysis of the relationship between power, sovereignty, and the state,

---

73   Ibid, p. 380.

74   Ibid, p. 412.

75   Ibid, p. 430.

Alekseev put forth the thesis that state power is the special will of the state-personality or state-individual.[76]

The topic of the personality and individual in Eurasianism was developed by Lev Karsavin, who came to be a fairly influential figure within the movement even though he was not involved in the movement in its origins. Being an anti-liberal philosopher and one of the founders of the Brotherhood of St. Sophia in Saint Petersburg in 1918, after emigrating Karsavin organically fell into Eurasian ranks. However, Karsavin's joining of the group coincided with the beginning of the second period, when the movement underwent an attempt at formalization. Although he joined only after Eurasianist journals had already published such renowned and authoritative theologians and culturologists as George Florovsky and Petr Bitsilli, Karsavin nonetheless became the "right-hand man" of Petr Suvchinsky who at the time led the Eurasianists' operations in Paris.[77]

Karsavin's first work was published in *The Eurasian Annals* in Berlin in 1925, but his most influential article would be his 1927 "The Church, the Personality, and the State." This article incited lively discussion, including between the organizers of the Eurasian movement, as the movement's methodological approach to such core concepts had not been finalized and many of its theoretical models had been of a polemical character. Although Karsavin was a well-known religious philosopher and expert on Eastern Church history before joining the Eurasian movement, there are grounds to consider that his several years of active work with the Eurasianists proceeded in an atmosphere of mutual influence. It was during his years of collaborating with the Eurasianists that "Lev Karsavin's notion of the conciliar personality and interest in political struggle as a means to achieve, in the words of the Byzantine canonists,

---

76   Ibid, p. 463.

77   Boris Stepanov, "*Spor evraziitsev o tserkvi, lichnosti, gosudarstve*" [The Eurasianists' dispute over the church, the personality, and the state], *Issledovaniia po istorii russkoi mysli* [*Studies in the History of Russian Thought*] (Moscow: Tri kvadrata, 2001/2002), p. 87.

the symphony as the perfectly coordinated action of church and state took distinctive shape."[78] For Karsavin, Eurasianism was the doctrine of the symphonic personality and the symphonic unity of cultures entailing processes of complex interactions whose result is the formation of a new cultural unit.[79]

One thinker who was drawn to the Eurasian movement at its first stage but who would later resign and turn to criticize it was Georges Florovsky (1893-1979), who is often cited as a case of the "inadequacy" of the consistency of Eurasianists ideas. Florovsky is alleged in some accounts to have been an "insider" whose later "revelations" saw Eurasianism to be an erroneous reaction to the revolutionary events in Russia. Florovsky himself was never an active member of the Eurasian group, instead preferring to focus on publishing lengthy reflections on culture, religion, and society, most often with regard to the revolution in Russia. In a letter to Petr Struve, Florovsky explained his motivations: "culturo-philosophical reflection seems to me to now be much more important and urgent of a national matter than the ongoing political struggle."[80] Florovsky called the Eurasian group "a Russian culture league" unified "only by the uniformity of tone in which we perceive and experience the impressions of the present."[81] In his article "Petrified Insensibility"[82], Florovsky expressed his support for Eurasianism despite not wishing to defend some of their theses, remarking that "the majority of opponents do not wish to search for any truth, while the Eurasians are condemned for none other than the restlessness of their search."[83] Florovsky argued

---

78 Vladas Povilaitis, *"Neizvestnye stat'i L.P. Karsavina"* [Unknown Articles by L.P. Karsavin], *Issledovaniia po istorii russkoi mysli* [*Studies in the History of Russian Thought*] 6 (Moscow: Modest Kolerov, 2003), p. 165-166.

79 K.B. Erimishina, *"N.S. Trubetzkoy i ego rol' v evraziiskom dvizhenii"* [N.S. Trubetzkoy and his role in the Eurasian movement], in Trubetzkoy, *"Pis'ma k P.P. Suvchinskomu 1921-1928,"* p. 9.

80 Georgy Florovsky, *Iz proshlogo russkoi mysli* [*From the Past of Russian Thought*] (Moscow: Agraf, 1988), p. 125.

81 Ibid, p. 126.

82 Published in *Put'* [Path] 2 (Paris: 1926), pp. 128-133

83 Ibid, p. 248.

that virtually all of the criticisms directed at the Eurasianists boiled down to unsubstantiated condemnations lacking any discussion. In 1928, however, Florovsky himself turned to criticize the Eurasianists, calling Eurasianism a "spiritual failure" in his article "The Eurasian Temptation." Florovsky posited that the Eurasianists "have heard the lively, acute questions of the day," but "they have been incapable of answering them."[84] Furthermore, Florovsky accused the Eurasianists of believing in an "infallibility" of history, of accepting the revolution as a deep renewal of stagnant life, and of misinterpreting the Petrine period of Russian history and reducing it entirely to "some kind of 'pseudo-morphism'" leading to a "rift between the state and the people" and Europeanization.[85] Florovsky also argued that the Eurasianists "are too fond of natural, geographical, and ethnic factors."[86] Florovsky held that the only clear defining line of the real cultural-natural borders of Russia-Eurasia as a "third historical world" was Orthodoxy, and even accused the Eurasianists of defending "naive paganism" and of sympathizing with sectarianism in their view of the "metaphysical pathos of genuine Russian religiosity."[87] Some of Florovsky's criticisms are easily explainable by his theological divergences with the founders of Eurasianism. Trubetzkoy, Savitsky, and Alekseev always opposed ecumenism, of which Florovsky was an active supporter.

Two other figures associated with Eurasianism who would emerge to be of global significance were the historian George Vernadsky (1887-1973) and the linguist Roman Jakobson (1896-1982). After emigrating from Russia, Vernadsky stayed in Europe for a relatively short period of time before moving to the United States in 1927, where he would become actively immersed in academia. Meanwhile, the Eurasianists' publishing house would release two books by him: *An Outline of the History of Eurasia* (1934) and *The Links of Russian*

---

84  Florovsky, *Iz proshlogo russkoi mysli*, p. 311.

85  Ibid, p. 315.

86  Ibid, p. 334.

87  Ibid, pp. 335, 337.

*Culture* (1938). The year of his move to the US saw the publication of his work *An Outline of Russian History from the Eurasian Point of View,* in which Vernadsky proposed an alternative view on the history of Russian statehood which aimed to overcome the generally accepted "Solovyov model." Vernadsky summarized his Eurasianist views in 1937 in the following terms: "...not only 'European Russia,' but all of Eurasia as a whole should be seen as a unified historical place-development... The process of the settling of the vast territory of Eurasia and its unification by the Russian people cannot be understood otherwise than on the basis of the concept of Eurasia as a special historico-geographical world. In this sense, the historical place-development of the Russian people should be seen in Eurasia as a whole."[88]

Vernadsky's Eurasianist views can be traced in many of his works which have since been recognized as classics. In his textbook on the history of Russia published by Yale University in 1927 and repeatedly reissued in new editions up to 1967, Vernadsky highlighted the integration of the European and Asian parts of Russia "into the only real unity possible, 'Eurasian Russia,'" the vast spaces of which had been occupied by the Russians "in the course of a long historical process."[89] Vernadsky posited that "the period extending from 1696 to the Revolution of 1917 saw the gradual expansion of the Russian state almost to the natural boundaries of Eurasia," in which Vernadsky saw that "the final unification of forest and steppe was achieved and the two great zones were finally welded into a single economic unit."[90] This historian also shared the Eurasianists' general view on the role of the Golden Horde in the formation of Russian statehood. In his work "The Two Feats of Alexander Nevsky" published in *The Eurasianist Annals* in 1925, Vernadsky wrote

---

88  Georgy Vernadsky, *Russkaia istoriografiia* [*Russian Historiography*] (Moscow: Agraf, 1998), p. 12.

89  George Vernadsky, *A History of Russia* (New Haven: Yale University Press, 1945), p. 5.

90  Ibid, p. 12.

that Alexander's 13th-century victory on the banks of the Nev and on the ice of Lake Peipus was an act of invective, whereas before the power of the East he was forced to humble himself, and it was under the protection of the Horde that Alexander Nevsky began to repel the West.[91]

Roman Jakobson collaborated with Trubetzkoy in the influential Prague Linguistic Circle, where Eurasianist ideas were brought into productive interaction with the structuralist linguistics of Ferdinand de Saussure (1857-1913). While Jakobson is predominantly well-known in the West for his contributions to formalism and structuralism, throughout his period of Eurasianist activism he sought to identify a Eurasian linguistic unity based on phonological criteria. Jakobson upheld the idea of soft correlation between languages and attempted to define concentric geographical zones on the basis of the juxtaposition of languages lacking soft correlation. Jakobson frequently employed the metaphor of an "oil stain" to describe the expansion of the zone of the phonological softening of consonants which, in his view, could spread through migration (as in case of the Turkic and Hungarian languages) or through the "local infection" of languages adjacent to the Eurasian place-development, a thesis which he demonstrated in the cases of the eastern dialects of Romanian, Bulgarian, and Estonian. According to Jakobson's theory, "the languages of the Eurasian association are characterized by the combination of two phonological features: (1) monotony, the absence of polytony, and (2) timbre differences between consonants."[92] Jakobson highlighted:

> In most cases, an extraordinary parallel can be observed between phonological and geographical indices. For example, the Armenian language and the Kartvelian group (Georgian, etc.) lack timbre contrasts, while geography and ethnography both testify to the

---

91  G.V. Vernadsky,"*Dva podviga Aleksandra Nevskogo*" [The Two Feats of Alexander Nevsky], *Nash sovremennik* [*Our Contemporary*] 3 (1992), p. 151-158.

92  "*O fonologicheskikh iazykovykh soyuzakh*" [On Phonological Language Associations], *Evraziia v svete iazykoznaniia* [*Eurasia in the Light of Linguistics*] (Prague: Eurasian Publication, 1931), p. 8.

fact that the region occupied by these languages is characterized as a transition point between Eurasia and neighboring place-developments. Similarly, the Paleo-Asiatic language confirms the geographer Savitsky's thesis that the Far East is outside of the Eurasian world. Both physical geography and phonology reveal a characteristic symmetry in the structure of the borders of Eurasia. In the far North-East and the far North-West, the Eurasian languages are adjacent to monotonic languages lacking timbre consonant differences: Chukchi, Yukagir, and others on the one side, and Suomi and Lopar on the other. In the North West and across the whole East, the Eurasian association borders polytonic associations such as the Baltic and Pacific. Finally, in the South-West and South the neighbors of the Eurasian association are once again monotonic languages which do not distinguish consonants by timbre, such as the main array of the languages of Europe, the Ottoman-Turkish, the Kartvelian groups, and the Indo-European languages of the Middle East (Armenian and the Indo-Iranian group).[93]

Without a doubt, Jakobson's interests were not limited to Eurasia. Jakobson held one of the tasks of phonology to be the development of a phonological geography and, ultimately, a phonological zoning of the world. This point directly correlated with the ideas of geopolitics, albeit on another plane beyond the level of geographical landscapes and institutions of power.[94]

Scholars have noted that in the field of linguistics the Eurasianists stood on the opposite pole from the Marrist school. The Eurasianists adhered to organic relativism while Nikolai Marr (1865-1934) and his followers were committed to evolutionary determinism. Although Trubetzkoy frequently criticized Marr's theory, there is no evidence that Marr ever negatively spoke of the Eurasianists in general or Trubetzkoy and Jakobson in particular. The Swiss-French linguist Patrick Sériot has suggested that Jakobson and Trubetzkoy "stood at a point of unstable equilibrium between two paradigms: between the theory of complex systems, whose access yields the

---

93    Roman Jakobson, "*O fonologicheskikh iazykovykh soyuzakh,*" p. 10.

94    History has seen striking interrelations between these three. For instance, the peculiarities of Cuban Spanish differ from the rest of the Carribean, and the national language of Pakistan, Urdu, is a hybrid mix of Farsi, Arabic, and Turkish based on the court dialect of the Mughals.

immaterial, and the theory of the One and the Whole, inherited from natural philosophy and Byzantine Neoplatonism."[95]

The preceding review of the different fields, theses, and collaborations of the major Eurasianists indicates that the Eurasianists genuinely attempted to develop a complex and holistic interdisciplinary approach based on rigorous scientific knowledge. Some of their ideas were, in terms of terminological apparatus, ahead of their time and would only come to be engaged by Western scholars decades later. In fact, this aspiration is evident from the reflections of Petr Savitsky, who wrote under the pseudonym "Logovikov":

> Alongside a geopolitical perspective, we can and should create a geo-economic, geo-ethnographical, geo-archaeological, and geo-linguistic doctrine of Russia-Eurasia. All of these can and should be combined into a single "picture-system." This is one aspect of the historic-geographical synthesis to which our time is called... Every Eurasianist publication is the result of collaboration between representatives of different fields on the resolution of a given problem... Every phenomenon within Russia-Eurasia should be included in the general system of Eurasian phenomena. But we cannot limit ourselves to this. Russian science should take on global horizons.[96]

This aspiration toward cultural analysis on a global scale shows that the Eurasianists did not limit themselves to Russia and Europe. They attempted to create an epistemological matrix that could be of value on a planetary scale. At the same time, although they did not directly speak of formulating an alternative political theory, such a theory was implied in the very breadth of their thinking and diverse interests.

---

95  Patrick Sériot, *Struktura i tselostnost': Ob intellektual'nykh istokakh strukturalizma v Tsentral'noi i Vostochnoi Evrope, 1920-30-e gg.* [*Structure and the Whole: The Intellectual Origins of Structuralism in Central and Eastern Europe*] (Moscow: Iazyki slavianskoi kul'tury [Languages of Slavic Culture], 1999), pp. 165, 168, 302. Later, revised English edition: *Structure and the Whole: East, West and Non-Darwinian Biology in the Origins of Structural Linguistics* (Berlin: Mouton/De Gruyter, 2014).

96  P.V. Logovikov, "*Nauchnye zadachi evraziistva*" [The scientific tasks of Eurasianism], *Tridtsatye gody sb. 1* [*The Thirties, Compilation 1*] (Eurasian Publications, 1931), pp. 56, 59.

A number of scholars have noted that Eurasianism resonated with the German Conservative Revolutionary movement as represented by some of the most prominent Germanic intellectuals of the time. One leading neo-Eurasianist author, to whom we will soon turn, has submitted on this matter:

> A comparison of the ideas of the Russian Eurasianists and the theories of the German Continentalist geopoliticians, who also attempted to construct their own geopolitical theory as an antithesis to the strategy of 'Sea Power', shows that the Germans only went halfway in this direction, whereas with the Russians, first and foremost Savitsky, we are dealing with a complete and consistent, fully-fledged view of the world. In this sense, we can deduce a certain law: The closer the German Continentalists' views came to Russian Eurasianism and the more fully they accepted *Ostorientierung*, the more consistent and logical were their doctrines and their political projects founded on geopolitics effective.[97]

For example, to the German National Bolshevik Ernst Niekisch (1889-1967) belongs the renowned geopolitical thesis of "Europe from Vladivostok to Vlissingen." Among these German thinkers, only this approach harmoniously fits with the consistent continentalism of Eurasianism. The Eurasianists themselves, especially Nikolai Alekseev and Petr Savitsky, affirmed that they were the "founders of a geopolitical approach to Russian history in Russian science."[98] It is well known that Trubetzkoy wanted the foreword to the German edition of his *Europe and Mankind* (published in Munich in 1922 and translated by Roman Jakobson's brother, Sergei Jakobson) to be written by Oswald Spengler.[99] However, there is currently no evidence of contact between the Eurasianists and Spengler, Niekisch, or Ernst Jünger (1895-1998).

---

97  Aleksandr Dugin, *Osnovy geopolitiki* [*Foundations of Geopolitics*] (Moscow: Arktogeia, 1997).

98  Savitsky, *Kontinent Evraziia*, p 126.

99  Krystyna Pomorska, Elżbieta Chodakowska, Hugh McLean, and Brent Vine (eds.), *Language, Poetry and Poetics: The Generation of the 1890s: Jacobson, Trubetzkoy, Majakowskij: Proceedings of the first Jakobson Colloquium Massachusetts Institute of Technology, 5-6 October 1984* (Berlin/New York: Mouton/De Gruyter, 1987).

It has become customary to distinguish from the preceding "classical Eurasianism" the emergence of "neo-Eurasianism" dating from the collapse of the USSR to the present. The latter is taken to include the ideas of the Soviet-era scholar Lev Nikolaevich Gumilev, largely because in the Soviet period in which he was active, Gumilev's ideas were not accessible to the general public and, moreover, could not claim any political-ideological legacy due to the author's imprisonment and disgrace by the Communist Party. Yet, according to Gumilev's own later testimony and in the words of Professor of Geography Sergey Borisovich Lavrov, "Lev Gumilev felt himself to be the successor and continuer of the works of the Eurasianists of the 1920s-'30s, to be rechecking and developing this concept."[100]

Gumilev is most known for his archaeological works on the history of the cultures of the steppes and, in connection with these studies, his complex theory of ethnogenesis. One of Gumilev's main perspectives resonant with the views of the classical Eurasianists was his emphasis on the forest-steppe zone as the ethnogenetic place-development of Eurasia.[101] Gumilev wrote: "The Great Steppe is a geographic totality, inhabited by diverse peoples with different economic structures, religions, social institutions, and more. Nevertheless, all its neighbors have always perceived it as a kind of unified entity, although neither ethnographers, nor historians, nor sociologists have been able to determine the content of the dominant principle."[102] Engaging in fresh archaeological and ethnological studies, Gumilev sought to demonstrate and develop to its logical culmination the

---

100 S.B. Lavrov, "*L.N. Gumilev i evraziistvo*" [L.N. Gumilev and Eurasianism], in *L.N. Gumilev, Ritmy Evrazii: Epokhi i tsivilizatsii* [*The Rhythms of Eurasia: Epochs and Civilizations*] (Moscow: ACT, 2005), p. 14.

101 See: L.N. Gumilev, *Tysiacheletie vokrug Kaspiia* [*The Millennium around the Caspian*] (Moscow: Airis Press, 2004).

102 L.N. Gumilev, *Khunnu: Stepnaia trilogiia* [*The Xiongnu: The Steppe Trilogy*] (Moscow: Kompass, 1993), p. 8. Translation from Marlène Laruelle, *Russian Eurasianism: An Ideology of Empire* (Washington, D.C./Baltimore: Woodrow Wilson Center Press/John Hopkins University Press, 2008), p. 71.

Eurasianist idea that the Great Russian ethnos was not merely a branch of the Eastern Slavs, but the result of a mergence between the Slavs and the predominantly Turkic cultures of the steppes. In Gumilev's thought, the unified diversity of Russia-Eurasia was thus the product of a process which he saw as rare and unique in the history of ethnic relations, namely, the formation of a symbiotic equilibrium or "positive complementarity" between *ethnoi* which yielded a new "super-" or "mega-ethnos." Central to Gumilev's theory of ethnogenesis was the idea of "passionarity," according to which over the course of their evolution ethnoi can reach an "acmatic" phase, when their accumulation of "passionary" energy results in immense feats and transformative developments. For Gumilev, Russia-Eurasia was the product of such "passionarity," and it might be said that he saw in Eurasianism a fresh attempt at understanding the factors and identity of this "passionate" civilizational construct.

In his theorizing of the phases of ethnogenesis and the patterns of ethnic relations, Gumilev emphasized the importance of landscape, meticulously synthesizing the sources of Soviet scholarship to substantiate the Eurasianists' intuitions of the central role of geography in the civilizational development of Eurasia.[103] Moreover, Gumilev saw the ethno-geographical synthesis of Eurasia as having been long established, remarking that "the peoples of Eurasia have up to our time already largely found their territorial state borders, intertwined into various conglomerates of *ethnoi*, and they cannot be arbitrarily severed."[104]

In his archaeological and ethnological works, Gumilev continued the Eurasianists' critique of what he called "the bias of Eurocentrism, according to which the whole world is only a

---

103 See: L.N. Gumilev, *"Etno-landshaftnye regiony Evrazii za istoricheskii period"* [The Ethno-Landscape Regions of Eurasia in the Historical Period"], *Doklady na ezhegodnykh chteniiakh pamiati L.S. Berga* [*Presentations at the Yearly Lectures in Memory of L.S. Berg*] VIII-XIV (Leningrad: 1968), pp. 118-134.

104 L.N. Gumilev, *Chernaia legenda: Druz'ia i nedrugi Velikoi stepi* [*Black Legend: The Friends and Foes of the Great Steppe*] (Moscow: Airis Press, 2006), p. 233.

barbarian periphery of Europe," which Gumilev criticized for dismissing the complex histories and cultures of the ancient and medieval steppes as "savage" and "backwards."[105] Not only did these cultures centrally contribute to shaping Russian-Eurasian identity, but the ethnohistory of Eurasia provides a vivid counterpoint to the unilinear and "exceptionalist" narratives of Eurocentric scholarship. To a definite extent, Gumilev's critique and the attention he devoted to the "Turanian" factor of Eurasia facilitated attraction to Eurasianist ideas outside of Russia, such as Kazakhstan, where he is regarded as a figure of national significance and the largest university in the capital bears his name: Gumilev Eurasian National University. Gumilev held Eurasianism to be particularly promising for the future of scholarship, stating in a 1992 interview: "it is thanks to Eurasianism and to the solid historical training which the Eurasianist theoreticians wielded that it is now possible to integrate such sciences as history, geography, and the natural sciences."[106] Although for the above-mentioned reasons Gumilev abstracted himself from political statements, at the end of his life he would emphasize the geopolitical and civilizational importance of Eurasianism with the following remark:

> The Eurasian thesis is that it is necessary to search not for enemies, of which there are so many anyway, but to seek out friends. This is the most important value in life. It is necessary to seek true allies. The Turks and Mongols can be true friends, but the English, the French, and the Germans, I am convinced, can only be cunning exploiters… If Russia is to be saved, it will be only as a Eurasian power and only through Eurasianism.[107]

Since Gumilev, the most significant contribution to the development of the ideas of Eurasianism has been the work of the Russian philosopher and geopolitician Alexander

---

105 Lev Gumilev, *Drevniaia Rus' i Velikaia step'* [*Ancient Rus' and the Great Steppe*] (Moscow: Eksmo, 2007), p. 404-405.

106 L.N. Gumilev, *"Skazhu Vam po sekretu, chto esli Rossiia budet spasena, to tol'ko kak evraziiskaia derzhava"* ["I'll tell you in secret that if Russia is to be saved, then only as a Eurasian power"] in Alexander Dugin (ed.), *Osnovy evraziistva* [*Foundations of Eurasianism*] (Moscow: Arktogeia, 2002), p. 482.

107 Ibid.

Dugin (1962-). Unlike Gumilev, many of Dugin's works have been of a pronounced political character, as Dugin has sought to formulate an explicit Eurasianist program for the contemporary Russian Federation as well as for reshaping international relations as a whole. In connection with this, Dugin has emerged to be the most prominent (as well as one of the most controversial) thinkers in the Eurasianist line, whose works and activism are inseparable from the recent resurgence of interest in and discourse on Eurasianism in its historical and contemporary experiences.

Dugin's advocacy of Eurasianism began in the early 1990s with the geopolitical journal *Elements*, the publication of numerous books on the cultural and political significance of the Eurasianist school[108], and the holding of lectures and seminars which disseminated Eurasianist thought on an unprecedented scale to both the broader public and Russian military and political circles, culminating in May 2002 in the founding of the political party "Eurasia." Against the backdrop of the indeterminacy of the foreign policy of the Russian Federation, Alexander Dugin proposed a strategic line founded on the geopolitical dichotomy between sea power and land power, Atlanticism and Continentalism, and globalism and Eurasianism. In effect, Dugin's Eurasianist theorizing and activism set the stage for the "rediscovery" of Eurasianist thought and present attempts at translating such into political reality.

In his programmatic work of 1999, *Our Path: Strategic Perspectives of Russia's Development in the Twenty-First Century*, Dugin articulated: "the logically following stage of Russia's state affirmation should be the era of the establishment of a geopolitical Eurasian State of a continental scope."[109] The

---

108 See, for instance, the anthology of classical and neo-Eurasianist texts edited by Dugin: *Osnovy evraziistva* [*Foundations of Eurasianism*] (Moscow: Arktogeia, 2002).

109 Aleksandr Dugin, *Nash put': Strategicheskie perspektivy razvitiia Rossii v XXI veke* [*Our Path: Strategic Perspectives of Russia's Development in the Twenty-First Century*] (Moscow: Arktogeia, 1999), p. 32.

"Eurasian Idea" was thus presented by Dugin as uniting two notions: "the specific uniqueness of Russian civilization, and a grand project for the creative affirmation of the whole span of the civilizational tendencies of the peoples of Eurasia (and, more broadly, the whole world) aspiring to uphold their own truths in the face of the leveling globalist offensive." "The new Eurasianism," Dugin put forth, "embodies the eternal Russian will toward a universal ideal, toward the realization of a lofty salvational mission to affirm the ideals of Good and Justice."[110] For this strategic Eurasian vision for Russia, Dugin proposed a political model integrating some of the key programmatic points of Eurasianist thought, advocating:

- the principle of organic democracy;

- the establishment of Eurasian centrism out of the unification of "left" and "right" elements (including a socially-oriented economy from the left spectrum and the conservatism of the right);

- federalism as opposed to the nation-state idea;

- economic pluralism and an autarkic, multi-layered economic system;

- a Eurasian financial system with the aim of gaining independence from the dollar;

- modernization without Westernization;

- a paternalistic model featuring an active role for the state in Eurasian integration;

- integration at varying paces;

- the establishment of a Eurasian civilizational trajectory through participation in planetary geo-economic processes;

- the preservation of the diversity of cultural heritages on the principle of "blossoming complexity";

- transitioning to the concept of "rights of peoples"

---

110 Ibid, p. 89.

or "rights of communities" instead of the Western individualistic philosophy of "human rights";

– an alliance of traditional religions;

– maintaining a positive or zero demographic balance with the aim of preventing the disappearance of *ethnoi*.

In his subsequent 2002 work, *The Eurasian Path as a National Idea*, Dugin expanded the Eurasianist vision thusly:

> By virtue of its geography, Russia is placed at the center of the continental landmass and has no other prospect than to serve as an axis for the consolidation of all state powers, civilizations, and cultures of a continental, land-based, Eurasian character... Eurasian civilization represents the antithesis to the Atlanticist civilization that is in its foundations the sum of the logic of the complex historical ensemble that was previously identified with Europe... The Eurasian project boils down to the consistent affirmation of the following geopolitical truth: reducing the diversity of cultures and civilizations to a single unifying model goes against nature. Every culture and every people has reason and the right to follow their own historical paths.[111]

In no small part in connection with Dugin's works, neo-Eurasianism has come to be considered a non-Western theory of international relations, one which has even begun to be developed and implemented as policy by several states since the 1980s and '90s. In Russia, the continued development of the ideas of classical Eurasianism has thus come to be seen in retrospect as an "indigenous" or "domestic" Russian theory based on an interdisciplinary approach. This underscores both the broad conceptual legacy of Eurasianism as well as its potential for practical implementation in the present and future.

However, the fact cannot be avoided that Eurasianism has largely not been understood in the West. Partially because of this, Eurasianism has remained unrevealed in all of its potential and subjected to targeted criticism, marginalization, and demonization under various pretexts. Such criticism generally

---

111 Aleksandr Dugin, *Evraziiskii put' kak natsional'naia ideia* [*The Eurasian Path as a National Idea*] (Moscow: Arktogeia, 2002), pp. 18, 46, 90.

comes from those sources and prejudiced authors who support the very neo-liberalism that has since been discredited on a global scale and whose core problematic presumptions have been profoundly deconstructed by the Eurasian perspective.

Nevertheless, it is likely that we are living in the era in which Eurasianism is destined to reveal and establish itself. As Petr Savitsky's son, the historian Ivan Savitsky, recalled his father saying, Eurasianism has the future ahead of it.[112] Perhaps the 20th century was not ready for such an at once innovative and conservative philosophy and the ideas of the first Eurasianists were ahead of their time. Now, however, the time has come to reconsider the ideas of the past century and to attentively study the numerous perspectives offered by Eurasianist authors who, after all, constituted a network encompassing nearly all of Europe, and even in cases in which there were no full branches or cells, Eurasianist ideas were still transmitted into the social environment, inspiring and encouraging critical and unconventional thinking. The 21st century might very well see the practical realization of Eurasianism in the spirit of the times.

*** 

---

112 Elena Patlatiya, "*O krivykh zerkalakh s I.P. Savitskim*" [On distorting mirrors with I.P. Savitsky], *Radio Prague International* (13/5/2005).

# EUROPE AND MANKIND

(selected excerpts)

## Nikolai Trubetzkoy[113]

...It is obvious that a shift has occurred in the thinking of many educated people. The Great War, and especially the ensuing "peace" (which to this day must still be written in quotes), shattered faith in "civilized humanity" and opened the eyes of many. We Russians, of course, find ourselves in a special position. We have been witnesses to just how abruptly that which we called "Russian culture" has collapsed. Many of us were struck by the speed and ease with which this was accomplished, and many have pondered the causes of this phenomenon. Perhaps the present pamphlet will help some of my compatriots to sort out their own considerations on this subject. Some of my points could have been abundantly illustrated with examples from Russian history and Russian reality, which would have rendered this exposition perhaps more intriguing and lively, but the clarity of the overall outline would, of course, suffer at the hands of such digressions. Meanwhile, in presenting the reader with relatively new thoughts, I value most of all that they are presented in the most clear and consistent form. Moreover, my thoughts concern not only Russians, but all other peoples which in one way or another have received European culture while being neither Romanic nor Germanic in their heritage...

...Any recognition of the correctness of the theses expounded in the present pamphlet obliges one to engage in further work. In adopting these theses, they must be

---

113 Pamphlet first published in 1920 by the Bulgarian-Russian Publishing House in Sofia, Bulgaria.

developed and concretized in application to reality, while a number of questions which have been and continue to be posed by life must be reconsidered from this point of view. Many people are now engaged in a "revaluation of values" in one way or another. Those who accept the positions I am defending will understand them to be one indication of the route such a revaluation should take. There is no doubt that the work which arises from adopting these main theses, both theoretical and practical, must be collective. One can toss out a certain thought or raise a certain banner on their own, but developing a whole system based on this thought and applying it in practice should be the work of many. I call all those who share my convictions to this collective work. I have been convinced that there are such people thanks to several coincidental meetings, they need only to rally together to engage in amicable cooperative work. If my pamphlet serves as an impetus or means for this unification, I will consider my aim to have been achieved...

## I.

The positions which any European might take on the national question are quite numerous, but all of them fall between two extremes: chauvinism on the one hand, and cosmopolitanism on the other. Any nationalism is, as it were, a synthesis of elements of chauvinism and cosmopolitanism, the experience of reconciling these two opposites. There is no doubt that for a European, chauvinism and cosmopolitanism are precisely opposites, and fundamentally different points of view from one another.

However, it is impossible to agree with such a formulation of the question. It is enough to look more attentively into chauvinism and cosmopolitanism in order to notice that there is fundamentally no radical difference between them, and that these are no more than two steps, two different aspects of one and the same phenomenon.

58

A chauvinist proceeds from the a priori position that the best of the world's peoples is none other than his own. The culture created by his people is better, more perfect than all others. To his people alone belongs the right to excel and dominate other nations, which should obey it, accept its faith, language, and culture, and merge with it. Everything that stands in the way of the ultimate triumph of this great nation must be swept away by force, the chauvinist believes, and he acts accordingly.

A cosmopolitan denies any difference between nationalities. If there are differences, then they should be eliminated. Civilized mankind ought to be united and have a single culture. Non-civilized peoples should accept this culture, join it and, entering the family of civilized peoples, go with them along the singular path of world progress. Civilization is the highest blessing, in the name of which national peculiarities must be sacrificed.

In this formulation, chauvinism and cosmopolitanism indeed seem to differ from each other. The first postulates the dominance of the culture of one ethnographic-anthropological species, while the second postulates the dominance of a culture above and beyond ethnographic humanity.

However, let us look at just what substance European cosmopolitans impart to the terms "civilization" and "civilized mankind." They understand "civilization" to be the culture jointly developed by the Romanic and Germanic peoples of Europe. By civilized peoples they mean, once again, first and foremost the Romanic and Germanic peoples, and then those other peoples which have adopted European culture.

Thus, we can see that the culture which, in the opinion of cosmopolitans, should dominate the world and abolish all other cultures is the very same culture of that ethnographic-anthropological unit whose dominance is the dream of the chauvinist. There is no fundamental difference here. In fact, the national, ethnographic-anthropological, and linguistic unity of any one people of Europe is only relative. Each of these peoples is a combination of different, smaller ethnic groups with their own dialectical, cultural, and anthropological particularities, tied together by kinship and a common history that has yielded a certain common stock of cultural values for all of them. Thus, in proclaiming his people the crown of creation and the sole bearer of all possible perfections, the chauvinist is in fact championing a whole group of ethnic units. If that were not enough, the chauvinist also wants other peoples to merge with his own and lose their national physiognomy. The chauvinist will treat all peoples who have already lost their national character and assimilated the language, faith, and culture of his people as if they truly are his own. Of course, he will only praise their contributions to his people if they have truly assimilated the spirit to which he is sympathetic and have managed to completely abandon their former national psychology. Chauvinists will always treat those assimilated by the dominant people with suspicion, especially if their communion was accomplished only recently. But no chauvinist will reject them in principle, as we know that even among European chauvinists there are quite a few peoples whose own surnames and anthropological traits clearly show that they do not descend from or fully belong to the people whose domination they so ardently preach.

If we now take the European cosmopolitan, we see that, in essence, he is no different from the chauvinist. The "civilization" and culture which he holds highest and before which, in his opinion, all other cultures ought to be swept away, also represents a certain stock of cultural values shared by several peoples connected by bonds of kinship and common history. Just as the chauvinist looks past the particular characteristics of the individual ethnic groups which make up his people, so the cosmopolitan rejects the cultural particularities of individual Romano-Germanic peoples, taking only that which fits into their common cultural stock. He also recognizes as a cultural value the activities of those non-Romano-Germanics who have fully received Romano-Germanic civilization, abandoned everything in themselves that contradicts the spirit of this civilization, and exchanged their national physiognomy for the pan-Romano-Germanic one. This is exactly like the chauvinist's acceptance as his "own" those strangers and foreigners who have managed to completely assimilate to the dominant people! Even the hostility experienced by cosmopolitans toward chauvinists and generally to those principles that separate the culture of individual Romano-Germanic peoples has a parallel in the worldview of the chauvinists. More specifically, chauvinists are always hostile toward any attempts at separatism among individual parts of their people. They try to erase and obscure all those local peculiarities that might violate the unity of their people.

The chauvinists and the cosmopolitans are thus completely parallel. They are in essence one and the same approach in the culture of the ethnographic-anthropological unit to which this person belongs. The only difference lies in the fact that the chauvinist takes a tighter ethnic group than the cosmopolitan, but in so doing, he still takes a group that is not homogenous, and the cosmopolitan, for his part, still takes a definite ethnic group. Thus, the difference is only one of degree, not principle.

In evaluating European cosmopolitanism, it is always necessary to remember that the words "mankind," "universal human civilization," and others of the sort are extremely inaccurate expressions behind which hide very particular ethnographic concepts. European culture is not the culture of mankind. It is the product of the history of a particular ethnic group. The Germanic and Celtic tribes, which were subject in varying proportions to the influence of Roman culture and which mixed together heavily, created a way of life out of elements of their national culture and Roman culture. By virtue of their common ethnographic and geographical conditions, they long shared a common existence in their everyday life and history, and thanks to constant interaction with one another, the common elements were so significant that the sense of Romano-Germanic unity always lived in them unconsciously. Over time, as is the case with so many other peoples, they developed a thirst to study the sources of their culture. Encountering the monuments of Roman and Greek culture brought to the surface the idea of a supra-national, global civilization, an idea which was peculiar to the Greco-Roman world. We know that this idea was based, yet again, on ethnographic-geographical grounds. In Rome, of course, the "whole world" was understood as *Orbis terrarum*, i.e., the peoples inhabiting the Mediterranean basin or those drawn to this sea who, in constant contact with each other, developed a number of common cultural values and ultimately united under the leveling effect of Greek and Roman colonization and Roman military dominance. At any rate, these ancient cosmopolitan ideas have been made into the foundation of education in Europe. Having found themselves on favorable ground for an unconscious sense of Romano-German unity, they gave rise to the theoretical foundations of so-called European "cosmopolitanism," which it would be more correct to call open pan-Romano-Germanic chauvinism.

These are the real historical grounds of European cosmopolitan theories. The psychological foundation of this cosmopolitanism is the very same as that of chauvinism. This is a variation of that unconscious prejudice, that particular psychology that is most accurately referred to as egocentrism. A person with a pronounced egocentric psychology unconsciously considers himself to be the center of the universe, the crown of creation, the best and most perfect of all beings. In comparing any two other beings, that which is closer and more like him is better, and that which is more distant, worse... To one extent or another, no one is free from this psychology. Science itself is not yet completely free of it, and any conquest of science for the sake of emancipation from egocentric prejudices presents the greatest difficulty...

Yet as soon as all of this reaches the consciousness of the sensitive and conscientious Romano-German man we have supposed, a collision takes place in his soul. The entirety of his spiritual culture and worldview are founded on the belief that

62

the unconscious life of the soul, and all the prejudices founded on it, should give way to the instructions of reason and logic, and that only on logical scientific grounds can any theories be built. His whole consciousness of justice is based on the rejection of any principles preventing free interaction between people. All of his ethics reject the resolution of issues by brute force... and suddenly it turns out that cosmopolitanism is based on egocentrism! Cosmopolitanism, this pinnacle of Romano-Germanic civilization, rests on foundations which radically contradict all of its central tenets. At the heart of cosmopolitanism, this universal-human religion, turns out to be an anti-cultural element: egocentrism. This situation is tragic, but there is a way out: the conscientious Romano-German must forever renounce both chauvinism and so-called cosmopolitanism, and consequently, all the views on the national question which occupy a middle position between these two extremes.

But what position toward European chauvinism and cosmopolitanism can be taken by those non-Roman-Germanic peoples, by the representatives of peoples which have not participated since the very beginning in the creation of so-called European civilization?...

European cosmopolitanism, which, as we have seen above, is no different from pan-Romano-Germanic chauvinism, is spreading among non-Romano-Germanic peoples with great rapidity and altogether negligible difficulties. There are already very many such cosmopolitans among the Slavs, Arabs, Turks, Indians, Chinese, and Japanese. Many of them are even more orthodox than their European brethren in their rejection of national characteristics, in their disdain for any non-Romano-Germanic culture, and so on.

What explains this contradiction? Why does pan-Romano-Germanic chauvinism have such undisputed success among the Slavs when even the slightest suggestion of Germanophilic propaganda is enough to make Slavs wary?

**63**

Why does the Russian intellectual indignantly reject the notion that they might be serving as a tool of German Junker nationalists while fearing subjugation to pan-romano-Germanic chauvinists? The answer to this riddle lies, of course, in the hypnosis of words...

The spread of so-called European cosmopolitanism among non-Romano-Germanic peoples is the product of pure misunderstanding. Those who have succumbed to the propaganda of Romano-Germanic chauvinists have been misled by words such as "mankind," "universal-humanity," "civilization," "world progress," and others. All of these words have been understood literally, whereas in actuality, very particular and altogether narrow ethnographic concepts hide behind them.

The "intellectuals" of non-Romano-Germanic peoples who have been duped by the Romano-Germanics must understand their mistake. They must understand that the culture which has been presented to them under the guise of universal human civilization is in fact merely the culture of a particular ethnic group of Romanic and Germanic peoples. This insight should, of course, significantly change their attitude toward the culture of their own people and compel them to think about whether they were right to impose a foreign culture upon their people and uproot features of a unique national identity in the name of "universal human" (which are, in fact, Romano-Germanic, i.e., foreign) ideals. They can resolve this question only upon maturely and logically examining the Romano-Germanic pretensions to being called "civilized mankind." Romano-Germanic culture can be accepted or not only upon the resolution of a whole number of questions, namely:

1. Is it possible to objectively prove that the culture of the Romano-Germanics is more perfect than all other cultures currently or once existing on Earth?

2. Is it possible for a people to fully assimilate to a culture developed by another people without the anthropological mixing of both peoples?

3. Is assimilation to European culture (as far as such is possible) a blessing or an evil?

Whoever is aware of the essence of European cosmopolitanism as pan-Romano-Germanic chauvinism is obliged to raise these questions. Only with an affirmative answer to all of these questions can universal Europeanization be recognized as necessary and desirable. In the case of a negative answer, this Europeanization should be rejected and new questions should be posed:

4. Is universal Europeanization inevitable?

5. How can one fight its negative consequences?...

## II.

We have already pointed out the fact that recognizing Romano-Germanic culture to be the most perfect of all cultures ever existing on Earth is founded on an egocentric psychology. As is well known, in Europe, the notion of the highest perfection of European civilization is alleged to be based on a scientific foundation, but the scientific nature of this foundation is only apparent. The fact is that the notion of evolution that exists in European ethnology, anthropology, and the history of culture is itself permeated with egocentrism. The "evolutionary ladder," the "stages of development" - all of these concepts are deeply egocentric. At their heart lies the notion that the development of the human race has and is proceeding along the path of so-called world progress. This path is thought of as a straight line. Humanity has proceeded along this straight line while individual peoples have stopped at different points and continue to stand at these points as if stagnating in place, while other peoples have succeeded in advancing somewhat further, stopping and "stagnating" at a subsequent point, and so on... Modern humanity as a whole is thus presented as a kind of developed and dismembered cinematography of evolution, and the cultures of diverse peoples differ from one another like different phases of general evolution, different stages of the universal path of world progress...

As a result, we are presented with a "ladder of the evolution of mankind." At the peak stand the Romano-Germanics and those peoples which have fully accepted their culture. A rung lower stand those "cultured peoples of antiquity," i.e., those peoples whose cultures came close to and exhibit similarities to Europeans. Further down are those cultured peoples of Asia, whose literacy, statehood, and other cultural factors allow them to be seen as similar to the Romano-Germanics to some degree. The same goes for the "old cultures of America" (e.g. Mexico, Peru): these cultures are somewhat less similar to Romano-Germanic culture and accordingly are placed somewhat lower on the evolutionary ladder. Yet all the peoples mentioned to this point harbor in their cultures a number of features with external similarities to the Romano-Germanics for which they are awarded the flattering title "cultured." Below them stand those "little-cultured" peoples and, finally, at the very bottom are the "uncultured," the "savages," i.e., those members of the human race who bear the least resemblance to the modern Romano-Germanics...

Like any culture, European culture has constantly changed and arrived at its modern state only gradually as the result of a long process of evolution. In each historical era, this culture has been somewhat different. Moreover, it is natural that in the epochs closer to the present, the culture of Europeans was closer to its present state than in more distant epochs. In these epochs, the culture of the ancestors of Europeans represented the maximum difference from modernity. Yet all cultures which maximally differ from modern European civilization are invariably treated by European scholars as belonging to a general group of "primitives." Therefore, naturally, the culture of the distant ancestors of the modern Romano-Germanics also fall under the same rubric. No positive conclusion can be derived from this. In view of the negativity of the notion of "primitive culture," the fact that the epithet "primitive" is applied by European scholars both to the culture of the Romano-Germanics' ancient ancestors and to the culture of modern Eskimos and Kaffirs does not mean that these cultures were identical to one another, but only that they are all equally dissimilar to modern European civilization...

We are told to compare the intellectual baggage of the cultured European with that of a Bushman, Botocudo, or Vedda, and that the superiority of the first over the second is clear. We, however, argue that what seems obvious is merely subjective. As soon as we take upon ourselves the labor of looking into the matter conscientiously and without prejudice, this obviousness disappears. A savage, a good savage hunter, possessing all the qualities his tribe appreciates in a person (and only such a savage can be compared with a real cultural European), keeps in his mind a huge reserve of all kinds of knowledge and information. He has perfectly studied the life of the nature surrounding him, he knows all the habits of the animals and those subtleties of their everyday life which escape the inquisitive gaze of the most attentive European naturalist. All of this knowledge is kept in the savage's mind not in chaotic disorder, but systematically, albeit not in accordance with the templates set by European scholars, but rather other, more convenient and practical templates pertinent to the life of a hunter. In addition to this practical-scientific knowledge, the mind of the savage contains what is often a complex mythology of his tribe, its codex of morals, rules, and regulations of etiquette, which are at times highly complex, as well as, finally, a more or less significant stock of the works of his people's oral literature. In a word, the head of the savage is "stuffed" thoroughly, despite the fact that the material "stuffing" it is completely different from that which fills the head of the European. By virtue of the heterogeneity between the materials of the mental lives of the savage and the European, their respective intellectual baggage should be recognized as incomparable and incommensurable, hence why the question of the superiority of one over the other must be considered insoluble.

They point out that European culture is in many respects more complex than the culture of a savage. However, that unbalanced ratio between the two cultures is not apparent in every aspect. Cultured Europeans pride themselves on the refinement of their manners and the subtlety of their politeness, but there is no doubt that the rules of etiquette and the conventions of communal life among many savages are much more complex and developed in detail than those of Europeans, not to mention that this code of good manner is obeyed by all members of the "savage" tribe without exception, whereas good manners are reserved only for the upper classes among Europeans. Moreover, in terms of preoccupation with appearance, "savages" often manifest much more complexity than many Europeans: we might recall the complex tattoo techniques of Australians and Polynesians or the most complex hairstyles of African beauties. Even if all of these complexities can be attributed to impractical eccentricity, there are still in the lives of some 'savages' various undoubtedly practical institutions which are far more complex than those of their European counterparts. Take, for instance, approaches to sexual life, family and marriage law. In Romano-Germanic civilization, this question has been elementarily resolved with the monogamous family which exists officially and is protected by law, while alongside it proceeds unbridled sexual freedom which society and the state theoretically condemn but de facto allow. Compare this with the detailed institution of group marriages among Australians, where sexual life is subjected to the strictest frameworks amidst which, in the absence of individual marriage, measures are nonetheless taken to provide for children and prevent incest.

Generally speaking, greater or lesser complexity says nothing of the degree of perfection of a culture. Evolution just as often moves in the direction of simplification as it does toward complication. Therefore, the degree of complexity can in no way serve as a measure of progress. Europeans are well aware of this and apply this measure only when it is convenient for the purposes of self-praise. In those cases where another culture, for example, the same culture of savages, is in some aspect more complex than the Europeans, the Europeans not only do not consider this great complexity a measure of progress, but even declare on the contrary that in this case, the complexity is a sign of "primitiveness"! This is how European science interprets the above-mentioned cases: the complex etiquette of savages, their concern for complex body decoration, and even the crafty system of Australian group marriage are all revealed to be manifestations of a low degree of culture... Much of what is held in modern Europe to be the final call of civilization or the height of still unreached progress can be found among savages, only to then be declared a sign of extreme primitiveness. The futuristic pictures drawn by Europeans are held to be signs of the high refinement of aesthetic taste, while altogether similar works by "savages" are naive attempts and the first awakenings of primitive art. Socialism, Communism, anarchism, and all "bright ideals of imminent higher progress," are only such when professed by the modern European. When these "ideals" are found realized in the everyday life of savages, they are immediately designated to be manifestations of primitive savagery.

There is not and cannot be any objective evidence of the superiority of the European over savages, because, in the comparison of different cultures, Europeans know only one measure: what is similar to us is better and more perfect than that which is different.

If Europeans are no more perfect than savages, then the evolutionary ladder of which we spoke at the beginning of this chapter must collapse. If its top is no higher than its base, then obviously its base is no higher than any of the rungs between it. Instead of a ladder, we have a horizontal plane. Instead of the principle of a gradation of peoples and cultures by degrees of perfection, we have a new principle of the equivalence and qualitative incommensurability of all cultures and peoples of the globe. The moment of evaluation must be banished once and for all from ethnology, the history of culture, and all evolutionary sciences, for such evaluations are always based on egocentrism. There are no higher and lower cultures, there are only similar and dissimilar. To declare those similar to us to be higher and those dissimilar to be lower is arbitrary, unscientific, naive, and, in the end, simply foolish. Only by fully overcoming this deeply ingrained egocentric prejudice and banishing its consequences from the very methodologies and theses constructed on it can the European evolutionary sciences, particularly ethnology, anthropology, and the history of culture, become real scientific disciplines. Until then, they are, at best, a means of deceiving people and justifying the imperialist, colonial policies and vandalistic Kulturträgerism of the "great powers" of Europe and America in the eyes of the Romano-Germanics and their stooges.

Thus, the first of the above-posed questions - "Is it possible to objectively prove that the culture of the Romano-Germanics is more perfect than all other cultures currently or once existing on Earth?" - must be answered in the negative.

## III.

Now let us undertake to answer the question of whether it is possible for a people to fully assimilate to a culture developed by another people. By full adherence, we mean a people assimilating a foreign culture to such an extent that it begins to see this foreign culture as its own, after which any further development occurs completely parallel to the developments of the culture it is borrowing from, to the point that the two merge into a single cultural whole.

In order to answer the question, one must know the laws of the life and development of a culture... The life and development of any culture consists of the continuous emergence of new cultural values. We understand "cultural value" to mean any purposeful creation of man that has become the common heritage of his compatriots. This can be a legal norm, an artistic production, an institution, a technological device, or a scientific or philosophical position insofar as all of these things meet certain physical or spiritual needs or are adopted by all or a part of a given people for the satisfaction of these needs. The emergence of any new cultural value can be termed with the general name "discovery" ("invention" in Tarde's terms). Each invention is a combination of two or more existing cultural values or their various elements, but the new invention is indissoluble into these component parts and contains a certain additional element in the form of, firstly, the means of the combination itself, and secondly, the imprint of the personality of the creator. Upon emergence, an invention is spread among other people by way of "imitation" (also Tarde's term), in which case this word should be understood in the broadest possible sense, starting with the reproduction of the cultural value itself or the reproduction of the means to satisfy a given need with the aid of this value, up to "sympathetic imitation," i.e. submission to the established norm, the assimilation of the given provision assumed to be true, or reverence for the dignity of the produced work. In the process of imitation, this novelty can encounter and enter into contradiction with other already recognized cultural values, in which case a battle for primacy ensues between them (Tarde's *duel logique*), as a result of which one of these values replaces the other. Only upon overcoming these obstacles and spreading to the entire social whole through imitation does such an invention become a fact of social life and an element of the culture. At any given moment, culture represents the sum of recognized inventions of the current and preceding generations of a given people. Thus, the essence of the development and life of culture boils down to two elementary processes: invention and propagation, along with the optional but nearly unavoidable "battle for recognition" (*duel logique*)…

Now let us try to clearly envision those conditions which are necessary for the continuous emergence of inventions, or, in other words, the development of culture. First of all, this requires the existence in the consciousness of a given cultural environment the entire stock of cultural values that have already been created and which have passed through the stage of struggle. This is necessary, firstly, because, as said above and in accordance with the principle of ex nihilo nihil fit, any new invention is always composed of elements from already existing cultural values. In addition, with the aim of satisfying a certain need, any new invention simultaneously triggers new needs or modifies old ones, thus making it necessary to search for new paths for the satisfaction of these new needs; all this makes it absolutely necessary to closely connect the new inventions with the already existing common stock of cultural property. This common stock of cultural values, or, in other words, the inventory of culture, must, for successful further development, be transmitted by way of tradition, i.e. every young generation must assimilate by means of imitating elders the culture in which the previous generation matured and which, in turn, the present generation has received from its predecessors. For each generation, the culture obtained by way of tradition is the starting point for further inventions, and this circumstance is one of the indispensable conditions for the continuity and organic development of culture. Finally, besides tradition, the most important role in the development of culture is played by heredity (a factor underestimated by Tarde). Heredity complements tradition and through it the tastes, predispositions, and temperaments of those who created cultural values in the past are transmitted from generation to generation, which contributes to the organic character of all of the development of culture. Of necessity to the propagation of inventions, which constitutes an equally essential part of development, are the very same conditions necessary for the emergence of such inventions. The presence of a common stock of cultural values is necessary in view of the fact that this stock determines the needs which an invention must meet and, meanwhile, an invention can be instilled only if the need which brought it to life is there already and precisely in the exact same form for both the inventor and society... But the presence of this identical stock of cultural values is not yet in itself sufficient for this. It is important for all of these values and their elements in the consciousness of both society and the inventor to be positioned in approximately the same way so that their interrelations are the same in the consciousness of one and the other, and this is possible only under the condition of there being one tradition. Finally, in order for an invention to be adopted by all or the majority, it is necessary that the tastes, predispositions, and temperament of the creator not contradict the mental mode of society, and this requires uniform heredity.

Following these preliminary reasonings from the field of general sociology, we can move to resolve the question of interest to us about the possibility of an entire people being fully assimilated into a foreign culture. Before us are two peoples, say people A and people B, each of which has its own culture (for without culture in the above-defined sense no people is conceivable), and these two cultures are different from one another. Now let us assume that people A borrows the culture of people B. The question is: can this culture continue in the same direction, spirit, and pace on soil A as on soil B? We know that this requires that A, in its borrowing, receives the same common cultural values, tradition, and heredity of B. However, none of these three are actually possible to receive. Even if people A immediately borrows from B the entire inventory of B's culture, both peoples' stocks of cultural values will not be the same, because A will adjoin to the stock of B, especially at first, the inventory of the former culture of A which was absent in the case of B. In the first period after such borrowing, this remainder of the former national culture will always continue to be alive, even if only in the memory of people A, no matter how diligently this culture has been uprooted. Because of this, the tradition of people A will turn out to be completely different than that of people B. Finally, heredity cannot be borrowed without the anthropological mixing of A and B, and even given such mixing the heredity of the hybrid A and B will be different than that of B itself. Thus, in the first period after borrowing, the conditions of people B's

73

cultural life will be completely different on the soil of people A than on the native soil of people B.

These first steps of culture being transferred onto new soil turn out to be fateful for further development. The lack of organic tradition will make itself felt in a most decisive way... As a result, the entire culture of people A will come to be based on the mixed tradition of two cultures, which means that any total cultural overlap between peoples A and B will nonetheless still fail. Finally, this is often complicated by differences in geographical conditions (for example, matters of attire) and anthropological types. Thus, it must be recognized that the complete assimilation of one people to a culture created by another people is an impossible matter...

Thus, the second of the above posed questions, "Is it possible for a people to fully assimilate to a culture developed by another people without the anthropological mixing of both peoples?," must also be answered in the negative.

## IV.

The third question asks: "Is assimilation to European culture (as far as such is possible) a blessing or an evil?" This question demands more precise framing in connection with the already obtained answers to the first two questions. First of all, we already know that Romano-Germanic culture is objectively not higher nor more perfect than any other culture, and secondly, that full assimilating to another culture is possible only under the condition of anthropological mixing with this people... any people which does not anthropologically mix with the Romano-Germanics cannot fully Europeanize, i.e. fully assimilate to Romano-Germanic culture.

However, we also know that despite this impossibility, many such peoples nevertheless strive with all their might toward assimilation and Europeanization. It is these peoples whom our question concerns: we ought to clarify the consequences which follow this aspiration for Europeanization and determine whether it is beneficial or desirable from their point of view...

Now let us substitute B with the Romano-Germanics and A with a Europeanizing non-Romano-Germanic people and take note of the special features which result from this position. The most significant features are introduced by that trait of the Romano-Germanics and their culture which we have characterized as egocentrism. The Romano-Germanic holds himself and everything identical to him to be higher, and everything that differs to be lower. In the field of culture, he recognizes as valuable only that which does or may constitute an element of his own modern culture, while all the rest has no value or is assessed by degree of proximity and similarity to the corresponding elements of his own culture. A Europeanized people or a people aspiring toward Europeanization is infected by this trait of the Romano-Germanic psyche but, not realizing its true egocentric lining, does not put itself in the place of the European, instead evaluating everything, including itself, its people, and its culture, from the Romano-Germanic point of view...

It is not difficult to understand what consequences all of this leads to. For the reasons described above, in any given span of time, a Europeanized people will manage to create only a small quantity of cultural values which can be adopted by other peoples of European culture. In the same period of time, the native Romano-Germanics will create many such values, and since all of them enter the common stock of Romano-Germanic culture and thereby acquire indisputable authority, the Europeanized people in question will have to accept them as well. Thus, this people will always receive more than it will give. Its cultural import will always exceed cultural exports, and this alone will put it in a dependent position in relation to the native Romano-Germanics.

In addition, it cannot go without note that the preponderance of imports over exports and the differences in the psychic heredity of the Europeanized people and the Romano-Germanics create extremely difficult conditions for the former in the assimilation and propagation of new inventions. The Romano-Germanics will generally assimilate only those inventions which bear the imprint of the common Romano-Germanic national psychology transmitted by way of heredity and tradition. They can simply discard everything that contradicts this psychology and brand it with the epithet of "barbarism." The Europeanized people finds itself in a different position: it is guided not by its own, but by the foreign Romano-Germanic national psychology and, without blinking, should accept everything that is created by or holds value for the original Romano-Germanics, even if this contradicts this people's national psychology or poorly fits their consciousness. This, of course, makes it difficult to assimilate and propagate imported inventions, given that such inventions, as we know, will always outnumber the Europeanized people's native ones. Needless to say, such constant difficulties in the field of assimilating inventions must have an extremely harmful impact on the economy of national forces of the Europeanized people, which already has to expend much labor on the unproductive work of reconciling two heterogeneous cultures... and developing the remnants of its own national culture...

All of these hindrances in cultural work are far from exhausting the disadvantage of the position of the Europeanized people. One of the most severe consequences of Europeanization is the destruction of national unity and the dismemberment of the national body of the Europeanized people. We have seen above that in borrowing from a foreign culture, each new generation must develop its own mixture, its own canon of the synthesis of elements of national and foreign culture. Thus, each generation of a people which has borrowed a foreign culture lives in accordance with its own particular culture, and therefore the differences between "fathers" and "children" will always be sharper than that among a people with a homogenous national culture. In addition to this, it is a very rare occurrence for a whole people to be subjected to Europeanization at once, to the point that the entire people equally embraces Romano-Germanic culture. This can happen only if the people in question is very small and poorly differentiated. Europeanization by and large proceeds from above to the bottom, first encompassing the social elite, the aristocracy, the urban population, and particular professions, and only then gradually spreads to the rest of a people. The process of this propagation is, of course, quite slow, and over its course a whole number of generations replace one another... Thus, at any given moment, different parts of the Europeanized people (different classes, estates, and professions) represent different stages of the assimilation of Romano-Germanic culture, different types of combinations of the elements of national and foreign culture in different proportions. These classes are not parts of a single national whole, but separate cultural units, as if they were separate peoples with their own cultures, traditions, habits, notions, and languages. Social, material, and professional differences among the Europeanized people are much sharper than among the native Romano-Germanics, precisely because they are adjoined by ethnographic and cultural differences.

The negative consequences of this phenomenon make themselves felt in the life of the Europeanized people at every step. The dismemberment of the nation aggravates class struggle and makes it more difficult to move from one class of society to another. This disunion of parts of the Europeanized people further hinders the propagation of innovations and inventions and obstructs cooperation between all parts of the people in cultural work. In a word, conditions are created which inevitably weaken the Europeanized people and put it in an extremely disadvantageous position in comparison to that of the native Romano-Germanics. Thus, the social life and cultural development of the Europeanized people are furnished with difficulties that are completely unknown to the native Romano-Germanics...

As a result, this people can always be seen as "backward" from the European point of view, and is forced to look at itself in exactly the same manner. By adopting European culture, it also embraces European standards for the assessment of culture... In comparing itself to the native Romano-Germanics, the Europeanized people comes to be aware of the former's superiority over itself, and this consciousness, together with constant lamentation over its inertia and backwardness, gradually leads to this people ceasing to respect itself. In studying its history, this people evaluates itself from the point of view of the native European: everything in its history which contradicts European culture is seen as an evil, an index of inertia and backwardness, while the highest points are when decisive turns toward Europe took place. Throughout the course of this history, everything that is taken from Europe is considered progress, while any deviation from European norms is seen as reaction. This people gradually learns to despise everything that is its own, unique, and national. If we add to this the above-mentioned dismemberment of the national body and the weakening of social ties between individual parts of this body as a consequence of the lack of a single culture and common cultural language, it becomes clear that the patriotism of a Europeanized people is always extremely poorly developed. The patriotism and national pride of such a people is the lot of mere individuals, and national self-assertion is by and large reduced to the ambitions of rulers and leading political circles...

All of these negative consequences are hinged upon the very fact of Europeanization: the degree of Europeanization plays no role. We know that with each generation the elements of the old "native" culture recede more and more into the background, so that over the course of time, the people striving toward Europeanization ultimately do so completely, which is to say, it obtains a culture consisting exclusively of elements of Romano-Germanic origin. This process is extremely long, especially since it proceeds very unevenly among the different parts and social groups of the Europeanized people. But even when this process is fully completed, the Europeanized people will still always have predispositions in its national psyche which have not been uprooted and have been transmitted by heredity, and these predispositions, differing from the elements of the innate psyche of the Romano-Germanics, will still, on the one hand, interfere with the fruitful creative work of this people and, on the other, prevent the successful and rapid assimilation of new cultural values created by native Romano-Germanics. Thus, even upon achieving the maximal degree of Europeanization, this people, already delayed in its development thanks to the long and difficult process of the gradual cultural leveling of all of its parts and the uprooting of the remnants of its national culture, will still be on unequal footing with the Romano-Germanics, and will continue to "lag behind." The fact that this people fatefully entered the zone of obligatory cultural exchange and interaction with the Romano-Germanics at the very beginning of its Europeanization makes its "backwardness" a fatal law.

However, there is no way to reconcile with this "law." Peoples who do not counteract this "backwardness" quickly become the victims of the neighboring or distant Romano-Germanic people, which deprives this lagging member of the "family of civilized peoples" of economic and then political independence, engages in its shameless exploitation, and extracts all of its vitality, turning it into mere "ethnographic material." Those who wish to fight against this law of perpetual backwardness will face an equally sad fate. In order to guard themselves from foreign danger, the "lagging" Europeanized people will have to, at the very least, maintain its military and industrial technology at the same level as the Romano-Germanics. But since the Europeanized people is, by virtue of the reasons pointed about above, not in a position to engage in creation in this field with the same rapidity as the native Romano-Germanics, this people will have to limit itself mainly to borrowing and imitating the inventions of others…

Not being able to keep up with the Romano-Germanics and gradually falling behind them, the Europeanized people will from time to time try to catch up by making more or less distant leaps. These leaps disrupt the entire course of historical development. This people must, in a short span of time, traverse the path which the Romano-Germanics trod gradually, over a long span of time. This people will have to jump over a whole number of historical steps and create at once, ex abrupto, what the Romano-Germanics have obtained as a result numerous historically continuous shifts. The consequences of this "leap of evolution" are truly terrible. Each leap is inevitably followed by a period of what seems (from the European point of view) to be stagnation, during which it is necessary to put culture in order and reconcile the results achieved by this leap in a certain sphere of life with the rest of the elements of culture. During this "stagnation," of course, this people will once again fall behind, and even further. The history of Europeanized peoples consists of this constant succession of brief periods of rapid "progress" and long periods of "stagnation." Historical leaps, in their disruption of the unity and continuous gradual pace of historical development, destroy the very tradition which is already poorly developed among the Europeanized people. All the while, continuous tradition remains one of the prerequisites for normal evolution. It is abundantly clear that such leaps and jumps, giving the temporary illusion of the achievement of the "European level of civilization" cannot, by virtue of the above-indicated reasons, lead a people forward in the true sense of the word. Leaping evolution even further squanders those national forces already overloaded by the very fact of Europeanization… And all of this comes without the people having faith in itself, without the reinforcing sense of national unity which has long since been destroyed by the very fact of Europeanization.

Thus, the consequences of Europeanization are so severe and terrible that it must be considered not a blessing, but an evil. Let us note that we have deliberately not even touched upon those negative sides of Europeanization which Europeans themselves frequently recognize with regret: vices and habits which are harmful to health, the particular diseases brought by European Kulturträger, militarism, and restless industrial life without aesthetic… We have spoken only of the consequences arising from the very essence of Europeanization which concern the very essence of the social life and culture of a Europeanized people.

As a result, we must answer all three of the questions posed above in the negative.

## V.

But if European civilization is no higher than any other, if full assimilation to a foreign culture is impossible, and if the aspiration to full Europeanization bodes a most pitiful and tragic fate for all non-Romano-Germanic peoples, then it is obvious that a people must fight this Europeanization with all its strength. But here arises the terrifying question: what if this struggle is impossible and universal Europeanization is an inevitable world law?

At first glance, there is much to suggest that this is indeed the case. When Europeans encounter any non-Romano-Germanic people, they bring their goods and their guns. If a people does not resist them, then the Europeans conquer them, make them into a colony, and Europeanize them by force. If a people does decide to resist, then in order to be in a position to fight the Europeans, it is compelled to acquire the guns and the improvements of European technology. This requires factories and mills on the one hand, and the study of the European applied sciences on the other. Yet factories are unthinkable without the socio-political mode of life of Europe, as are the applied sciences without the "pure" sciences. Thus, to battle Europe, the people in question must assimilate the contemporary Romano-Germanic civilization step by step and Europeanize voluntarily. This means that in either case, Europeanization is, it would seem, inevitable…

Everything we have just said may give the impression that Europeanization is an inevitable consequence of the European's possession of military technology and the factory production of goods, but military technology is a result of militarism, and factory production of capitalism. Militarism and capitalism are not eternal, they arose historically and, as European socialists predict, will soon perish and give way to a new socialist system. It turns out that the opponents of universal Europeanization should be dreaming of the establishment of a socialist system in European countries... However, this is nothing more than a paradox. Socialists insist even more than all other Europeans on the Internationale, on militant cosmopolitanism, the true essence of which was already revealed in the beginning of this work. And this is no accident. Socialism is possible only under universal Europeanization, the leveling of all nationalities, and their subordination to a uniform culture and single common mode of life...

The negative consequences of Europeanization which we discussed above remain under a socialist system in exactly the same way as under a capitalist system. Moreover, all of these consequences are actually aggravated under a socialist system, as the demand for uniformity in the socio-political life of all peoples, without which socialism is unthinkable, further compels Europeanized peoples to "reach out" to the native Romano-Germanics...

In fact, let us note that the need to maintain a single general level of "civilization" among all peoples under a socialist system will compel the Romano-Germanics to "spur" and "drive forward" the "backward" peoples. Insofar as "national prejudices" are supposed to disappear by this time, having submitted to triumphant cosmopolitanism, it is obvious that under a socialist system, primary roles such as educators and even rulers will be held in all Europeanized states by representatives of purely Romano-Germanic peoples or peoples which have been fully assimilated to Romano-Germanic culture. In the end, the Romano-Germanics will retain the privileged position of aristocrats in the "family of socialist peoples," while the other "backward peoples" will gradually fall into the position of slaves.

Thus, the nature of the socio-political system of Romano-Germanic states plays no role in the question of the inevitability of Europeanization and its negative consequences. This inevitability remains independently of whether the system of Romano-Germanic states will be capitalist or socialist. It depends not on militarism and capitalism, but on the insatiable avarice inherent to the very nature of the international predators, the Romano-Germanics, and the egocentrism which permeates their entire notorious "civilization."

## VI.

How can this nightmare of the inevitability of universal Europeanization be fought?...

The situation is not so hopeless. We said above that one of the main conditions which renders universal Europeanization inevitable is the egocentrism which permeates the entire culture of the Romano-Germanics. It is, of course, impossible to hope that the Romano-Germanics themselves will correct this fatal flaw in their culture. But Europeanized non-Romano-Germanic peoples, in their reception of European culture, can fully purge themselves of this egocentrism. If they succeed in doing so, then the borrowing of certain elements from Romano-Germanic culture will not have the same negative consequences of which we spoke above, and will only enrich the national culture of these peoples. In fact, if the peoples in question in their encounter with European culture will be free from the prejudices which compel them to see something absolutely higher and more perfect in all of this culture's elements, they will have no need to borrow absolutely all of this culture or to strive to eradicate their native culture in favor of European culture, and finally, they will in no way see themselves as "backwards" and stalled in their development among the human race. Seeing Romano-Germanic culture as only one possible culture, they can take from it only those elements which they understand and are convenient, and in the future they will be free to change these elements in regard to their national tastes and needs regardless of how such changes will be evaluated by the Romano-Germanics from their egocentric standpoint.

That such a turn of affairs is in fact quite conceivable and possible, there can be no doubt. Against this possibility there is no point in referring to historical examples. History does teach us that no Europeanized people has been capable of maintaining such a sober point of view toward Romano-Germanic culture. Many peoples which have borrowed European culture initially intended to take from it only the most necessary, but in the further course of their development, they gradually came under the hypnotism of Romano-Germanic egocentrism and, forgetting their original intentions, began to borrow everything indiscriminately and strive toward full assimilation to European civilization. At the beginning of his activity, Peter the Great wanted to borrow from the "Germans" only their military and maritime technology, but he was gradually drawn toward the process of borrowing and adopted many superfluous things with no direct relation to this main goal. Nevertheless, he did not cease to realize that sooner or later, having taken everything that it needs from Europe, Russia must turn its back on Europe and continue to develop its culture freely, without "aligning with the West." But he died without preparing worthy successors. All of the eighteenth century passed for Russia with the unworthy, superficial copying of Europe. By the end of this century, the minds of the echelons of Russian society were already saturated with Romano-Germanic prejudices, and the nineteenth and the early twentieth centuries were spent striving toward the full Europeanization of all aspects of Russian life, during which time Russia assimilated those techniques of "leaping evolution" which we discussed above. The very same history is ready to be repeated before our very eyes in Japan, which initially wanted to borrow from the Romano-Germanics only military and naval technology, but has gradually gone much further in its imitative aspirations to the point that at the present time a significant portion of "educated" society there has assimilated the methods of Romano-Germanic thinking. It is true that Europeanization in Japan has thus far been tempered by the healthy instinct of national pride and loyalty to historical traditions, but who knows whether the Japanese will hold to this position for long.

Nonetheless, even if it were to be admitted that the solution which we have proposed for this question has not yet had historical precedent, it does not follow that this solution itself is impossible. The whole point is that the true nature of European cosmopolitanism and other European theories based on egocentric prejudices have not yet been disclosed. Not realizing the unfoundedness of the egocentric psychology of the Romano-Germanics, the intelligentsia of Europeanized peoples, i.e. the part of these peoples which has embraced the spiritual culture of the Romano-Germanics most fully, has hitherto been unable to fight the consequences of this aspect of European culture, and has trustfully followed Romano-Germanic ideologies oblivious to the pitfalls ahead on their path. This whole picture shall radically change as soon as this intelligentsia begins to consciously approach the matter and approaches European civilization with an objective critique. Thus, the entire center of gravity shall move into the realm of the psychology of the intelligentsia of Europeanized peoples. This psychology must be radically transformed. The intelligentsia of Europeanized peoples must tear from their eyes the blindfold imposed on them by the Romano-Germanics and liberate themselves from the spell of Romano-Germanic psychology. The intelligentsia must understand altogether clearly, firmly, and irrevocably that:

- They have been deceived;

- European culture is not something absolute, and is not the culture of all of mankind, but merely the creation of a limited and definite ethnic or ethnographic group of peoples sharing a common history;

- European culture is mandatory only for the particular group of peoples who created it;

- That this culture is no more perfect and no "higher" than any other culture created by any other ethnographic group, for there are no "higher" and "lower" cultures and peoples, there are only cultures and peoples which are more or less similar to one another;

– Therefore, the assimilation of Romano-Germanic culture by a people which did not participate in its creation is not an unconditional blessing and does not wield any absolute moral force;

– The complete, organic assimilation of Romano-Germanic culture (or any foreign culture in general), an assimilation which makes it possible to further create in the spirit of this culture in step with the those who created it, is possible only as a result of anthropological mixing with the Romano-Germanics and the anthropological absorption of this people by the Romano-Germanics;

– Without such anthropological mixing, only a surrogate form of the full assimilation of culture is possible, one in which only the "static" of this culture can be assimilated, not its "dynamics," i.e. a people assimilating the modern state of European culture will turn out to be incapable of developing it further and each new change in this culture's elements will have to be borrowed once again from the Romano-Germanics;

– Under such conditions, this people will have to completely abandon independent cultural creation, live in the reflected light of Europe, and become a monkey constantly aping the Romano-Germanics;

– As a result, this people will always "lag behind" the Romano-Germanics, i.e., will always assimilate and reproduce different stages of their cultural development with a definite delay and will find themselves in a disadvantageous, subordinate position to the native Europeans, as well as in material and spiritual dependence on them;

- Thus, Europeanization is an absolute evil for any non-Romano-Germanic people;

- This evil can and, as follows, must be fought by any means. All of this must be recognized not on an external level, but inwardly; it must not only be recognized, but felt, experienced, and suffered. It is necessary that the truth appear in all of its nakedness without any embellishments, without any remnants of the great deception from which it must be purged. The impossibility of any compromises must be made clear and obvious: if there must be a struggle, so be it.

All of this presupposes, as we have said above, a complete pivot and revolution in the psychology of the intelligentsia of the non-Romano-Germanic peoples. The main essence of this revolution is consciousness of the relativity of what has hitherto seemed unconditional - the blessing of European "civilization." This must be carried out with ruthless radicalism. Accomplishing this will be difficult, extremely difficult, but absolutely necessary nonetheless.

The revolution in the consciousness of the intelligentsias of non-Romano-Germanic peoples will inevitably prove fatal to the cause of universal Europeanization. After all, until now, it has been none other than this intelligentsia that has been the conduit of Europeanization, and it is they who, believing in cosmopolitanism and the "blessing of civilization," regretted the "backwardness" and "stagnation" of their people, and thus attempted to assimilate them to European culture by forcefully destroying the centuries-old foundations of their own unique culture. The intelligentsias of Europeanized peoples have gone further in this direction and engaged in drawing into European culture not only their own peoples, but their neighbors as well. Thus, they have been the main agents of the Romano-Germanics. If they now understand and deeply realize that Europeanization is an absolute evil and cosmopolitanism an impudent deception, they will cease to help the Romano-Germanics, and the triumphant march of "civilization" will have to stop - the Romano-Germanics alone, without the support of already Europeanized peoples, will be in no position to continue their cause of spiritually assimilating all the peoples of the world...

In this great and difficult work of freeing the peoples of the world from the hypnosis of the "benefits of civilization" and spiritual slavery, the intelligentsia of all non-Romano-Germanic peoples who have already entered or intend to embark on the path of Europeanization must act amicably and in unison. Never for a moment can sight be lost of the true essence of the problem. There can be no distraction by individual nationalisms or individual solutions such as Pan-Slavism and all the other "pan-isms": these particulars only obscure the essence of the matter. One must always and firmly remember that confrontations between Slavs and Germanic peoples or Turanians and Aryans do not provide a true resolution to the problem, for there is only one true confrontation: that between the Romano-Germanics and all other peoples of the world, between Europe and Mankind.

***

# EUROPE AND EURASIA

## (On Nikolai Trubetzkoy's *Europe and Mankind*)

### *Petr Savitsky*[114]

***

### I.

Prince Nikolai Sergeyevich Trubetzkoy's recently released pamphlet, *Europe and Mankind*, poses with great determination the question of the relationship between Western European culture, which Prince Trubetzkoy designates in the racial terms of the main peoples of Western Europe as "Romano-Germanic" culture, and the cultures of the rest of mankind. To the question "Is it possible to objectively prove that the culture of the Romano-Germanics is more perfect than all other cultures currently or once existing on Earth?," Prince Trubetzkoy gives a decidedly negative answer and proceeds: "If Europeans are no more perfect than savages, then the evolutionary ladder... must collapse...Instead of a ladder, we have a horizontal plane. Instead of the principle of a gradation of peoples and cultures by degrees of perfection, we have a new principle of the equivalence and qualitative incommensurability of all cultures and peoples of the globe." Prince Trubetzkoy presents this "new principle" with great expressiveness and tenacity. But it would be appropriate to ask: is this principle really new? Does

---

114 Article authored in Narli, Turkey on 8 January 1921, first published in the journal *Russkaia Mysl'* [*Russian Thought*] No. 1-2 (Sofia: Bulgarian-Russian Publishing House, 1921).

the thought advanced by Prince Trubetzkoy not lie in the very definition of culture as exists in modern cultural studies? Culture is the totality of "cultural values," and a "cultural value" is that which, according to Prince Trubetzkoy's formulation of "Romano-Germanic" and following that of the sociologist Gabriel Tarde, "is adopted to meet the needs of all or a part of a given people." Therefore, for the emergence of "cultural value" as such, it is not at all necessary that it be accepted to meet the needs of all subjects of the human race, all intelligible humanity. For the emergence of cultural value, the recognition of a certain social group, even a small one, is sufficient. In other words, the notion of a "cultural value" and the related concept of "culture" do not appeal in their very existence to any universal recognition or universal obligation. The very determination of such a value entails the indication that there is no common measure by which the "cultural values" of one people might be recognized as "better and more perfect" than the cultural values established by another people. In this sense, a cultural value is a "subjective" value, not an "objective" one, and the very idea of a subjective value precludes the question of "objective evidence" of its perfection or imperfection.

The field of cultural evaluations is a domain of "philosophical freedom," and it is in light of such "freedom" that Prince Trubetzkoy is absolutely right when, for example, he praises the institution of group marriage among the Australians, presenting its advantages over "elementary European monogamy," or when he puts on par the works of the savage and the "futuristic pictures drawn by Europeans." But so too would the "conscientious Romano-German" be completely in the right to prove the supremacy of monogamy and futuristic pictures. After all, both are created and affirmed in their own being as "cultural values" by the social environment to which he belongs, and a "subjective" value in its first collectivistic expression cannot, as a general rule, seem to him "more perfect and better" than the corresponding creations of other peoples.

It is indisputable that there exists a number of "cultural values" with regard to which Prince Trubetzkoy's idea of "equivalence and qualitative incommensurability" is absolutely right. But are all "cultural values" qualitatively incommensurable with each other? Prince Trubetzkoy speaks of all "cultures" while perceiving "culture" to be some kind of single totality: "Such could be a norm of law, an artistic work, an institution, a technological device, or a scientific or philosophical work." But is such generalizing acceptable? Would the view of "equivalence and qualitative incommensurability" between cultures be substantiated if we take some "technological device" as an object of comparison, for example, if we were to compare a boomerang and a 3-line rifle as weapons of attack and defense? Can we speak here of any absence of a general measure of "perfection" which we find in discussing "institutions" or "works of art?" Does the necessity not arise at this point of some kind of generally binding judgement, just as all homo sapiens would recognize the rifle to be "more perfect" than the boomerang as a weapon for attacking and defending? Savages already acquainted with glass might think that the vault of heaven seen above us is made of glass; can this view be attributed "qualitative equivalence" with the "Romano-Germanic" knowledge of the atmosphere? Prince Trubetzkoy does not seem to deny the general binding of the logic (or, in other words, "perfection") created by the Romano-Germanics and, at any rate, expressing hope that the ideas he defends will be "proved logically," he offers no exposé of any new, non-Romano-Germanic logic. Meanwhile, from the point of view of logic, certain categories of "cultural values" are "commensurate" and "inequivalent," as some correspond to the requirements of logic while others do not. Insofar as this is the case, is Prince Trubetzkoy right to apply his notions of "equivalence" and "qualitative incommensurability" not to one or another category of "cultural values," but to "cultures" taken as a whole?

Among the inventory of culture, it is necessary to distinguish between two orders of cultural values: one concerns the definition of major directions, goals, and "ends in themselves" in both indigenous life and in the life of mankind in general; the other sets the means for realizing the aims of human existence. This difference can be unfurled into an opposition between ideology on the one hand, and technological and empirical knowledge on the other. Legal norms, works of art, "institutions" concerning spheres which are undoubtedly of an "end in itself" character in human existence, such as sexual life, as well as philosophical provisions, belong to the sphere of ideology. Scientific postulates and technological devices naturally fall into the second group. It is conceivable that there are cases in which doubt may arise as to just which sphere one or another "cultural value" belongs, but the possibility of such doubt does not annul the importance of this distinction. Even if we consider Prince Nikolai Sergeyevich Trubetzkoy's "principle of equivalence and qualitative incommensurability" to be applicable to the sphere of "ideology," it still must be decidedly pointed out that in the field of technology and empirical knowledge, by the very nature of its subject, it is impossible not to recognize the existence of some generally binding principle and measure for evaluating the relative perfection of one or another technological or scientific-empirical achievement, for ascertaining their inequality and, at the same time, qualitative commensurability.

This idea which we have fixed in the form of a contrast between the ideological elements of culture on the one hand and the technological and empirico-scientific elements on the other, as well as the related contrast between differences in the reception and principles of evaluation - this thought can, of course, be clothed in different words and other, more precise formulas than we have done here. But it seems to us that, in clarifying the relation of one or another people, and moreover of all of "mankind" to Western European (or any other) culture, it is completely erroneous to pass over in silence the cardinal difference which exists between separate groups of "cultural values" with regard to their conceivable equivalence and qualitative commensurability. There are circumstances which, it seems to us, demand with particular insistence that precisely such a fallacy be pointed out in the discussion of Prince N.S. Trubetzkoy's ideas. Without a doubt, Trubetzkoy's work poses, among other things, a call for some kind of practical action in the field of culture. It is even imbued with a certain irritation with "Romano-Germanic" culture. Prince Trubetzkoy speaks of "the delusion of Romano-Germanic ideology," of "the impertinent deception of cosmopolitanism," and of a "hated yoke." He calls the intelligentsia of non-Romano-Germanic peoples to revolution: "The main essence of this revolution is consciousness of the relativity of what has hitherto seemed unconditional - the blessing of European 'civilization.' This must be carried out with ruthless radicalism." Prince N.S. Trubetzkoy is no stranger to the understanding that this "ruthless radicalism" should not apply to all attributes of European civilization. It is not for nothing that he calls "universal" some "productions of Romano-Germanic material culture," e.g., "military equipment and mechanical devices for movement," and, evidently, recognizes the necessary universality of their dissemination. Also along this line is the recognition that, given certain conditions, "the borrowing of certain elements from Romano-Germanic culture will not have...negative consequences." Yet calling for the overthrow of the "hated yoke" of Romano-Germanic civilization cannot be limited by certain hints and reservations in regard to the basic distinction between "cultural values" and in the sense of the relativity of some and the non-relativity of others. We do not find any clarification of this difference with the aid of the systematic categories of cultural studies in Prince Trubetzkoy's pamphlet. This creates the possibility of a "universal" interpretation of his calls for consciousness of the "relativity of the good of European civilization."

It is wholly understandable that every people ought to aspire and strive to gain their own ideological face, and not face ideology in the wake of other nations. But what position would a people find itself in if, upon listening to sermons on the "relativity of the good of European civilization," it wished to change out its rifles for boomerangs and modern physics and chemistry (with their technological applications not only in the field of "military equipment" and "devices for movement") for the physical and chemical knowledge of a savage? From a proper point of view, the only vital formula for national existence in this field can be the following: one must have their own ideology, regardless of whether they have their own or someone else's technology and empirical knowledge

Insofar as Prince Trubetzkoy's model can be interpreted as a rejection of, among other things, European technology and science - and this interpretation finds confirmation in a variety of Prince Trubetzkoy's judgements, such as how he considers "the creation of factories and mills and the study of European sciences" to be a stage in his hated "Europeanization" - such ideas, despite the healthy principle embedded in them, may become dangerous to the peoples to whom they are addressed. For it is quite obvious that if a people were to heed calls in the likes of Prince N.S. Trubetzkoy's and be indifferent toward ideology, technology and science, this people would reduce by many times its capacity for economic and political action and, quite likely, would even perish as a national whole under the pressure of other, economically and politically stronger peoples and cultures...

In the general structure of Prince Trubetzkoy's ideas, his excessively generalized formulas which lend themselves to ambiguity (for example, the principle of the "equivalence and qualitative incommensurability of all cultures and peoples of the globe" and the "relativity of the blessing of European civilization") might perhaps not deserve detailed analysis: they could be perceived as casual slips of naivety. If we have dwelled on them in any detail, it is exclusively because we should like to, by way of systematic distinctions, contribute to clarifying the idea of the cultural-ideological emancipation of the non-Romano-Germanic peoples, that thought which lies at the heart of Prince Trubetzkoy's work, and contribute to a realistic and empirical posing of the problem. Such a posing of the problem is impossible without consciousness of the fact that alongside the positive aim of the ideological-national "self-assertion" of non-Romano-Germanic peoples, the lives of the latter remain faced with the full significance of an equally positive goal: the need to use the technical and empirical-scientific achievements of the Romano-Germanics to meet the needs of these peoples. Insofar as Prince Trubetzkoy does not categorically and intelligibly address this, the idealization of the "savage" as well as remarks about the "relativity of the good of European civilization" draw close to preaching cultural weakness.

## II.

From the point of view of methodological analysis, it is completely clear why these ambiguities and naivety from which Prince N.S. Trubetzkoy's pamphlet *Europe and Mankind* suffers emerged. Prince Trubetzkoy's constructs are closer in character to the preaching of cultural weakness because the author ignores the significance of power as a driving factor in cultural and national life. [Trubetzkoy writes:]

> The simplest and most widespread evidence [of the greater perfection of Romano-Germanic civilizational in comparison to the culture of "savages"] is that Europeans defeat savages. The crudeness and naivety of this proof should be clear to any objectively thinking person. This argument clearly demonstrates how the worship of brute force that constitutes an essential trait of the national character of those tribes which created European civilization is alive to this very day in the consciousness of every descendant of the ancient Gauls and Germanic peoples...It is, of course, not worth analyzing the logical inconsistency [of this proof]...Europeans constantly have to admit that victory altogether often falls to the share of "less cultured" peoples than the natives over whom they've prevailed.

This tirade over the "crudeness and naivety" of the cited evidence is worthy of a place in any of Lloyd George's speeches on the "aims of the war" against Germany - speeches which, in historical perspective, can be considered incomparable paradigms of human hypocrisy. But is such a tirade appropriate in reasoning claiming to be philosophically impartial? In order to answer this question, we should return to that circle of thought on which we have already partially touched in our analysis of the "principle of equivalence and qualitative incommensurability of all cultures and peoples of the globe." We should establish that the greater or lesser "perfection" of one or another civilization can be evaluated from different points of view. For example, this could be done from the point of view of the moral idea of Good and Evil, insofar as this idea is realized in phenomena of culture. From this standpoint, the inconsistency of referencing actual victories of Europeans over "savages" as a measure of "perfection" is clear without further explanation: from this point of view, such references are downright ridiculous. But if the domain of judgements of Good and Evil is recognized to be a realm subordinate to the principle of "philosophical freedom," then it must be stated that this domain does not allow for the existence of any universal, logically binding judgements.

The matter would stand differently if we were to evaluate the degree of a culture's perfection, for instance, from the point of view of the development of empirical science. From this viewpoint, a gradation of cultures in terms of the wealth of empirically-cognized material accumulated by each culture is permissible. It is also possible to assess the "perfection" of cultures in terms of the relative stability or strength which they exhibit in contact with one another. All the "great cultures of antiquity" recognized by European science were destroyed by none other than "barbarians." It ought to be added that in these cases in which "great cultures" were destroyed by "barbarians," the latter in turn experienced the influence of the culture they "destroyed." From all of this it follows that the measure of greater force is set differently in different branches of human culture. In some cases, one culture may wield military-political predominance as well as predominance of cultural influence with regard to another, as has been the case in contact between modern Europeans and "savages." In other cases, one culture may be stronger in military-political terms but weaker in terms of cultural influence, as was the case with the "barbarians" who destroyed the "great cultures of antiquity." The actual victories of Europeans over "savages," as evidence of greater "perfection" of European culture compared to savage cultures, should be interpreted in the sense of greater "perfection" from the standpoint of force. In such a sense, this argument contains nothing more than a simple statement of a fact, but a fact that is extremely substantial in the general structure of human culture.

The essentiality of this fact lies in that it is only those cultures which survive and gain historic significance which, in coming into contact with others, prove to be strong enough to uphold their existence in at least one of the above-mentioned relations, whether military-political or cultural influence. Otherwise, the culture disappears, as have such diverse cultures as the Incas, the Aztecs, the Fuegians, and the Tasmanians. Also, the maxim of national being which we formulated earlier as "one's own ideology, regardless of one's own or someone else's technology and empirical knowledge" is applicable only to those peoples that have shown stability and vitality in their cultural existence. After all, is it even possible for a people to have its "own ideology" when it is incapable of militarily defending its independence or, to the same extent, confronting foreign cultural influences?! Moreover, with regard to defense and confrontation, the peoples of the world have never and do not now find themselves in identical positions, but rather are organized more along the principle of a "ladder" than a "horizontal plane."

This condition determines our assessment of the conceptualization of relations between the Romano-Germanic and non-Romano-Germanic cultures which we find in Prince N.S. Trubetzkoy's work. Prince Trubetzkoy speaks of "Europe and Mankind," by which "Europe" refers to the Romano-Germanics, while by "Mankind" is meant the totality of "Slavs, Chinese, Indians, Arabs, Negroes, and other tribes...without distinction of skin color." [Trubetzkoy writes:] "One must always and firmly remember that confrontations between

Slavs and Germanic peoples or Turanians and Aryans do not provide a true resolution to the problem, for there is only one true confrontation: that between the Romano-Germanics and all other peoples of the world, between Europe and Mankind." Thus, the call to fight the "nightmare of universal Europeanization" is addressed to "Mankind." Such is the posing of the problem in the work of Prince Trubetzkoy, who, as we have seen, ignores the standard of strength in matters of relations between human cultures. Can such a postulate be recognized as correct from a point of view which recognizes force as the main driving factor in this branch of human existence? From this point of view, in order to fight the "nightmare of Europeanization," it is not enough for a people to simply exist as one component part of "Mankind"; it is necessary to have the capacity to oppose Romano-Germanic culture with one's own equal culture - a culture which would help a given people to deflect manu militari the political attempts of the Romano-Germanics and negate the predominance of their cultural influence. In other words, in order to overthrow the "yoke" of Romano-Germanic culture, it is necessary to have not only the desire, but the strength and force to do so. The appeal to "Mankind" to free itself from the hypnosis of "the blessings of civilization" can have real empirical significance only if it is proven that all the peoples which constitute "Mankind" really wield the power needed to do so. It seems to us that, at the present moment, finding such proof is impossible. Very many peoples, not to mention the Australians and Papuans and even the Negroes and Malays, have altogether little chance of successfully resisting Romano-Germanic aggression. Since the hitherto established mutual ties between all parts of the globe have not been broken, only one possibility exists for these peoples: replacing the Romano-Germanic yoke with another one. Thus, from a real empirical point of view, the call for cultural emancipation, insofar as it is addressed to all of "Mankind," is a mystical *desideratum*, not a program with grounds for realization in the near future.

And yet there is no smoke without fire. Every phenomenon, including in spiritual life, is tied to the empirical situation amidst which it arose and which it reflects. Therefore, even if from a completely abstract point of view, the question should be asked: is the appearance of calls for emancipation in the likes of Prince Trubetzkoy's not a sign that in some empirical, national environment, namely the one in which such a call is being sounded, conditions have arisen which are determining the possibility of realizing such emancipation? For thinking that takes into account empirical possibilities, the opposition of "Europe and Mankind" is an empty program in the struggle for cultural emancipation. But does some other opposition not stand behind Prince Trubetzkoy's constructions? If we delve into Prince Trubetzkoy's idea, it seems to us that there can be no doubt that such a reality indeed stands behind them. This reality is the confrontation between Europe and Russia. Prince Trubetzkoy recognizes that some of his provisions could be "abundantly illustrated by examples from Russian history and Russian reality," but that the "clarity of the overall plan" would suffer as a result. Meanwhile, some parts of Prince Trubetzkoy's pamphlet are written not merely about Russia among others, but about none other than Russia. These include, for example, the observations on the results of familiarization with European culture. It was the Russians who in the 18th and 19th centuries evaluated "their people and culture...from the standpoint of the Romano-German." Other "Europeanized" peoples, such as the Japanese in Prince Trubetzkoy's recognition, have not been complicit in such depreciation of their own spiritual identity. It was among the Russian people in the 18th and 19th centuries that "every generation lived its own special cultural life and the difference between 'fathers and children' was stronger" than among other peoples. We all know the "fathers and children" of Russian life and literature. But does Prince Trubetzkoy point out something of the sort, for instance, with respect to Japan? The list of the negative consequences of Europeanization which Prince N.S. Trubetzkoy offers primarily relates to

Russia. Yet, if Prince Trubetzkoy's constructions were to be the object of various observations from the outside, then would these constructions, perceived as empirical phenomena of Russian intellectual life, not be a sign that processes are maturing within the Russian national body whose trajectory is oriented toward turning "Europeanization" into a stage of Russian national life which has been overcome? If it cannot be expected that "Mankind," perceived as a totality, will turn out in the present to have sufficient cultural potential for eliminating "Europeanization," then are there not signs that such potential does exist in one part of "Mankind" (as understood by Prince Trubetzkoy), namely, in Russia?

Two facts of empirical reality appear to us to be particularly substantial in this regard. On the one hand, in the very process of "Europeanization," Russia has asserted itself in the field of fine literature and visual arts. This self-affirmation has become such an indisputable fact that by the end of the 19th and by the early 20th century Russia's spiritual "export" in these fields was, one must think, no less than its spiritual "import." On the other hand, as a result of the First World War and the Revolution, it is precisely in Russia that the historical phenomenon called Bolshevism has presented itself. One can fully understand how horrific the terror inflicted by the Bolsheviks has been, how ridiculous has been the destruction of Russian economic life arising from their economic experiments. But at the same time, it seems to us that we need to recognize that Bolshevism, in the form in which it has come to life, at its core rejects the mentality which left Russians assessing "their people and culture from the standpoint of the Romano-German." Surely, without a doubt, influences hailing from the West played a major role in the Bolsheviks' act. But popular Bolshevism, Bolshevism in practice, has essentially diverged from what its original leaders, the "Westernist"-Marxists had devised it to be. In practice, the Bolshevik social experiment in its ideological and spatial scales is without precedent in the history of the West, and in this sense is uniquely Russian.

**102**

For the Bolsheviks, in their striving to reshape Russia, the Romano-Germanic world no longer serves as an unquestionable model. On the contrary, they are characterized by an aspiration to reshape all of "capitalist" Europe along their own, essentially Russian model. For Bolshevik ideology, the non-historical centers of the West - Paris, Rome, or London - are lights of the universe, but they are cities which cannot be recognized as such from the traditional "Romano-Germanic" point of view. [The German poet Max Barthel writes in his 1920 poem "Petrograd":]

> Petrograd! You are a red flame, the dawn beacon of the universe,
>
> Your people, having broken their shackles, are forging their own destiny...
>
> Rus', for now you are alone, but the blissful moment will come,
>
> Petrograd, your standard of victory shall gather all under your flag!

Even for the non-Bolshevik it seems certain that the phenomenon of Bolshevism, with the world-significance which it has assumed, marks a significant shift in culturo-historical relations between Europe and Russia. In the course of this phenomenon, the West is no longer playing the role of the active factor, and Russia is no longer acting as an imitator belatedly following the path already traversed by other peoples. In this case, Russia is not repeating, as per usual, what has already happened in the leading centers of the world, first and foremost in "Romano-Germanic" Europe: it is itself, with its own destiny, in the most direct manner, determining the destiny of the world. Bolshevism will, of course, sooner or later be replaced by a different system. Whatever system may replace it will very likely recognize the change in the historico-cultural relations between Europe and Russia which Bolshevism has brought. For the essence of this change consists not in opposition between the socialist system in its Bolshevik interpretation and the capitalist system of the West. Russia's conceivable world-culture cannot be reduced to a certain uniform content any more than can other world cultures. The essence of this change consists of a new coordination of the elements of activity and passivity, creativity and imitation that recently defined relations between Europe and Russia.

## III.

Such is the reality which we feel in the constructions of Prince Trubetzkoy. We have reduced his opposition between "Europe and Mankind" to an opposition between "Europe and Russia." However, the latter formula sits uneasily from a logical and, we would say, geographical point of view. The fact of the matter is that according to generally accepted definitions, Russia in one significant part constitutes part of Europe, while at the same time, in its other part, Russia extends well beyond Europe. Tomsk and Irkutsk are just as much Russia as Penza and Kharkov. In other words, European Russia figures in both elements of the opposition of "Europe and Russia," which obliterates the logical and geographical clarity of the latter formula. It should be noted that, in a purely geographical sense, Russia in its 1914 borders, or more accurately in its parts lying to the East of the Pulkovo meridian (we take such artificial borders since there is no natural border), represents its own unique world different from both "Europe" as the totality of countries lying to the West of the Pulkovo meridian in the direction of the Atlantic Ocean, and "Asia" as the totality of the lowlands of China, Hindustan, Mesopotamia, the mountain countries lying between them and the islands adjacent to them. Russia is the most continental world of all the geographical worlds of such spatial scale that could be carved out on the continents of the globe.

The main topographical element of Russia as a geographical whole is its three plains: the main Russian plain (which with respect to its ends could be called the "White Sea-Caucasian" plain), the Siberian plain, and the Turkestan plain, which together, by virtue of the insignificance of the borders separating them from one another (the Urals and the Aral-Irtysh watershed), constitute in many respects a single whole plain-space. Russia is a combination of these plains with a portion of the mountain countries bordering its plain-space from the East and the South. Across nearly its entire expanse, Russia has a climate that is uniform in many of its main features and at the same time significantly different from the prevailing climates of "Europe" and "Asia." Nearly all of its space receives less than 600 mm of precipitation yearly, while the predominant part of its expanse has more than 300 mm of rainfall. Meanwhile, Europe is differentiated into climatic types with a quantity of precipitation of more than 600 mm yearly, while Asia is a combination of regions receiving more than 600 mm with others receiving less than 300. An even more characteristic trait of the "Russian" climate, and at once quite an extraordinary one with regard to the general rule regarding the climates of "Europe" and "Asia," is its altogether wide amplitude of temperature fluctuations during the year, with an extremely significant deviation of average temperature between the hottest month and the coldest. In Russia, in the vast majority of cases, this deviation exceeds 25 °C, and in the Yakutia region it sets world records, reaching up to 65 °C. In "Europe" and "Asia," only as an exception does it reach 25 °C. Only very small districts of Russia deviate from this uniform type in their climatic character and come close to those climatic types distinctive of "Europe" and "Asia." It is not difficult to list these areas. The climate of the southern coast of Crimea resembles that of the regions around the Aegean and Marmara Seas. The climate of the foothills of the North Caucasus (Ekaterinodar, Vladikavkaz) is close to that of the Danubian countries (Romania, Hungary). The climate of the Caucasus-Black Sea coast reproduces the climatic type of Central China and Southern Japan. We might also call the climate of the Murmansk coast similar to that of the countries of the North-Eastern basin of the Atlantic Ocean - Northern Norway, Iceland, and the Faroe Islands. In all of the above cases, the climatic types which cover vast spaces outside of Russia dominate within Russia only on narrow strips of land stretching along mountain ranges or sea coasts; they are not the climates of significant geographical areas, but rather "for the collection." The differences between the prevailing types of Russian climate on the one hand, and the climates of "Europe" and "Asia" on the other, can to some extent be reduced to the traditional difference between "continental" and "oceanic" climates. It ought to be noted just how grandiose the totality of "continental" climates Russia is, and at the same time caution against the view, by no means foreign to our elementary geography textbooks, that the "continentality" of its climates constitutes some kind of geographical "deprivation." The question of the "advantages" of an oceanic climate is much more complex than is commonly thought. But since we are not writing a study of geography, we cannot enter into such details. With regard to soils, the brace which firmly connects Russia's parts lying on one and the other side of the Ural range is the black earth that spans from Podolia to the Minusinsk steppes and which, at the same time, has no analogues among the soils of "Europe" and "Asia."

Russia, in its spatial scale and geographical nature, is largely uniform across the entirety of its space, and at the same time differs from the nature of the adjacent countries: it is a "continent in itself." It seems to us that this continent, bordering both "Europe" and "Asia" yet at the same time unlike either of them, is befitting of the name "Eurasia." This designation is habitually applied to the whole continent of the "Old World." In this case, we want to apply it to the middle part of this continent, to that vast area whose center is the mediastinum between Europe and Asia in their traditional division. Instead of the usual two on the mainland of the "Old World," we distinguish three continents: Europe, Eurasia, and Asia...The borders of "Eurasia" cannot be determined as indisputable according to any one standard, just as such a border cannot be established with respect to the habitual division between Europe and Asia. In the latter case, Europe's limits are conditionally held to be the eastern borders of the Arkhangelsk, Vologda, Perm, Ufa, and Orenburg provinces and the Ural region. Similarly, the limits of "Eurasia" might be considered the borders of the Russian State, or its parts lying East of the Pulkovo meridian. Thus, we identify Russia with Eurasia.

In connection with this, the opposition of "Europe and Russia," containing as it does a definite geographical incongruity, is revealed for us in the opposition of "Europe and Eurasia" which, given some modification of habitual geographical definitions, seems to us to sound more precise and clear. These modifications do not, of course, preclude the name Russia in all of its historical and ethnographic significance. However, it is not merely in geographical definitions that the meaning of this proposed change of formulation lies. This change is also oriented toward certain culturo-historical circumstances. Given the fact that the concepts of "Europe" and "Asia" are associated with various culturo-historical ideas, we include in the name "Eurasia" some of the compressed culturo-historical character of the world which we would otherwise call "Russian" - its character being a combination of the culturo-historical elements of "Europe" and "Asia" which is, at the same time in full analogy with geographical nature, neither Europe nor Asia.

The parallels between geographical and culturo-historical conditions could be taken further. In this regard, it is precisely the comparison of "Europe and Eurasia" that is particularly of interest. Europe knows neither such high nor such low temperatures as those that are the general rule in the climate of Russia-Eurasia. Is it possible to ascertain a renowned parallel to this breadth of the amplitude of thermal fluctuations in the spiritual life of the latter? Is it not characteristic of Russian-Eurasian culture, is it not a distinguishing trait of the Russian-Eurasian soul, to bring such soulful darkness and lowness together with such intensity of enlightenment and impulse in a manner inaccessible to the European soul and unknown in European culture, balanced and closed in its relatively narrow spiritual amplitude?

The substitution of the name "Russia" with the name "Eurasia" is also of significance to us in relation to that concrete historical opposition between "Europe and Russia" and "Europe and Eurasia" about which we have spoken in the preceding. It is completely obvious that in the non-Romano-Germanic world which we call into question, "Eurasia" or "Russia" is that force which is capable of dethroning its own unconditional subordination to "Romano-Germanic" culture and rectifying the blind imitation of the "European" model, the "nightmare of universal Europeanization," and it is completely obvious that in this world ethnographic Russia plays a central and decisive role. However, it would be absolutely incorrect to reduce the culturo-historical confrontation, whose rise we can feel in the present, to an opposition between Europe and Russia as ethnographic wholes. This opposition is fueled both ideologically and militarily by forces not of ethnographic Russia alone, but of the whole circle of adjacent Turanian, Mongol, Aryan, Iverian, and Finnish peoples. The forces of these peoples partially contributed to the creation of Russian might and culture, and they are active in the phenomenon of Bolshevism. Indeed, in the latter phenomenon, despite its repulsive and savage face, there are without a doubt elements of a kind of protest by the non-Romano-Germanic world against the Romano-Germanic cultural and other "yokes." Even with the exclusive aim of taking into account the participation of non-Russian elements in some kind of common action with ethnographic Russia, it would be correct to call Russia "Eurasia" in contrast to "Europe." In essence, however, the question at hand is even broader. A number of peoples and countries along Russia's borders, while not belonging to Russia and in most cases striving to preserve their full political independence, are nevertheless tied to Russia by a certain commonality of spiritual composition and partly by racial and ethnographic characteristics. These countries are not "Romano-Germanic" but in a number of cases have, like Russia, served or still serve as objects of "Europeanization."

At the same time, many of them, in their pasts and at present, harbor the surety of a unique spiritual identity. It is altogether likely that these peoples and countries might become Russia's allies or join it in its culturo-historical opposition to "Europe." It cannot be ruled out that this will happen (and is partially already taking place) in the case of some Slavic peoples, the Turks, Persians, Mongols, and walled China. It is interesting to note that these peoples occupy territories which, in large swathes of their expanse, are close to the geographical character and nature of Russia-Eurasia. For example, the climates of the plateaus of Asia Minor, Iran and North-West China closely match the climatic types of Eurasia in terms of precipitation or the amplitude of thermal fluctuations. These countries figure among the mountain regions that separate the plains of Eurasia from the lowlands of Asia - some of which are part of Russia. Their closeness in geographical character to the nature of Russia-Eurasia illustrates the fact that there are no definite natural borders between Eurasia and Asia. The existence of these countries in their geographical and culturo-historical convergence with Russia gives us new grounds in our analysis of the relations between the Romano-Germanic and non-Romano-Germanic cultures to speak not of Russia, but of "Eurasia."

It is not at all improbable that the opposition between "Europe and Eurasia" will draw into its fold some of the peoples of "Asia" as well. However, while admitting the possibility of such an extension of the scope of world protest against Romano-Germanic aggression, it should be qualified that the extension of this framework to such peoples as the Indians or Chinese does not mean an extension up to the point of all of "Mankind." For the Indians or the Chinese, in terms of their potential for culturo-historical opposition, are not of the same character as, for instance, the Negroes, the Australians, or the Papuans.

Nevertheless, the extension of this framework, a possibility which we allow for, is quite enough to substantiate the question: insofar as Russia in its opposition to "Europe" will involve in its camp a whole number of other, non-Russian peoples, does this not mean for these peoples a simple change of yoke from "Romano-Germanic" culture to one of Russian culture? In responding to this question, it should first of all be noted that the peoples of Eurasia are not identical to one another; their cultural potential is different and, for example, what may apply to the Tungusic peoples may not to the Bashkirs or the Kirghiz, let alone to the Turks and Persians. Life is cruel, and the weakest peoples of Eurasia may be drawn into a Russian yoke of the same character as the Romano-Germanic one. But with regard to those peoples which are not deprived of cultural potentials, the most important fact characterizing the national conditions of Eurasia is that of the difference between the structuring of relations between the Russian nation and the other nations of Eurasia and those relations found in the regions drawn into the sphere of European colonial policy, that is, between the Romano-Germanics and native peoples. Eurasia is a region of a certain equality and a certain "fraternization" of nations which has no analogues in the international relations of the colonial empires. "Eurasian" culture can be imagined as a culture that is to some degree the common creation and common heritage of the peoples of Eurasia. Is such a community of cultural creation and heritage conceivable in the case of the Romano-Germanics and, for instance, the Bantu Negroes or the Malays?

## IV.

In what real forms can that "revolution in psychology" and the "struggle without any compromises" to liberate the non-Romano-Germanic peoples from the "delusion of Romano-Germanic ideology" take place? As we have striven to show in the preceding, Romano-Germanic technology and science must be extracted from this "revolution in psychology" in order for such a struggle to be realized. Otherwise, Romano-Germanic guns would altogether quickly and radically send the self-asserting people back under the "hated yoke." In other words, the "revolution in psychology" can only and must concern "ideology"... Prince

Trubetzkoy speaks of an "ethnocentrism" that "permeates the entire culture of the Romano-Germanics" and which compels one "to see something absolutely higher and more perfect in all of this culture's elements." Trubetzkoy sees the "fatal flaw" of Romano-Germanic culture in this egocentrism. His program for "struggle without any compromises" boils down to the postulate that the "Europeanized non-Romano-Germanic peoples, in their reception of European culture, can fully purge themselves of this egocentrism." In accordance with what has been said above, this "purge" can only be a matter of ideology. Therefore, if we raise the question of the real implementation of Prince N.S. Trubetzkoy's "program," then it should be asked: is it possible to liberate the national ideology of one or another people from egocentrism? Let us recall that ideology, like any other "cultural value," exists insofar as it is accepted to meet a certain kind of needs "by all or part of a given people." Is it conceivable that a people, or some among it, affirming by recognition the very being of such an ideology, could refuse any "egocentrism" in evaluating the latter? Is it not completely obvious that people for this reason adopt one or another ideology to satisfy their spiritual needs, and that they see in it something "supreme and perfect?" Does recognizing a foreign ideology to be higher or more perfect than one's own, or just as high and perfect as one's own, not mean abandoning one's own ideology and thereby eliminating its very existence? It seems to us that the stamp of "egocentrism" is fixed in the very notion of "ideology." Insofar as Prince Trubetzkoy wishes to bring about the overthrow of the "severe oppression" of Romano-Germanic culture by means of cleansing culture from "egocentrism," his ideas are just as unreal and alienated from empirical reality as is his idea of the possibility of the cultural emancipation of all of "Mankind." Is not the best proof of the correctness of this recognition Prince Trubetzkoy's own approach to his professed ideology of fighting against the "nightmare of universal Europeanization"? In the field which his constructions concern, he believes that all "oppositions" hitherto discovered "do not provide a true resolution to the

**111**

problem, yet only one confrontation is true" namely, of course, the one beheld by Prince N.S. Trubetzkoy: "that between the Romano-Germanics and all other peoples of the world, Europe and Mankind." Does this not show that the very author of the pamphlet under examination recognized the ideology created by him to be "higher and more perfect" than any other on these questions? One wonders how he will prove the possibility not only of individuals, but of whole peoples rejecting "egocentrism" when he himself in his ideology is completely at the mercy of this "fatal flaw."

It must be categorically recognized that the realistic and empirical posing of the problem of emancipation from the "inevitability of universal Europeanization" is not tied to any rejection of "egocentrism" by those peoples heading toward such emancipation. It is not the end, but the beginning of "Europeanization" that is associated with such a rejection. Only when a people begins to "strive to eradicate their native culture in favor of European culture," when a people's intelligentsia begins to "see themselves as 'backwards' and stalled in their development among the human race" and evaluates "their own people and culture from the point of view of the Romano-German" - only then does a people fully renounce egocentrism and truly ceases to think that its own "native" culture is something "absolutely higher and perfect." At this moment, the number of self-asserting national ideologies in the world is reduced to one. Romano-Germanic ideology eliminates the unique, original ideology of a people and replaces it with its own. This phenomenon took place in Russia under Peter the Great and later, when Russia ideologically prostrated itself before "Europe." The opposite must happen in the cultural "emancipation" of a people. A people thus returns to consciousness of the fact that it is not some foreign, imported ideology but its own that is "supreme and perfect." It is imbued with "egocentrism," it extols its ideology and its superiority, and is ready to effectively uphold itself in the face of foreigners.

This by all means applies to the imaginable cultural emancipation of Russia-Eurasia. This emancipation can be achieved not by way of the opposition of "Europe and Mankind," which exists only in mystical aspirations, and not by means of purging non-Romano-Germanic cultures of elements of "egocentrism," but by completely real confrontation between European egocentrism and Eurasian egocentrism. The pledge to realizing such emancipation lies in the creation, conscious and unconscious, of an effective and creative "egocentrism" of Eurasia, one which would rally forces and raise them up toward a sacrificial feat.

\*\*\*

# PREMONITIONS AND FULFILLMENTS: THE AFFIRMATION OF THE EURASIANS

*Petr Savitsky, Petr Suvchinsky, Georges Florovsky, and Nikolai Trubetzkoy*[115]

\*\*\*

The articles of the present anthology claim neither exhaustiveness on all the issues which they address nor unity in the sense of complete unanimity of opinions between the authors. These articles were written by people who think quite differently from one another on certain issues. But there is something common to them, and the following lines are aimed at establishing the essence of this commonality.

The articles included in the present compilation took shape in an atmosphere of a catastrophic world-sense. We experience the period of time in which our lives have passed since the outbreak of the war not merely as a time of transition, but as a turning point. In that which has happened and that which is happening we see not only shock, but crisis, and we expect from the ensuing profound change in the conventional shape of the world.

---

115 Text first published as the foreword to the first collective Eurasianist manifesto, *Iskhod k Vostoku. Predchuvstviia i sversheniia. Utverzhdenie evraziitsev* [*Exodus to the East: Premonitions and Fulfillments - The Affirmation of the Eurasians*] (Sofia: Bulgarian-Russian Publishing House, 1921).

In the catastrophic nature of current events we see signs of an imminent, accelerating resettlement and rebirth of culture. We conceive culture as being in constant motion and ceaseless renewal. Culture does not linger on beyond its span within one or another historico-cultural settlement. Furthermore, culture cannot be fully exhausted by any concrete achievements, as culture cannot fully fit into the predetermined frameworks of devised formulas. We do not believe that there are peoples forever destined to serve as the bearers of culture; we deny the very possibility of any "last words" or final syntheses. For us, history is not a confident ascent toward some kind of pre-historically determined absolute end, but a free and creative improvisation, every moment of which is fulfilled not for the sake of some invented, general plan, but for the sake of its own meaning and significance.

The culture of Romano-Germanic Europe is marked by a definite commitment to the "wisdom of systems" and a certain striving to turn the present into an immutable norm. We honor the past and present of Western European culture, but not all of this culture will be relevant in the future. Instead, trembling both with joy and in fear of the risk of indulging in devastating pride, we feel, together with Herzen, that henceforth "history is pressing at our gates." History is at our gates not for the sake of creating some kind of zoological "self-determination" on our part, but so that, in its great feats of labor and achievements, Russia can reveal to the world a universal truth that has been revealed by her greatest.

Contemplating the present situation, we feel that we are in the midst of a cataclysm comparable to the greatest upheavals known in history, one comparable to the fundamental pivots in the fates of Cultures, such as Alexander the Macedonian's conquests of the Ancient East, or the great migrations of peoples. Such pivots could not and cannot happen in an instant. The processes which resulted in the dilution of the Ancient East amidst the Hellenistic world have their origins as early as the period of the great Persian Wars. Cyrus the Younger's campaign

**116**

toward the East, including as many as 10,000 Greeks, directly anticipated the intentions of the later Macedonian conqueror. But Cyrus the Younger fell, and Alexander could claim to have established the dominion of Hellenic culture in the East only some decades after his death. We do not know which of Russia's uprisings against the West will prove to be like Cyrus the Younger's attempt and which will be akin to the deed of Alexander. But we do know that an historical spasm separating one era of world history from the next has already begun. We have no doubts that change for the Western European world will come from the East.

Here, there is no need to demand evidence. Those who think otherwise have the right to call us madmen, just as we may call them blind. We are more concerned with looking into the features of the cultural upheaval that is presenting itself to us in the storms and shudders of the present.

Any contemporary reflection on the future destinies of Russia should be guided in a certain way with respect to the already existing methods of solving, or, more precisely, the very formulation of the Russian problem: that of the Slavophiles and the Narodniki on the one hand, and the Westernizers on the other. The point is not in one or another separate theoretical conclusion or concrete historical evaluation, but in the very subjective-psychological approach to this problem. To look upon Russia, as some Westernizers do, as some kind of cultural "province" of Europe belatedly trailing after the latter, is in our days now possible only for those operating with templates of thought claiming to prevail over the authority of historical truth. Russia's fates have crashed into world history too deeply and uniquely, and much that is nationally Russian has been recognized by the Romano-Germanic world. But, following the Slavophiles, we assert that Russia's national element is an independent value and, receiving the tone of the Slavophile approach to Russia, we reject the Populist identification of this element with certain concrete achievements or, so to speak, predominant forms of life. In accordance with our historiosophical principle, we believe

**117**

that it is impossible to determine once and for all the content of the Russian life of the future. Thus, for instance, we do not share the Populists' view that the village commune is the form of economic life to which, as the Populists' held, the economic future of Russia belongs and should belong. In the economic sphere, Russia's existence may turn out to be most "Western." We see no contradiction here with the actual and impending cultural uniqueness of Russia. After all, for those who do not count themselves among the followers of historical materialism, culture is not the "superstructure" of an economic base.

We do not combine historical individualism with economic collectivism, as has been the case in other past currents of Russian thought (e.g., Herzen), but rather we affirm the importance of the sovereign personality in, among others, the economic sphere which, it seems to us, would be the point of view of consistent individualism. Yet not all of us attach equal significance to the matter of Russia's powerful economic development. Still, none of us are hostile toward this development - whereas Populism, in its concrete expression, harbored an elemental hostility toward the creative flourishing and flowing of Russian economic forces. We combine the Slavophile sense of the world-significance of the Russian national element with both the Westernists' sense of Russia's relative cultural primitiveness in the economic field and their aspiration to eliminate this primitiveness.

Nevertheless, we do not refrain from defining - at least for ourselves - the content of the very truth which, in our opinion, Russia has revealed through its revolution. This truth is the rejection of socialism and the affirmation of the Church.

We have no other words besides those of horror and disgust for characterizing the inhumanity and abomination of Bolshevism. But we recognize that it is only the Bolsheviks' fearless posing of the question of the very essence of that which exists now, only their daring, historically unprecedented in terms of scope, that has explained and established what would have otherwise long remained obscure or led to temptation:

**118**

that is, the material and spiritual squalor and repulsiveness of socialism, and the salvational force of Religion. In its historical fruition, Bolshevism is coming toward denying itself, in turn setting the stage for the vital overcoming of socialism.

We know that epochs of volcanic shifts and exposures of the mysterious, black depths of chaos are in essence and at once epochs of grace and insight. Humbled before the revolution, as before a natural catastrophe, and forgiving all the misfortunes of its unrestrainable forces, we curse only its consciously evil will so boldly and blasphemously rising against God and the Church. Only through the repentance of the whole people can the sinful madness of this rebellion be atoned. We feel that the secret of our inspirited era is being revealed not only in the vast flood of mystical sensations, but also in the strict forms of Church life. Together with the great majority of Russians, we see that the Church is coming to life with a new force of Grace and is regaining the prophetic language of wisdom and revelation. The "Age of Science" is being replaced by the "Era of Faith" - not by the destruction of science, but through the recognition of the powerlessness and blasphemy of attempting to resolve the main, ultimate problems of existence by scientific means.

In worldly affairs, our attitude is that of nationalism. But we do not wish to enclose such in the narrow framework of national chauvinism. Moreover, we think that organic and creative nationalism, which Russian nationalism is by its very nature, dissolves and breaks down all the constraints of the "nationalisms" of the Western European scale. Russian nationalism, even in an ethnic sense, stretches and covers the earth just as far and wide as Russia's forests and steppes. In this sense, we once again draw near to Slavophilism, which spoke not of the Russian people alone, but of Slavdom as a whole. Of course, before the court of reality, as such seems to us, the notion of 'Slavdom' did not substantiate those hopes which Slavophilism placed in it. We turn our nationalism toward the subject of not only the Slavs, but of the whole circle of peoples of the "Eurasian" world, among which the Russian people occupies the central position. It seems to us that this communion of the whole circle of Eastern European and Asiatic peoples in the conceptual sphere of the culture of the Russian World stems both from that innermost "affinity of souls" which has rendered Russian culture understandable and close to these peoples and which, from the other direction, has determined the fruitfulness of these peoples' participation in the Russian cause, as well as from the commonality of economic interests and economic reciprocity between these peoples.

Russians and the peoples of the "Russian World" are in essence neither Europeans nor Asians. Immersed in the native elements of culture and life surrounding us, we are not ashamed to recognize ourselves to be Eurasians.

***

# THE PIVOT TO THE EAST

*Petr Savitsky*[116]

❦ ❦ ❦

There is a certain constantly noticeable analogousness between the situation of the world of France in the time of the Great Revolution and of Russia in the present time. However, apart from details and particulars, there is a fundamental difference that might harbor the future. Then, just as now, there was Europe, and one of the countries of Europe brought a "new Gospel": this country, having left its old political borders in a revolutionary burst outward, conquered nearly the entire continent; however, when it faltered in its conquests, the rest of Europe (by then united into a coalition) managed to bridle and occupy it.

Before both the war and the revolution, Russia "was a modern civilisation of the Western type, [although] the least disciplined and most ramshackle of all the Great Powers…" (H. G. Wells). During the war and the revolution, however, the "Europeanness" of Russia fell away, much like a mask falls off a face, and when we saw the image of Russia that was not covered by the fabric of historical decorations, we saw a Russia with two faces. One of her faces was turned to Europe - that of Russia as a European country. As France had in 1793, she is bringing Europe a 'new Gospel', this time that of the 'revolution of the proletariat', of Communism made manifest. The other face, however, is turned away from Europe. Wells speaks of how "Gorky is obsessed by a nightmare and fear of Russia going East…"

---

116 Text first published as the first chapter of *Exodus to the East* (1921).

"Russia going East" - but is Russia itself not "the East?" Can one find many in Russia through whose veins there does not flow Khazar or Polovtsy, Tatar or Bashkir, Mordvin or Chuvash blood? Is the mark of the Eastern spirit (its mysticism, its love for contemplation, and, finally, its contemplative laziness) alien to many Russians? One notices a certain sympathetic attraction to the popular masses of the East among the Russian masses of the common people, and through the organic fraternisation of the Orthodox with the Asian nomad or pariah, Russia truly is an Orthodox-Muslim, an Orthodox-Buddhist country.

The Bolsheviks launched a campaign of persecution against Orthodoxy and engaged in the mockery of all religion. This is true. At the same time, however, the religious attitude and direction of those Russian and non-Russian masses by whose movements and breath Bolshevism lives is coming to the forefront with even greater clarity, emphasised by the full force of contrast. The Bolshevik mockery of, or indifference toward religion are of as much use for understanding Russia as the Bolsheviks' attempts to implement the eloquent prophecies of Marx in practice.

It is for this reason that Russia is not just "the West," but also "the East," not just "Europe," but also "Asia," and not even Europe at all, but "Eurasia." For this very reason, the historical essence that was embodied in the Great French Revolution is joined by another, far from unveiled essence in the Russian Revolution. The French Revolution was a revolution that took place in a European country with a population of 25 million and an area of 540 thousand square kilometers. The Russian Revolution is taking place in a country that is not entirely European, or not even European at all, with 150 million inhabitants and an area of 20 million square kilometers. France is a part of Europe. Russia on the other hand is a "continent in itself" that is (in a certain sense) "equal" to Europe. The allies of 1814-1815 managed to pacify and occupy France. How great must the new coalition be for it to gain the opportunity to pacify and occupy Russia? The Great French Revolution

**124**

was one of the episodes of European history. The Russian Revolution is no mere episode of European history.

In the present period, two problems have become intertwined. One touches upon deep questions of being and cultural creation; the other translates the terms of ideological denominations into the concrete language of cultural-geographic, cultural-historic reality.

Through immense suffering and deprivation, hungry and covered in blood and sweat, Russia has taken upon itself the burden of finding the truth from all and for all. Russia is mired in sin and godlessness, covered in filth and dirt; however, Russia is searching and struggling in a quest for an otherworldly city. The pathos of history will not stay its hand against those who are calm in their knowledge of the truth, those who are self-content and full. Fiery tongues of inspiration will not descend on the *beati possidentes*, but on those who are restless of spirit: the wings of the angel of the Lord have disturbed the water of the fount.

It seems as if the world has not changed, except for the fact that Russia is now absent from the accommodating civilised world. In this absence lies the change, for in her special kind of "non-existence," Russia is becoming in a certain sense the ideological center of the world.

Translating what has been said above into the language of reality, this means that a new cultural-geographical world that has not yet played a guiding role has appeared in the arena of world history. An intense gaze looks onto the future with disdain: might the goddess of Culture whose little tent had been put up among the valleys and hills of the European West leave for the East? Might she leave for the hungry, the cold and the suffering?

We are under the spell of a premonition. And in this premonition we can obtain a source of contentment of a special kind: the contentment of the suffering. To surrender to contentment means to die. It is not permissible to hide that which is considered to be the truth. However, it is also not permissible to relax amidst this premonition. It is not by quietism, but by the achievement of self-perfection that the affair of history is formed. Those who become prideful will be abandoned by the grace of seeking, and the curse of infertility will strike the self-confident. There is no inevitability, there is possibility. Only by way of intense creativity without any fear of confessing one's mistakes and acknowledging one's weaknesses, only at the price of constant efforts that are realised within the limits of this 'plastic' world that is open to will, does possibility become actuality.

\*\*\*

# THE STRENGTH OF THE WEAK

*Petr Suvchinsky*[117]

\*\*\*

What happens if one has not yet begun to be disturbed,

while another has already come up against a bolted door

and violently beaten his head against it?

The same fate awaits all men in their turn unless they walk in the

saving road of humble communion with the people.

– Dostoevsky ("Pushkin Speech")

At the present time, an event of global importance is unfolding, the true essence and consequences of which are impenetrable even to the most perceptive. This event is the Russian Revolution, not in its socio-political sense and significance, but rather in its national-metaphysical essence. As a manifestation of a socio-political order, it is most likely obediently following the course of revolutionary legitimacy. Its secret lies in its national and global outcome.

In endeavoring to encircle Russia with its outposts, the West is not afraid of the Communist contagion alone. Europe has understood, albeit unclearly and unassuredly, or rather felt the future result of the Russian Revolution, it has already shuddered before it and taken defensive measures. Europe has understood that this outcome is not being determined by the revolutionary energy of Russian Communism, but by the

---

117 Text first published as the second chapter of *Exodus to the East* (1921).

historical predestination of the entire Russian people. It has understood that before everyone's eyes, a former European province is growing and gaining strength, a province which it will inevitably have to engage in combat, a province that will strike first, without waiting for a lofty challenge, and engage itself in a war of conviction, reproach and anger at its recent and, it seemed, eternal metropolis.

Russia has been a great power but never in a governmental sense. The governmental capability of every people is determined by the resultant state-consciousness of all the individuals who make it up. This great-power essence is the predestined potential of the authority, scope, and outpouring of the entire essence of a people. It is the subconscious feeling of power, the fateful weight of the entire mass of the people, a mass that dislodges and moves the environment that surrounds it. It is involuntary self-confirmation, the droit sacré of one's own being. This great-power essence sometimes arrogantly sprouts up, and sometimes weakens, disintegrates, thereby transforming the apparently strong flesh of the state into a crumbling, weak, collapsing human substance. Sometimes, the gift of great-power essence coincides with developed aptitudes for the building of a state; sometimes, however, they are mutually exclusive.

The glory of Russia is not consciously dependent on the governmental capabilities of her people. The glory of Russia has been blindly endowed with its great-power essence. This essence defines the whole history of the collective Russian people, the Russian personality is completely subordinate to it, it determines the qualities of the Russian soul and will; even the qualities of the masses follow from the quality of this distinct personality. Similar to the ebb and flow of the great-power essence of the Russian state collective, the Russian personality is on the path to spiritual ascension, on the path of a vital test, all the while wavering, reeling between rise and fall, ascending and stalling. Ascension astounds with its rising force, as if an unseen hand extends from heaven and swoops it up. Stalling is always horrific through the void of the fall, through the loss of the image of God.

And then humility and obedience border on servility, cowardliness, the dirty feeling of personal lostness: at times, bravery turns into insanity, yielding pride. In this wavering lies the law of the history of the Russian people, as does the law of the life of every individual person among the Russian people. In this interchange of exaltation and humiliation, popular, elemental Russia lived, at times limitlessly like a great power, at times powerless and enslaved when the mysterious forces of popular effort and elasticity suddenly dried up, ran out, were pushed together like the gigantic wings of a frightened bird.

The Russian intelligentsia has long been accustomed to perceiving European culture not in terms of equality, but on the conviction of its superiority, commitment, exclusivity and rightness. This timidity and subordination is undoubtedly rooted in the very essence of Russian nature: if one acknowledges oneself as unequal and allows someone's superiority to take hold of them, then it is necessary to submit and acquiesce, cowardly rejecting one's own. This is a kind of servility, even self-betrayal. In relation to other peoples, elemental Russia was either like a great power i.e. dominant, or it spasmodically compressed itself, collapsing, involuntarily submitting and surrendering, while simultaneously hiding its covenants in the depths of the popular soul.

Universal ideas are reflected by different peoples in the forms of diverse cultures. By developing within itself the genius of universal ideal capacity, the Russian intelligentsia actually combined and absorbed within its conscious all varieties of alien European cultures to the level of total congeniality, thereby harming the self-discovery and affirmation of Russia's own culture. As a result of this, the Russian intelligentsia was internationally enlightened, but de-personalized.

The "intelligentsia" does not, of course, deplete Russia as a whole. In the manifestations of dominant great-power statehood and in the creative work of culture, Russia stores, as a precious asset, examples of a singular, exclusive and genuine national will.

In the present time, in this era of the greatest tragedy of decline, of the paralysis of the sovereign forces and will of the Russian people, in an era in which the whole congregation of Russian statehood has been weakened and blurred, leaving all its internal relations to be reborn and rebuilt, the popular element has unconsciously but imperiously risen to exact persecution, revenge, and denunciation on its conscious part for being unable to provide a familiar, comprehensible, popular, national culture during the great moment of tribulation. It cannot be said that the entire intelligentsia has been expelled, but it can safely be said that, with few exceptions, only the intelligentsia has been expelled.

This exile issued a formidable verdict on that form of perception of Western culture which since the time of Peter the Great has been recognized by Russian consciousness as immutable and true. As far as the creative, oracular genius of Russia has been free and true to its uniqueness, so has this oracular, masterful genius revealed itself in all its timidity and subordinate conditioning. The intelligentsia has been dispersed throughout the world. At the same time, the popular element is once again, through tortuous battles and passions, regaining its mysterious, great-power forces that will sooner or later spread and spill out in all of its former glory and strength. The Russian intelligentsia, which has for the first time been confronted face-to-face, personality-to-personality with the civilized peoples of the world, must thereby, finally, deservedly self-assess its capabilities, and most importantly, its national, popular roots and begin to experience the redemptive process of belated self-discovery and self-confirmation. Only in an effective, actual opposition, not from the "beautiful far" and not in the process of blind assimilation, did the Russian intelligentsia really feel the line that passed between it and its former spiritual idol. It has understood and remorsefully shuddered as its own has turned out to be too invaluable and precious, and the foreign too obsolete and poor. Powerless and banished, the intelligentsia has begun its rebirth and, if it does not interrupt this process, then in the near future it will regain its true strengths and rights. The people gather their strength in collective struggle, while the intelligentsia(s) does so in the experience of personality. At this moment they are enemies because, in thirst for self-expression and liberation from other people's forms of consciousness and life, the people put the intelligentsia on the side of their European enemies. However, it would be a great mistake to think that the Russian people are fighting Europe and the intelligentsia with the sword of Communism. On the contrary: Communism is the final likeness that the intelligentsia has taken in its fanatical defence of the principle of equalization and universality.

Having expelled its false ideological leaders in a burst of hatred, in its search for conscious truth, the Russian people have, in their habitual submissiveness, put their fate in the hands of another and subjected themselves to slavery once again, to the dictatorship of that very same intelligentsia that had ruled up to the very moment the revolution actually manifested outside the realm of fanatical will where it had formerly resided. The unaccountable, rebellious forces of the intelligentsia, selected in a blind drive toward global socialist ideas, have focused a terrifying, painful energy into the unhealthy, overheated atmosphere of the émigré community and the underground. This will is fiery, merciless, vengeful, and without any restraint; it has now grabbed the popular masses, which have lost their guiding star while in its grasp. However, its guiding truth is alien and hateful toward the true Russia as much as its predecessor; after all, the Bolshevik international is but a volitional consequence of the cosmopolitan errors and temptations of the godless, sinful spirit of the Russian intelligentsia – sinful, because the dream of the global and true cannot be righteous outside of the Church. All will understand this sooner or later, after which the strong-willed dictatorship of the intelligentsia will be wiped out with the very same elemental fury. Then the great covenant

**133**

of Russia will be fulfilled and her prophetic mystery will come into being: the wisened and calmed people and the enlightened intelligentsia will, reconciled, unite under the single great and all-solving cupola of the Orthodox Church.

***

# BREAKS AND TIES

## Georges Florovsky[118]

***

Why? saith the Lord of hosts. Because of mine house that is waste,
and ye run every man unto his own house.

- Haggai 1:10.

Yet now, if thou wilt forgive their sin; and if not, blot me, I pray thee,
out of thy book which thou hast written.

- Exodus 32:32.

For many long years, 'revolution' has been the Russian
ideal. The image of the 'revolutionary' has appeared to social
consciousness to be the highest kind of patriot who combines
within himself eminence of intention, love for the people, the
destitute, and the suffering, and a readiness toward oblational
self-sacrifice on the altar of common happiness. However
different the contents that different men put into these concepts
may have been (from the monarchic to the anarchic), all versions
have been similar to each other in one respect: in the faith
that, be it through organised civil society, the good sense of the
people, or by the selfless courage of 'those dying for the great
cause of love', they had the strength to and, by way of exerting
their will, they could break the ties of the social and political
evil that had ensnared Russia and establish the highest and
most perfect form of social-cultural life. In this faith in
themselves, in the glorious essence of their inner being, in
the true goodness of their internal constitution concurred all
men, from inveterate Zimmerwaldians to rabid reactionaries.

---

118 Text first published as the third chapter of *Exodus to the East* (1921).

**137**

They thought that it was necessary and sufficient to put on a mask and change into costume à l'européenne; others thought it enough to tear off the Western clothes they had so quickly put on, while yet others sought recourse in a restructuring of classes. There were debates about who the true people were; however, almost everyone was a *narodnik* deep down: all believed in the messianic calling of the entire people or some part of it. Gorky's 'prayer' was close to them all to a greater or lesser degree: "...and I saw her master, the all-powerful, immortal people and I prayed: There shall be no God but thou, for thou art the one God, the creator of miracles."

It is in this sentiment that we entered and 'accepted' the war, placing it in the magnanimous scope of utopian, 'progressive' humanism. Misanthropy and fratricide were seen under the mark of the "greatest happiness for the greatest number of people"; the mysterious contradictory nature of the task (buying and securing a thousand lives at the price of a thousand murders and a thousand deaths) was hidden with hypnotising words about this war being "the last," a "war for peace," for "universal disarmament, internal overcoming, the self-exhaustion of belligerence."

The severity of the moral anguish every one who raises the sword must go through was mitigated by the transfer of pathos to the plane of formal duty - to the homeland and fellow tribesmen, to the good of humanity and civilization. It was truly believed that "the cross and sword are one," that the revealing of the bestial elements of human life would magically enlighten them, and that the war would be followed by the blessed time of "eternal peace." Men would make themselves perfect to such a degree that it would be possible to turn swords to plough-shares. It is for this alluring dream that men happily went off to kill and die.

In its name, the ecstatic hymns of the "magnanimous and merciful" revolution sounded four years ago. When from beneath the 'bloodless' image, which was known from legend and dear from tradition, the demonic contours of the growing collapse started to brazenly make themselves manifest among the carbon-black and wandering wafts of incendiary catastrophe, when beneath the reddening smoke before our very eyes chaos was "startled into action," the uncomprehending societal mind started to speak of some mistakes and miscalculations, about prematurity, about tardiness, about the confusion of the idea, about the uncouthness of the masses, all the while not losing its faith in an easy and possible correction, and, as if it were seeking to defend itself, it concentrated its gaze on squabbles of daily life, on all kinds of crisis, from that of production to that of paper, all in order to not see the all-encompassing, terrible dash into bottomlessness, the rupture of body and soul.

There, where death and disease
have been passed by the slashing gauge –
disappear into space, disappear
Russia, my Russia…

And Russia has disappeared. Not only has Russian "statehood" disappeared, not only has our hereditary way of life disappeared: national unity has collapsed, all social bonds have disintegrated, and, as was the case with the Tower of Babylon of old, a mixing of the tongues has taken place within our consciousness. Into the currents of this historical maelstrom has been drawn everything that Russia had become through the ages, everything She was when we first started loving Her, a "strange love" though it may have been.

Peering into the mouth of the "silent Russian sphinx" with its wise smile, we suddenly, unexpectedly see the ghoulish image of an "enormous, disgusting beast, a-hundred maws and barking," and, what is most horrifying, we recognise within it the concretion of our own, ancient, ancestors' hopes. The longer we stare at this terrible riddle, the clearer we feel that these old dreams have not yet lost their power over our souls as well, and that we still believe, or want to believe in a "successful conclusion," in a "natural sequence of things," in the creative power of lofty ideals.

In this great cataclysm, all fissures and crevices have opened, primordial stocks have been carried up the surface, the depths have been laid bare. We have felt the bifurcation of the Russian national element. And we have seen Russia standing:

at a crossroads,

neither daring to take up the sceptre of the Beast,

nor the light yoke of Christ

And we have seen that we love Russia precisely for this two-facedness of hers, for her endlessness in which two abysses, above and below, are joined. Atavistically enchanted by the straining of raging forces, we once again dream of strength and glory on an elemental scale, of human strength and glory.

There is truth in the fact that this 'disappeared' Russia is stronger than the West, which persists until now; however, the truth of repudiation does not redeem the possible mendacity of affirmation. This is precisely the reverse of the pink optimism of the author of the "Theodicy": all are right in the fact of their affirmation and only err in their repudiations; only someone who believes in his omnipotence, in his inborn goodness, one for whom evil is an error and not a sin could speak that way. Of course, no one 'made' the revolution, and no one is guilty of its horror and sorrow. It created itself, it was irresistibly born as the result of the entire Russian historical process that preceded it. Everything in the revolution is irresistible, everything is marked with the seal of Judgement. However, out of what did it grow? Out of the good, holy, eternal, sacred elemental forces of our people, from its 'idea', from the fact that "God thought about it in eternity," or from a spiritual lie, a crookedness that was put at the foundation of our historic existence by human will?

We will comprehend the past and become worthy of the future only when it does not become a sweet hope for us, but a duty, when hopes are reborn into a thirst for victory, when the thickened, almost apocalyptic atmosphere of our days pours streams of true religious pathos, of the 'fear of God' into our souls, when behind the collisions of finite human will with the blind occurrences of the 'great Faceless Nothing' we comprehend the Christian tragedy of internal bifurcation: I do not do the good that I wish to do, but the evil that I wish not to. When we understand that only:

> With the Lord Creator
>
> there is the eternal obliteration
>
> of all earthly suffering…

We are not speaking of "repentance." There has been a great deal of repentance in Russia, a very great deal, even to an excessive and exuberant degree. Repentance managed to become so habitual that it became a pose, a caricature, transforming into prideful self-deprecation, into the most exquisite and refined form of spiritual delusion. The accounting and all-national confession of our own sins (as well as those of others at the same time) became not the laborious achievement of providential rebirth, but a stylised sentiment, and good deeds and worthy penitence were replaced by the overexertion of a self-flagellating and self-exposing voice. We are now speaking not of the arithmetic of sin, but rather about the need to feel horror in the face of current events, to feel the entire mystery of life that is splitting into two, to see through the reality of evil and temptation.

"Imagine that you are creating a fabric of human destiny for the sake of making men happy in the end, giving them peace and rest at last, but that it was essential and inevitable to torture to death only one tiny creature—that baby beating its breast with its fist, for instance—and to found that edifice on its unavenged tears, would you consent to be the architect on those conditions?" This is the question Dostoevsky posed to himself, and he shuddered in agony as he did not understand, did not accept this harsh world.

However, it is not by the tears of one tortured child, but by the hands of tears and blood that the "fabric of human destiny,"

**141**

the fabric of the fate of Russia is founded and created. It is now being forged by bloodied hands, there, in deserted spaces. For years upon years we have lived in hatred, rage, a desire for vengeance, a desire for victory and punishment. Some kill, others die, all hate. There are even those who dare to call their hatred 'sacred,' who dare to speak of the "sweetness of hating one's homeland," as in the old days. All kill: some with words, some with looks, some with swords. There is no love in anyone. There is no way out, as there is no desire for repentance. We are suffering. We even cry, bitterly and inconsolably. However, our tears are still those of an offended child, not the tears of a man who has stood face-to-face with his 'second death.' We are confidently capable of justifying our lowest means with a 'higher' goal: we still hope all too stubbornly that pride will melt away entirely. The downfall of our 'geographic fatherland' is hiding the horror of the dying of human souls from us. It is not terrible that men die, but rather that they cease to be human. There is only one exodus from this horror and fear. Our hearts should burn not only for our 'Great Russia', but above all else for the cleansing of the darkened Russian soul. It is not in prideful guesswork, nor in prophesies, nor in the enjoyment of the outpouring of national forces, nor in the contemplation of the superhuman strength and power of elementary popular forces, but in repentance created by tears, burning prayer, and providential forgiveness from Above that will we acquire the right to believe, hope, prophesy, and call out.

\*\*\*

# THE MIGRATION OF CULTURE

*Petr Savitsky*[119]

\*\*\*

The evolution of culture can be examined from, among others, the point of view of the geographical movement of its centers, i.e. the focal points of the cultural life of those peoples which in one era or another have exerted the greatest influence on the surrounding historical environment. If we turn to the cultural life of the "Old World," particularly that environ whose historico-cultural tradition is today imprinted in the culture of Western Europe, we see that the process of the geographical shift of the leading cultural centers within this environment has been marked by a definite tendency. We will focus our attention on this part of the Old World which we call "Western" in contrast to the Southern and Eastern parts, Hindustan and the Far East, which had and have their own unique civilizations.

The culture by which Europe lives today, having, of course, changed over many millennia, drew what is for us its tangible beginning in the civilizations of Mesopotamia and Egypt. If this fact is translated into climatic-geographical language, and if we assume an unchanged climate, which would be generally correct since our historical periods are negligibly short in the process of cosmic changes, then it is the case that in this period the cultural focal points were to be found within those regions having an average annual temperature of around 20 degrees

119 Text first published as the sixth chapter of *Exodus to the East* (1921).

celsius and higher: Nineveh (Mossul) having an average annual temperature of +20.4°, Babylon (Baghdad) +23.3°, and the ancient Egyptian Thebes (Kosseir) +24.6°.[120] Insofar as in this era the regions of significance were those lying beyond anterior Asia, and first and foremost the region of the Aegean world, these regions were the extreme southern limit. Cretan culture existed on a territory with an average annual temperature approaching +20° (+18.2° in Capea in Northern Crete). This was the case until approximately 1000 BC, around which time we can regard the central and northern regions of the Aegean-Hellenic world as having begun to play a major role.

The era around 1000 BC was the era of the so-called Mycenaean-Trojan culture. Subsequently, by way of a long historical process, the predominance of cultural influence shifted from the countries of the ancient East to the countries of the Greco-Italic North-West, first and foremost to ancient Hellas and later Rome. This evolution marked the shift of cultural centers from regions with a warmer climate to those with a more moderate one. It can be said that starting around 1000 BC, the most important cultural focal points of the Western part of the Old World lay in climates with an average annual temperature of around +15° and higher, ancient Troy with +15°, Athens +17.3°, and Rome +15.3°. Soon after the Birth of Christ, these culturo-climatic relations underwent further transformation. Gaul began to advance in the arena of cultural creativity, gradually to become the bearer of Latin culture and, as such, would partially replace Italy and Rome. At the turn of the eighth and ninth centuries, this process acquired a certain political formalization by the fact of the restoration of the Western Roman Empire in the form of the Frankish Empire of Charlemagne. The role of Italy in the development of Western-European culture did not henceforth lose significance, just as the role of Egypt (e.g. Alexandria) did not diminish amidst the emergence of more northern centers. But in itself, the very

---

120 Here and throughout we have borrowed such data on average annual temperatures from Dr. Julius Hann's work, *Handbuch der Klimatologie* (Stuttgart: 1883).

emergence of Gaul-France undoubtedly marked the transition of cultural focal points to a sphere of a more severe climate. The climate of Gaul-France is characterized by an average annual temperature of less than +15°, Avignon having +14°, Paris +10.3°, and Brussels +9.9°. Yet this rise was not tied to any decline in the cultural role of its more southern neighbor. Simultaneously with the emergence of the cultural significance of Gaul-France in the West, in the East, the hegemony of cultural influence shifted from the central and northern regions of the Aegean world to the even more northern capital of Constantinople, with an average annual temperature of less than +15° (+14.1° to be precise). Taking into account that the most important *fait nouveau* or "new event" in the history of culture of the first millennium AD was the birth of the cultural significance of Gaul and the emergence of "Frankish" culture, whose centers were located in regions with an average yearly temperature of around +10°, we think that there are grounds to contend that between the Birth of Christ and 1000 AD the leading centers of the culture of interest to us came to be localized in regions with average annual temperatures of approximately +10° and higher (the Arab civilization of this era flourished in climates with an average of approximately +20°).

In what direction did the focal point of culture shift over the course of the second millennium AD? It seems to us indisputable that over this period the culture of the Western part of the Old World continued its advance northward (which had begun several thousand years before), or more precisely, toward those lands with a harsher climate. It is impossible to ignore the cultural significance of the peoples inhabiting the British Isles already in the first millennium AD (the culture of Ireland and Anglo-Saxon cultures) amidst an average yearly climate of +10° and slightly lower (London being +10.3°, Hull at +8.8°, and Edinburgh +8.2°). In the second millennium AD, and especially in its second half, this significance increased to an enormous extent. Around 1000 AD, Norman culture loomed as one of the most active factors in the cultural being of Europe, and it inhabited lands with an average annual temperature slightly exceeding +5° (Bergen +6.9°, Christiania +5.2°). Around the same time, the Frankish civilization of the Carolingian era split into several differentiated national branches. In the cultural existence of one of these nationalities which took shape and would acquire major significance, the Germanic, a prominent role fell to the eastern regions of its territory, the "Eastern Marches," e.g. Brandenburg and others. The Germanic Eastern Marches and Scandinavia lie within a thermal region with temperatures lower than +10°, the average yearly temperature being at +8°, +7°, and even +6° (with Königsberg, the former capital of Prussia and the birthplace of Kant, being at +6.6°). We will not venture any further into the examination of the geographical-climatic distribution of the centers of modern culture. Instead, we will state our conclusion directly: in the second millennium AD, the culture of the Western part of the Old World's leading focal points rose northward, up to regions with an average temperature of approximately +5°. Such a brief examination of this question leads us to establish the following schema of cultural-geographical shifts, according to which the cultural focal points of the Western part of the Old World were located:

- up to 1000 BC in regions with average annual temperatures around +20° and higher;

- from 1000 BC to the Birth of Christ in regions with average annual temperatures around +15° and higher;

- from the Birth of Christ to 1000 AD in regions with average annual temperatures around +10° and higher;

- from 1000 AD to the present in regions with average annual temperatures around +5° and higher.

We do not ascribe absolute accuracy to this schema. In particular, by the designation "around" we bear in mind the possibility of deviations in average annual temperatures below the specified values with a margin of up to 2.5°, i.e. half of the thermal value that separates the neighboring historical-climatic

**148**

groups of this model from each other. It is also completely obvious that this schema sets only the lower thermal limit of these regions in which the leading centers of culture came to be distributed in corresponding eras. This limit has moved over time toward harsher climates, which has meant an increase in the relative cultural significance of colder countries. This shift does not exclude the possibility and fact of powerful cultural life existing in each of these eras in countries even significantly south of this limit, as well as individual cases of the shift of cultural focal points from colder to warmer countries. Our model aims rather to establish the cultural-climatic fait nouveau of each of the eras in consideration, and this fait nouveau invariably turns out to be the spread of culture in its leading manifestations to countries with successively colder climates.

With regard to the more recent era, we wish to recall the following: in the second half of the second millennium AD, the culture of the Western part of the Old World, represented in this period as "Western-European," was as such no more than one culture existing on the planet, one which coexisted in all previous eras indeed with a multiplicity of other cultures but which, upon fully or almost fully differentiating itself from them, turned out to be capable of establishing, whether for long or briefly, for the first time in the observable period of human history, a system of connections between the peoples of the entire globe. In this process, this culture gained predominance both militarily and in terms of cultural influence over the cultures of all other peoples, and thereby conditioned the possibility for Europeans to colonize vast regions beyond Europe, including all of America and Australia and parts of Africa. This fact most substantially expanded the geographical sphere within which the centers of "European" culture could shift. This is a question of both the present and the future. With regard to the past, we have seen that the focal points of culture underwent a process of historical evolution toward regions with harsher climates. Beginning migration from countries close to the maximal average annual temperature known on the planet (in upper Egypt reaching around $+25°$, the maximal known being approximately $+28°$), culture moved to colder regions and reached the countries of Central and Northern Europe. We observe this process exclusively in relation to that specific culturo-historical world which we call the "Western part of the Old World," leaving as an open question the nature of geographical tendencies in the development of other culturo-historical spheres which have existed and are extant on the planet. Nonetheless, we attach to this designated process of geographical-cultural movements a certain world-historic significance, because in light of the above it is precisely this concrete historical culture, being the bearer of these shifts, that at a certain moment in the second half of the second millennium AD found within itself the potential to break the fetters of intra-planetary disconnection and to subjugate to greater or lesser extents the whole world to its influence. Thus rising to world-historic significance, this culture, in reaction to the past, overshadowed with this significance both the very culturo-historical evolution that nurtured it and, among other things, the very evolution of cultural-geographical shifts which we have examined. We have established this tendency of evolution altogether empirically. We cannot and do not set before ourselves the task of offering a causal interpretation of it. We shall note only in comparison, for which we wholeheartedly refer to the proverb *"comparaison n'est pas raison"* ("comparison is not explanation"), that in this process of geographical movements, which has taken place in what on a cosmic scale is but an infinitesimal interval of time, a certain parallelism can be seen with the processes of the organic evolution of the world that unfolded over an infinitely more vast span of time.

> "The middle of the secondary period was, apparently, a uniformly warm and humid period during which the entire face of the planet was more or less dominated by climatic conditions similar to those of the present equatorial zone... The Cretaceous period saw the beginning of the differentiation of a polarized world.... The warm zone with its reefs of zoological origin became increasingly narrow... On the continents, increasing cooling and drying was accompanied by the formation of biological zones, the extinction

of various biological groups, and the birth of new ones. In the secondary period, cold-blooded creatures were gigantic in size; there existed species adapted to diverse forms of existence: amphibians, reptilians, and running, swimming, and flying creatures. Cooling led to their extinction, and predominance passed to hot-blooded creatures: birds and mammals…"[121]

It is interesting to compare with this evolution the process of the migration of culture to more severe climates as we have noted with regard to the cultural destinies of the Old World. Just as "later" species of living creatures were born with the cooling of the planet, so have "later" cultures been born in colder countries. Cold - if this cooling which affects the Earth's climates, insignificant in the structure of the cosmos, can even be called 'cold' - is a defining factor of evolution. It conditions modifications in the forms of the organic world. Does it not also ensnare human culture in its most intense manifestations? And will the existence of both the organic world and human culture not end sooner or later with its icy touch? This is a topic which offers food for thought.

Yet no trend, no matter how clearly it may have expressed itself in the past, can justify predictions of the future, and no comparison can grant it this quality. However, the existence of a tendency conditions the emergence of expectations.

The second millennium AD is elapsing. If the forces which have been active in the cultural development of the Western part of the Old World over the past millennia will continue to operate with the same intensity, then it would be legitimate to anticipate that in the third millennium AD, continuing at the same pace as in the past their movement toward the cold, the cultural focal points of the world will move toward climatic zones with an average annual temperature of around 0°. Among the regions of the globe which are punctuated by average annual temperatures reaching between +5° and 0° and which are at the same time inhabitable by modern man, the only regions

---

121 Emmanuel de Martonne, *Traité de géographie physique* (3rd edition; Paris: 1920), pp. 741-742.

of significance are those of Canada (with Winnipeg at +0.6°, localities in central Saskatchewan at 0°, and Fort Chipewayan on Lake Athabasca still in the realm of wheat culture at 2.5°), the adjacent areas of the United States of America (northern Minnesota at +3°), and those regions of Northern, Central, and Far Eastern Russia, including both European Russia and Siberia (with Moscow at +3.9°, Kazan +2.9°, Yekaterinburg +0.5°, Krasnoyarsk +0.3°, Irkutsk 0.1°), i.e. those regions which are parts of the geographical sphere which we call "Eurasia." Thus, the persistence of this tendency of geographical-cultural shifts into the future would seem to suggest that the cultural focal points of the world whose culture was borne in recent centuries by Western Europe will move to Russia-Eurasia and North America...

Within these geographical worlds, and along its path, culture is heading not only toward areas with lower annual averages, but also to countries that are much warmer; for instance, New York, not to mention the southern states, has an average annual of + 11 ° C. Culture is settling and asserting itself in these warmer regions as well. In the system of cultural-geographical thought, or more precisely the cultural-climatic concept expounded here, this fact can be seen as one of those phenomena accompanying the process of the migration of culture toward the "poles of the cold" in the depths of North America and Eurasia. It would be ridiculous to argue for the scientific certainty of such a concept. Furthermore, from the point of view of the principle of freedom of philosophical conviction, which, according to the nature of things, should prevail wherever an attempt is made to predict the future on the basis of rough estimates and empirical trends, it is perfectly acceptable, for example, to believe that, having reached the present limit, the leading centers of culture will once again move to the South.

For those who are inclined to think that the processes of geographical-cultural shift will proceed in the future in the same direction as in the past, the possibility arises for seeking out signs that the cultural centers of our time are really moving and have moved in the direction of Russia-

Eurasia and North America and for attempts to connect the expectations arising from the observation of the trend of culturo-geographical shifts with the living impressions of the present. Here we could cite the advantage which North America has gained in recent years in the economic life of nearly the entire globe, in large part thanks to the intense economic activity of those harsher-climate regions whose development is most significant from the point of view of the geographical-cultural trend established here. We could also point to the ever-growing political significance of the United States of America. On the other hand, let us recall the in some sense central position which Russia has occupied in the ideological life of the world in recent years by the fact of the turmoil and strife of its revolution, as well as, to a certain extent, by the totality of its culture. Meanwhile, in one of the processes of its cultural evolution, Russia is by way of agricultural colonization and the relocation of centers of industry leaving the former cultural territory of its Center and North-West, moving evermore to the East, to the vast spaces and steppes on the margins of European and and Asian lands, to those regions where the average annual temperature reaches 0°.

> "Oh, my Rus'! My wife!
>
> Our long path is painfully clear to us.
>
> Our path - the arrow of ancient Tatar will
>
> Has pierced our breast.
>
> Our path is the steppe…"
>
> - Alexander Blok

One might think that the leading centers of culture and their most influential focal points are now no longer solely in Western Europe, as was the case until recently, but in Russia-Eurasia and North America, and that these two regions, or rather, two continents, are emerging to be on par with Western Europe and are "replacing" it in the sense of taking upon themselves part of the endeavor of cultural creativity (which, of course, does

**153**

not mean the culturo-historical "elimination" of the previously active world).

We come to the prediction of such a "change" by establishing a certain tendency of culturo-geographical movements, a tendency which, in our opinion, is essential to understanding the fate of culture, but which determines only the outer frame of the culturo-historical process. Our point of view is, in a certain sense, a formal-geographical one. Our immediate task is to indicate the perspectives which open up from this point of view. Following the geographical movements of cultures, we see that the Anterior-Asian, Mediterranean, and Western-European cultures replace one another. Here we pose the question: will their heirs and, in particular, the heirs of Western-European culture (or its coexisting "companions") be North American culture on the one hand and Eurasian culture on the other? The name "Eurasia" expresses for us, among other things, the conjunction of the Russian element with various non-Russian ethnic elements in its surrounding environment. If we were asked how we would translate this geographical schema of cultural shifts into the language of ethnography, then, following the establishment of the Chaldean-Egyptian, Greco-Italic, and Romano-Germanic periods, we would designate the cultural existence of North America as the continuation of the Romano-Germanic period, and on the matter of Russia-Eurasia we would speak of a Slavic-Mongolian, Slavic-Turanian, or already Russian-Mongolian or Russian-Turanian period.

How does the situation of the process of cultural-geographical and culturo-ethnographic evolution stand in regard to changes in the content of culture? Our concept implies, of course, that this content undergoes historical changes, and that such changes correspond to the stages of geographical and ethnographic shifts. In this concept, the forms of the geography and ethnography of culture are at once the bearers of the specific content of the latter: religion and philosophy, poetry and art, statehood and economy, technology, and everyday life. It would be of importance to establish a gradation of the intensity of these changes in the content of cultures accompanying individual stages of culturo-geographical and ethnographic shifts. Unfortunately, not possessing a yardstick with which to measure the differences in intensity, we are compelled to confine ourselves to the empirical postulation of the existence of the latter, the existence of differences between, for instance, the shift of cultural focal points such as from the Argolis of King Agamemnon to the Attica of Pericles and their shift from the countries of the ancient East to Hellas as a whole. The question thus arises: is the conceivable shift of culture from Western Europe to Russia-Eurasia and North America similar to the shift of focal point from Argolis to Attica or approximate in character to the shift of culture from the ancient East to Hellas? If this question is formulated with regard to Russia in particular, then it could be posed thusly: Is Russia's advance the advance of one "European" country in the sphere of "European" culture, similar, for instance, to the growth of significance of Gaul-France alongside that of Italy and the replacement of the conceivable "Italic" period with a French one, or is this emergence of a new culture (albeit genetically associated with the culture of Western-Europe) representative of such a radical change of tradition as, for example, that which Hellas accomplished with regard to its "inheritance" of the ancient East, or the New World with relation to the ancient world?

The process of the shifts of cultural focal points from Argolis to Attica and from the ancient East to Hellas were extreme cases. History provides examples of culturo-geographical shifts which are moderate in terms of radicality, such as the replacement of the Hellenic world by the Hellenistic world. The question could be asked: with regard to the culture of Romano-Germanic Europe, do the cultures of Russia-Eurasia and North America not exhibit some kind of likeness to the relations of the intermediate type?

This problem is adjoined to yet another. The emergence of a leading cultural role for "young" countries does not in itself mean that the centers of the "old" culture lose their significance.

**155**

Indeed, in the organic world, newborns, young people, adults, and the elderly all coexist. But in general, the young outlive the old. Similarly, in the world of culture, the "younger" centers will obviate, albeit gradually, the significance of the "old." There are exceptions: for instance, the culture of Ancient Egypt outlived many other "younger" cultures. But the general rule is otherwise.

How will Russia-Eurasia and North America relate to "Europe"? Will *le déclin de l'Europe, der Untergang des Abendlandes,* the death of the West, proceed? Or will Europe, in all of its cultural fermentation, prove to be more stable in its cultural significance than the others entering the historical arena of the world, together or alone? We shall set aside the ideological abyss of potential divergences. Instead, we will confine ourselves to some brief indications of the differences with respect to Western Europe between the individual positions of North America on the one hand and Russia-Eurasia on the other, both on the scale of the geographical "leap" associated with conceivable cultural-geographical evolution and the nature of the cultural tradition which they both possess.

The emergence of powerful cultural life in North America is a kind of "revolutionary" fact of cultural-geographical evolution. The relocation over the ocean of those centers of culture which at their roots composed the culture of the "Western part of the Old World" eliminates this culture's qualitative belonging exclusively to the "Old World" and imbues it with an essentially new geographical configuration. Yet, an equally new cultural-geographic fact is the appearance in the broad culturo-historical arena of the regions of North-Eastern Europe and North Asia which have been mastered by the Russian element. These regions remain within the "Old World." It can be said that in an external-geographic sense, North America is further away from Western Europe than Russia-Eurasia is, and for this reason, if the future does not belong to Western Europe, then in the perspective of conceivable cultural-geographical evolution, it is Russia-Eurasia that is the direct heir of the cultural continuity of the "Western part of the Old World." The situation stands differently with regard to the content of cultural tradition. North America is a country populated entirely by way of immigration from Western Europe, and in some sense it is the flesh of Western Europe's flesh and the blood of its blood. Over the course of time, America is developing and will develop its own tradition as a matter of course. However, at its core, America's traditions are fully derived from Western European culture. Russian culture, meanwhile, encompasses not only traditions taken from Western Europe, but also others, such as the cultural tradition it inherited directly from Byzantium.

If we perceive Russia in light of this expanded interpretation, and if we foresee and ascribe significance to the participation of Tatars and Sarts, Georgians and Armenians, Persians and Turks in Russian culture, then it can be said that the Russian element, in its spiritual being, dwells at the intersection of the Western-European tradition and the traditions of the old, "pre-European" East. While the culture of Romano-Germanic Europe is enjoying unprecedented expansion with the rise of North America, in the 'Old World' a new world is rising to cultural prominence whose cultural tradition has a different and in some sense more complex constitution than that of North America.

***

# ON NON-HISTORICAL PEOPLES: THE FATHERLAND AND CHILDREN'S LAND

## Georges Florovsky[122]

"The process of history is combustion." - Novalis

The idea of culturo-historical inequality and, as follows, inequality between peoples, has its origins in deep antiquity, in the times when Israel distinguished itself to be "God's chosen people" among the motley masses of "gentiles," when the "free" Hellenes contrasted themselves to the "barbarian-slaves." In the consciousness of the generations closest to us, this thought has taken upon itself the form of an antithesis between "historical" and "non-historical" peoples, between those peoples who have lived through long series of historical transformations and therefore harbor a vast amount of consistent cultural layers, and those new, hitherto mute, culturally-virgin peoples "lacking heritage" and ancestors. Here the problem of nationality has been refracted through the prism of the global historical scale of life and has found resolution in the perspective of the singularity of the historical process and the linearity of its path. It is not with a beam of rays or a bundle of parallels, but with a single line that the destinies of mankind are directed, as a single whole, toward the realization of a single, universal task. Slowly, by continuous steps, mankind moves toward its cherished goal. But not all of humanity at once enters the world arena,

---

122 Text first published as the seventh chapter of *Exodus to the East* (1921).

**159**

as some peoples are replaced by others and one hoists over the others ever newer and higher tablets. They do not annul one another, but steadily accumulate and deepen the heritage of wisdom. As Hegel said, all past centuries are combined in the present. The riches of "universal human civilization" grow and gain strength. But, so it seems, the limited number of "historical" peoples who have inherited from others the leadership of universal life has already been exhausted, and that people to whom the last turn has fallen is called upon to forever preserve for itself the right to cultural hegemony and the significance of being the center of the world. Such is the enviable lot of "Europe," the "Romano-Germanic" world which took shape out of the ruins of the ancient Roman Empire and inherited from its predecessors their statesmanship, religious revelations, and cultural predispositions. A "change of peoples" occurred within this world which eventually led to the Germanic people becoming the "heart" and "capital" of world culture. During a time of patriotic grief, state humiliation, and popular despair, Fichte convinced the "German nation," in a fit of religious enthusiasm, that it alone constituted a "people" in the authentic, strict - and messianic - sense of the word, and that only to it was that genuine "love for the Fatherland" of enlightened ideals accessible. In nearly the same years, in striving to reconstruct a complete model of the successive destinies of mankind, Hegel came to the conclusion that none other than the "folk spirit" of the Germanic tribe, its *Gemüth*, is the highest point of the development of world Reason. After a series of attempts, the latter had at last found an adequate form for its self-revelation.

The series of culturo-historical migrations has ended. And those peoples who, like the unwise virgins of the Gospel parable, have still not managed to take on leading roles in the "past" are now doomed to forever remain in the cast of historical extras who may not ever be given the opportunity to come out from behind the curtain of historical life, condemned to the darkness of oblivion into which more than one people that has lived its course has already departed. The right to participate in the historical drama is thus granted by descent, nobility, and, so to speak, purity of blood, with rootless and forgotten kin having already been excluded. Unable to find any creative force, the only thing left for them to disclose is an ability to quickly assimilate. The higher their relative importance in the world turnover and the closer they are to the original in the process of imitation, the more accurate copies of it they will become.

The stock of "new" words has already been exhausted. Everything available to human achievement has already been fitted in the treasuries of "eternal and absolute wisdom." The key to the world mystery has already been found. The all-conciliating and all-resolving word has been uttered. Henceforth, the problem of production is to yield its place in the economy of cultural life to the problem of distribution and exchange. The matter to be taken further is not the creation of new values, but the assimilation of what is already at hand, what has been achieved, and "communing" with the wisdom of the ages. The type of the self-sacrificing seeker of truth is to be replaced by the *Kulturträger* type, the enlightener and preacher of paternal precepts. Between the "beneficent hand of Providence," the dialectical self-realization of world Reason, the iron laws of the biological and economic "struggle for existence," and the "most immutable laws of physiology" - there is no difference insofar as the fatal necessity of historical development has forced human life to cast itself into final, unalterable forms held standard for all of the anthropological genus of bipeds.

The "uniformity of nature" is the basic law of both world and historical life. The number of active cosmic factors is constant, and the laws governing them are unchanging. So it was, so it shall be - this is the main, pervasive idea of the "evolutionary" worldview. The forces active in nature have always been in operation, and they alone, in accordance with the necessary laws revealed by the modern investigators of nature and observers of the lives of people and human societies. "The future," as Herzen said with his usual ruthlessness, "has been given into bondage before birth." Those fears which filled the timid humid heart in the old "catastrophic" worldview of the time of Vico, of the disputes between the "Neptunists" and "Plutonists," and even of the time of Cuvier, have been dispelled. Those "laws of nature" which varied once upon a time can change once again, the cosmic process can turn onto new paths, new forces can unexpectedly disrupt global harmony, and everything that has hitherto existed will fall into oblivion. But the "theory of progress" insures against such a possibility. And along with this risk the sense of "personal responsibility" is abolished as completely superfluous to the wheel of the well-established mechanism of the "system of nature." Thus, behind the culturo-historical opposition between historical and non-historical peoples lurks another, deeper opposition, that of the culturo-philosophical opposition between two tones of life, two understandings of life, the retrospective and prospective, which Zarathustra so soulfully condensed into his volatile words on the "country of fathers" and the "country of children," the *Vaterland* and *Kinderland*:

> Indeed, you couldn't wear a better mask, you people of today, than that of your own face! Who could recognize you! Written full with the characters of the past, and even these characters painted over with new characters: thus you have hidden yourselves well from all interpreters of characters! And even if one were to give you a physical examination, who would even believe you have a body? You seem to be baked from colors and paper slips glued together. Motley, all ages and peoples peek from your veils; motley, all customs and beliefs speak from your gestures.[123]

But they do not have their own living face, nor their own convinced word. They have only the wisdom of their fathers, only their forefathers' testaments. Their faces are turned to the past - there, and not in the present, they seek provisions for

---

123 All quotations of Nietzsche are taken from *Thus Spoke Zarathustra: A Book for All and None* (translated and edited by Adrian del Caro and Robert Pippin; Cambridge: Cambridge University Press, 2006) - Ed.

the future, striving to catch on to the "trends of development." A kind of pride is forged over the years around the quantity of past generations. The most ancient is considered the strongest. Genealogy replaces the principled justification and substantiation of the essence of the trial of time, the test of ideals. Thus is created the type of the "Western old believer." "It was laid down before our time—let it lie so forever and ever."[124] Everything that is not rooted in deep, subterranean layers becomes a chimera, and "groundless dreams" are contrasted with "primordial beginnings," "successive traditions of the human race" with the "fulfillment of higher possibilities." Herzen grasped the very essence of this ideology when he wrote to Chicherin:

> You know a lot. You know well. Everything is fresh and new in your head, and most importantly you are sure that you know and are therefore calm. You firmly await the rational development of events to confirm the program unveiled by science. You cannot be at odds with the present, for you know that if the past was so-and-such then the present should be such-and-so and lead to such-and-such a future. You know for certain whither to go and whither to lead.

The philosophy of progress is oriented entirely toward the past. It is from the past that all programs of action are deduced and on the basis of the past that historical predictions are made. The future itself is projected into the past, either in the form of the everlasting idea of world-ruling Reason, or in the form of hidden potentialities of the extant which unfold of immanent necessity in time, or in the form of a conscious choice of will to life. Besides, "history repeats itself." All "peoples" pass through one and the same cycle of transformations, the difference being only in tempo and rhythm and in the counting of generations. In terms of the history of one people, we can read ahead into the history created by another. "*Historia est Magistra vitae*" - in this aphorism, Cicero merged all the culturo-philosophical hopes of the "fathers." Turgenev wrote to Herzen: "We, Russians, belong by language and species to the European family, *genus Europaeum*, and as follows in accordance with the invariable laws of physiology we ought to follow the same path. I have yet

124 Quote of Avvakum Petrov - Ed.

**163**

to hear of a duck belonging to the duck species which would breathe with gills like a fish." And thus he mocked the Russian "riddle," the "Russian Sphinx" with years of silence, seeing in it the familiar traits of the Yaroslav peasant downtrodden by need and unbearable labor with his stench and heartburn. He likely measured the latter with the scales of the "magnificent edifice of majestic civilization composed over the ages" - composed in the West, that is.

It was in this ideological atmosphere that the first attempt at a "philosophy of Russian history" was born. Russian historiosophy began at once with escape. The dreary, cheerless, discouraging pessimism of Chaadaev's "First Philosophical Letter" was invoked by none other than the statement that "we have never advanced along with other people; we are not related to any of the great human families."[125] "Our history is not linked with anything and neither explains or demonstrates a thing," Chaadaev said, for we did nothing "as the edifice of modern civilization was arising out of the struggle between the northern people's energetic barbarism and the lofty religious thought [of Christianity]," and "nothing that was happening in Europe reached us." "While the world was being completely rebuilt, nothing was being built in our land: we remained squatting in our hovels made of small joists and thatch." "We Russians, who have come into the world like illegitimate children without a heritage, without a link with the men who preceded us on earth, we possess within our hearts no teachings prior to our own existence...Our memories do not go back beyond yesterday." And thus, having "given nothing to the world, taken nothing from the world, bestowed not even a single idea upon the fund of human ideas," having "no inner development," we, according to Chaadaev, "all resemble travelers," "we grow but we do not mature." "We move so peculiarly through time that, as we advance, each preceding moment escapes us irrevocably...new ideas sweep away the old," and "the indelible

---

125 All quotations of Chaadaev are taken from: *Philosophical Works of Peter Chaadaev* (translated and edited by Raymond McNally and Richard Tempest), *Sovietica* 56 (University of Fribourg/ Springer Science+Business Media, 1991) - Ed.

characteristics which a movement of progressive ideas engraves upon men's mind and gives them power, does not even make an impression upon our intellects." As naturally follows, "not one useful idea has germinated in the sterile soil of our fatherland; we have launched no great truth," for we completely lack the "hereditary patrimony of ideas." "We are one of those nations," Chaadaev declared, "which do not seem to form an integral part of humanity," and it is in this sense "it can be said that we are an exceptional people." Even if we wanted to get away from this dubious and painful vantage, even if we wanted to enter history, and "if we wish to take up a position similar to that of other civilized peoples, we must, in a certain sense, repeat the whole education of mankind" - newly and briefly. Thus, with these words, Russian "Westernism" was born on the soil of the universal plan of human history. Such was no longer the common sense of the "Tsar-Craftsman," nor a spontaneous *Drang nach Westen*, nor an ordinary Europeanization, nor an authentic historiosophy of national fate. If there are no blood-ancestors, then they must be procured; one needs to achieve access to "one of the great families of the human race" by adoption. These families are somewhat akin to Noah's Ark, and "those who do not make it inside are doomed to death, obscurity, and sterility."

Yet Chaadaev's patriotic anxiety immediately softened into fertile hope, into anticipation of the future, as soon as he realized that being an historical newborn does not at all mean being doomed to the lot of perpetual infancy, and that having nothing of note in one's past is far from equivalent to the prospect of eternal insignificance. On the contrary, "We have never lived under the rule of historical necessities," Chaadaev wrote in his "Apologia of a Madman," "never did an omnipotent law precipitate us into the abysses which the times dig in front of nations." "Let us rejoice in the immense advantage of... obeying only the voice of enlightened reason with a deliberate will." Thus, lack of historical heritage turns from shameful poverty into priceless wealth. Old soil is too full of "memories," too littered with the refuse of long centuries of life. New shoots will have to sprout on "depleted soil" and make their way through the crowding of aged ones. The weight of age-old acquisitions, of inherited prejudices and fulfilled and broken hopes, always opposes and burdens thought, always paralyzes the fearlessness of a creative quest. The power of a crystallized, apperceptive mass hinders an open-minded view and complicates the straightness of original, unique identity with intricate fractures. As Herzen wrote:

> The past of the West binds him. His life forces are shackled by the shadows of the past... The bright, humane sides of modern European life grew in narrow medieval alleys and institutions; they are fused with old armor, cassocks, and dwellings designed for a completely different life - and separating them is dangerous, for the same arteries run through them. Amidst the inconveniences of inherited forms, the West respects its memories and the will of its fathers. Its way forward is blocked by stones, but these stones are monuments to civil victories or tombstones.

The West is the "land of only the past," a land that has already been established and is therefore no longer moving, a land in which efforts are allocated to protecting ancestral riches and cleaning museum treasures.

But no amount of cultural wealth can replace the irrepressible impulsiveness of youthful growth. "*Sero venientibus ossa*" - this Western European proverb harbors false wisdom: latecomers receive as a gift the reserves of a crystallized life-experience, thus avoiding the painful burden of experiencing it themselves and being freed from a good half of historical temptations and sinful falls. Such a line of thought has found recapitulation in Russian consciousness on more than one occasion since the times of Chaadaev, Solovyov, and Dostoevsky, dispelling the merciless specter of "non-historicity." The "Slavophiles" felt to no worse degree than the "Westernizers" how "beautiful and majestic is the West," where "inspiration and faith merge in bright rainbows and the fire of the living stream of light poured forth."[126] It is no wonder, then, that Slavophile mouths dropped the winged words "land of holy miracles." They passionately professed

126 Quote of Aleksey Khomyakov's 1835 "*Mezhdu*" [Between] - Ed.

**166**

"Europe" as their "second fatherland." But they also knew that "all this has long been a graveyard and nothing more" - albeit, "a most precious graveyard": "Precious are the dead that lie there, every stone over them speaks of such burning life in the past, of such passionate faith in their work, their truth, their struggle and their science, that I know I shall fall on the ground and kiss those stones and weep over them."[127] The very same words were said almost literally by Herzen in his address to Turgenev as a representative of Russian "Westernists": "You love European ideas - and I love them too - these are ideas for all history. They are a tombstone on which is written the testament not only of yesterday, but of Egypt, India, Greece and Rome, of Catholicism and Protestantism, and of the Romanic and Germanic peoples." All of this is but "a rarity, a sarcophagus, a magnificent trace of a past life." All "European culture," all of the brilliance and noise of "civilization" that stuns and strikes the senses, is of the past, not the future. "The wind from the West brings tears," Solovyov would say several decades later. Not only tears, but tears of tender gratitude for a world that has since passed on and died, tears of reconciliation. "The heart has not returned from the land of the dead"; it will await new "imperious thought and word" from another, a new country, while the old will give impetus to action only as a point of contrast.

It has long since become cliché to affirm that poets are not created by education, they are born. But no one has yet managed to convince the human masses that culture cannot be taught, it cannot be "learned," "adopted," "inherited," that it can only be crafted, created by the free exertion of individual forces. In the expression "cultural tradition" lies a fatal ambiguity. Historically, "*Natura non facit saltus*" is a lie. On the contrary, all of history consists of "leaps." Cultural succession is continued only by he who renews it, who remakes traditions into his own, into an integral element of his personal being and, as it were, creates them anew. "You creators, you higher men!," Zarathustra spoke, "One is pregnant only with one's own child." When historical

---

127 Quote of Dostoevsky's 1880 *The Brothers Karamazov* - Ed.

"mutations" and the unforeseen arising of new forms of existence cease, then culture dies, and only stagnant everyday life remains. And this "everyday life" is indeed inherited. "Everyday life" is frozen culture, objectified ideas. In their objectification, ideas lose their unique spirit, their autonomous rhythm. Everyday life does not immediately form, it is sometimes forged over the course of centuries. But when it has finally taken shape, this means that life has exhausted itself along this line of development and pushed up against some kind of inner limit. Culture is none other than that which has not crystallized into "everyday life" in *statu nascendi*. Herzen wrote:

> Wherever a species has already taken form, history ceases, or in the very least becomes more modest and develops leisurely in the same form our planet did: having matured to a certain period of cooling down, its crust changed little by little. There are floods, but no global deluges; there are earthquakes here and there, but there is no universal upheaval... Species stop and consolidate different capacities to a greater or lesser extent unilaterally in one or another direction; they satisfy them, can hardly step over them, and if they did, then this would be in the same one-sided direction. A mollusk does not covet becoming a crawfish, nor does the latter seek to become a trout. If it were possible to presume animal ideals, then the ideal of the crayfish would be a crayfish with a perfect body... A species which has taken shape, after bursting above its strengths and falling below its capacities, little by little balances itself out, moderates itself, and loses its anatomical eccentricities and physiological wildness, acquiring instead fecundity and beginning to repeat, in the form and likeness of the first settling down of the forefather, its designated appearance and individuality... A generation later, there are no more impulses; everything takes its usual order, personality fades, and changes in specimens are hardly noticeable in the ongoing routine of life... While some are satisfied with what they have achieved, unformed species continue to develop near and around the finished species that has completed its cycle.

In this lies the only "law" of life: the young incessantly displace the old. That is what makes it life. If the number of "historical peoples" has indeed been exhausted, and if the "change of peoples" has indeed stopped, then this would mean that life itself has ended in the face of imminent death. If the dream of a golden age and blessed island could ever become a fact, then this would mean the onset of an endless era of eternal hibernation, of eternal stagnation. With the achievement of all aims, the very notion of movement would lose any meaning. We, the forerunners of this imaginary era, an era that is at times so passionately desired and called for, could not even in our dreams invent such a "future human" for whom the contrast of the given and the norm, the sought for and the present, would seem so meaningless. Yet, if nature is only a system, then this kingdom will come against our will. The second law of thermodynamics, that upon which all our calculations of the physical world are based and that to which human struggle with nature and the "conquest of nature" for human goals is subordinated, holds that the entropy of the world increases, i.e. all the irregularities in the world smooth out and the number of cosmic transformations is constantly decreasing, with less and less space for them - in a word, the world tends toward rest. The rest of death is, after all, only another expression for the elimination of all disharmonies and the quenching of all inequalities. If the world is ruled only by "laws," then we are digging our own graves and preparing to fill them ourselves.

But what are the laws of the world and in what sense can we speak of their domination over all that exists? The "reality" of such, in the sense that they represent, so to speak, an exact copy of the relations between the forces of nature as they exist in and of themselves, *an und für sich*, is something which no one could dare to assert. The perspective that these laws are a means for understanding the world has already deeply taken root, which is to say that the laws of nature known to us are in essence the laws of existence as passed through the prism of our understanding of the world and our ways of thinking about the world. Thus, the question is: are these means immutable and unchanging? The only grounds for a positive answer are presented by the proverbial "uniformity of nature," which expresses nothing more than a dogmatic, volition-affirming faith in the notion that the future is an unambiguous function of the

**169**

past. We try to create with our intellectual imagination such an ideal image of the world that the forces acting in it generate exactly those phenomena that we are observing now and, as we know, have been observed before us. We try to explain certain factual materials and certain concrete historical facts in such a manner. By constructing a "plan" of historical progress, we mean to establish a causal inevitability for the present, and we proceed from the tacit presumption that the past rests in the present as if at a dead end. And if, in the end, it begins to seem to us that historical life is governed by iron laws of fatal predestination, then this is only because we started with such a premise. After all, the human mind will always find in things whatever it vests in them to begin with. In actuality, historical prospects have slid and changed more than once. It once was customary to divide history into ancient, middle, and new, but this habit had to be parted with as soon as antiquity was revealed to have had its own "middle ages" and as soon as it became clear that what we considered to be one period of a single world-historical process was in essence a complete whole, an autonomous culturo-historical unit with its own beginning, acme, and end. Other such closed historical cycles were discovered outside of the Mediterranean cultural world. Regardless of how long the Book of Daniel's schema of four kingdoms held, in the end, the complete unsuitability of this model became clear.

Our historico-genetic models have always rested, at one end, on a certain present and, on the other, a certain past. We can make forecasts and predictions with confidence only under the condition that we initially exclude the possibility of surprises, fractures, and bends  - in a word, if we exclude creativity. Calculations are to be carried out as if there is only everyday life, and no culture. From there we derive a new everyday life from the old one while forgetting about the link between them: the human personality. Seized by ominous foreboding, Vladimir Solovyov claimed it was no longer possible to see history as a straight line divisible into ancient, middle, and new. All that remains is to play out the epilogue of this great drama, though it might drag on for many acts. But was the specter of "pale death" which stood before this thinker as he neared his grave the specter of universal death, or only a sentencing of the past? Is the death of Europe the death of mankind? To make this assertion, one would need to equate Europe with mankind. Can this be done without violating the facts? Is European culture the first ever? Are we not aware of the extinction of "cultures" no less magnificent?

"It will not be overly long, "Zarathustra predicted, "and new peoples will originate and new wells will roar down into new depths. An earthquake, afterall – it buries many wells, it causes much dying of thirst: it also brings to light inner powers and secrets. An earthquake reveals new wells. In an earthquake of ancient peoples new wells break out."

"The general course of evolution," Herzen wrote to Turgenev, "allows for an endless number of unpredictable variations... What is there that has *not* developed out of the same matter: dogs, wolves, foxes, hounds, greyhounds, swimmer-dogs, and pugs?... Common origin does not condition only one biography. Cain and Abel were siblings, and yet what different careers they had..." Recalling Turgenev's comparison, Herzen continues:

> A duck does not breathe with its gills, and it is even more true that it does not fly like a hummingbird. You are right to know that in the life of the duck there was a moment of hesitation, when the aorta did not bend down but branched out with a tendency to forming gills. However, having physiological inheritance, habit, and the capacity for evolution, the duck did not stop at the level of the poorest respiratory organ, but evolved lungs. This means simply that the fish has adapted to the conditions of life underwater, and that gills do not walk, but the duck does... We are now faced with finished, settled types which are so far apart from one another that any transition between them is impossible. Behind every animal shines a long history of aspirations, progress, *avortement*, and balancing over the course of which its forms finally calm down, not realizing a vague ideal but stopping at the possible, at the level of the Russian saying 'and yet it lives'... Some parts of the human race have achieved their appropriate form and have, so to say, conquered history. Others are creating their form in the midst of activity and struggle. Still others,

**171**

like the recently dried bottom of the sea, are ready for all kinds of seeds, for great sowings, and present all an inexhaustibly rich soil.

As if anticipating the contemporary theorists of "creative evolution," Herzen laid the foundations for a new sociology - alas, still unconstructed - based not on the notion of the monophyletic evolution of life, but rather on the idea of a fan-shaped divergence of life's paths.

The "fatherland," the country of legend and succession, is replaced by "the land of children, undiscovered in the furthest sea"... to which the prophet of the *Übermensch* deliriously called the "higher people." But where is it, this new "land of the blessed"? What compass will indicate where to sail? The answer is clear: toward the land of "non-historical" peoples.

The young Kireevsky wrote in his "Westernist" *Lehrjahren* of 1830 that, among the European peoples, "every one of them has already fulfilled their purpose, each has already expressed their character" and thus, as if having vented and taken their respective turns at being the pan-human "heart" and "capital of enlightened peoples," they have fallen into an old man's slumber. "Hence why Europe gives the impression of being in some kind of stupor" with its "belated opinions and dilapidated forms, like a dammed river, a fertile land turned into a swamp where only forget-me-nots bloom and a cold, wandering twinkle occasionally flashes." "Out of all of enlightened humanity," Kireevsky wrote, "only two peoples are not part of the general lull, only two young, fresh peoples are blooming with hope: the United States of America and our fatherland." Hegel himself deemed America the country of the future, in which in future times "world-historic value shall be revealed" - a value different and separate from the soil on which world history has hitherto developed. He recalls the proud words of Napoleon: "Cette vieille *Europe m'ennuie!*" In the 1860s, having passed through the painful temptation of revolutionary contemplation, Herzen found beyond Europe "only two active lands: America and Russia, and perhaps Australia, which is only at its beginning." True,

America is the same as Europe, only still young and growing. Herzen wrote:

> Wave after wave, influx after influx is brought to its [America's] shores, and they do not remain in place but move on further. This movement continues within America itself, as new immigrants seep through the main population and sometimes carry it away. Everything is striving, pushing, and hurrying…The United States, like an avalanche taking off from its mountain, pushes everything in its way."

Herzen wrote to Turgenev:

> Russia encircles the tribes on all sides, enclosing them like water… And what youthful plasticity! At what was Joseph II laughing at the founding of Yekaterinoslav when he said that the empress laid the city's first stone, and he the last? Was it not a city that was built there, but a state… and all of Siberia? And the new settlements on the banks of the Amur, where will the star-spangled flag of the American republics be raised in coming days? And what of the easternmost provinces of European Russia? Reading the annals of the Bargov family, I was struck by the similarity between the elder who moved to Ufa province and the "settlers" who moved from New York to somewhere in Wisconsin or Illinois?… When Bargov gathered people from all corners to fill up the dam for a mill, when the neighbors carried the earth with song and when he first solemnly walked along the defeated river, it seems as if you are reading Cooper or Irving Washington.

Thus, Russia's "geographical physiology" itself testifies to Russia's power and strength, the "indefatigability" of its people, and prophecies a future which will handsomely compensate for the absence of a past.

These optimistic forecasts were, of course, based not on "youthful plasticity," but were underpinned by a certain sociological basis, albeit not that of Kireevsky and Herzen. The difference between them was conditioned not by the opposition between "Slavophilia" and "Westernism," between conservative nationalism and liberal cosmopolitanism, but by the fact that only Herzen took his destructive critique of historical prejudices to a conclusion, while the views of the early Slavophiles remained in the same circle and lapsed into

**173**

internal splits. They essentially only added another people to the ranks of those considered "historical" and justified so doing with the restoration of a forgotten "tradition" that was in many cases obviously fictitious. Alongside the "Western" track of the world-historical path originating in Rome, they established an "Eastern" one originating in Byzantium, perhaps from Hellas itself and Jerusalem. The Slavic tribe was included in the plan of historical predestination in the very same place of the "apex" on which the "German nation" was placed in the West. In both cases, culture was confused with everyday life, and achievements with ideals. The future was deduced from the past, all hopes were pinned on it and on us having a history no worse, and perhaps even better than the Western, on us having a rich and old heritage. Instead of accounting for present forces, a review of ancestors was once again made. Only Herzen fully overcame the notion of an "historical people," and only his historical predictions were based on the idea of the non-definiteness of the historical process, on the idea of the "disheveled improvisation of history" which knows neither monopolies nor prerogatives. Only Herzen did not erect historical props, looking only ahead.

Sociology, no matter of what kind, cannot substantiate creative premonitions, it can only reveal the possibility of the birth of "new" cultures, the possibility of a culture being ever-renewed above everyday life. All the Russian visionaries asserting a Russian or Slavic future beheld before their spiritual eyes an altogether clear image of an impending cultural type.

"Orthodoxy" and "socialism" - these are the two landmarks by which Russian foretellers have usually oriented themselves. "Holy Rus," the "God-bearing people," the "land community," and the "choral element" - such are the incessantly repeated slogans of the advocates of Russian "unique identity." Yet these words should not be packed with fixed content, and they should not be understood as referring to concrete historical forms. Rather, they have always been understood first and foremost as "ideas," and if one takes a closer look at the context in which

174

they have usually been thought, then it becomes completely clear that these seemingly incompatible ideas have intersected in the notion of the "whole life" or "free unity" as Vladimir Solovyov put it. It is not for nothing that Dostoevsky called universal Orthodox ecclesiality "our Russian socialism." No matter how often the "due" and the "present" were fused in the consciousness of the Russian intelligentsia into an ugly ingot of nationalist utopia, and no matter how often attempts were made to issue apologia for an entirely specific historical Russian - and Byzantine-Slavic in general - path, the driving thought has always been the idea of overcoming "organization," the idea of the creative personality. The Russian soul has yearned not for system, but for spirit. And with such yearning it has believed that life can be built outside the "narrow framework of legal principles," that all written legislation can be replaced with an unwritten law imprinted in the human heart, and that power and coercion can be replaced by the sincere profession of truth. It has believed in such because it knows that only such a life would be a true fulfillment of the great covenant of God-mankind, the realization of the prophetic prayer of the Eternal High Priest: "that all may be one." Vladimir Solovyov expressed this hope most clearly of all in the early, still purely "Slavophile" period of his work. "Such a people," he said of the messiah-people, "should have no specific limited task. It is not called to work on forms and elements of human existence, but only to convey the living soul, to give focus and wholeness to torn and dead humanity through its union with the whole divine principle. Such a people does not need any particular advantages, for it acts not of its own accord and fulfills something that does not belong to it." This people is the authentic instrument of God, the creative bearer of divine and universal life, of "pan-human and universal culture." Is there any bitter taste for national "self-aggrandizement" here, has "love for the fatherland" been distorted into "national pride"? Are there elements of exaltation in this true messianism whose foundations were laid by the promise given from above to Abraham with the call to leave the land of the ancestors "not for a year, not for many years, but for eternal ages"?

But more than that, the very attempt to recreate a "past" for an impending culture harbored a true grain and *conditio sine qua non.* These unsuccessful "apologetics" wanted to show the possibility of such an ideal being realized by none other than the Russian people or the whole Slavic tribe. "Whoever had to create," Zarathustra preached in the "land of education," "also always had his prophetic dreams and astrological signs - and believed in believing!" Hence the urgent need for historical retrospection, for immersion into the bosom of the popular element in order to check the correspondence between ideas and the forces for their incarnation. Historical exceptions require reference points in the past and present. Here there is no contradiction with revolt against paternal traditions and calls to look only ahead. The notion of "tradition" in the field of "culture" and in the field of "everyday life" is far from one and the same.

When we say that the legal norms of contemporary Europe rest on Roman law, we can trace step by step all the stages of this continuous succession and show the nodal points of its intersecting threads. We can point to the material monuments into which this tradition has been cast and to all the directly interrelated links in the chain stretched from the Licinian Rogations to the Digest and to the Napoleonic Code and the later Germanic codex. We can show that there has been conscious "assimilation and "reception" in the strict and precise sense of the word. The very same could be said of the everyday Hellenization of the Roman world, the Europeanization of modern Japan, etc. But would this be in the sense of how Dostoevsky understood "tradition" when he quite rightly claimed that the utopian socialism of Fourier and the Icarians breathes the spirit of Roman Catholicism? Do we employ the notion of "continuity" or "succession" in the same sense when we say that the philosophy of Europe is saturated with reminiscences of Platonism?

The streams of cultural and everyday "tradition" can diverge sharply and drastically. This is why the face of the Far West, America, is so enigmatic. In terms of everyday life, America is a repetition and exaggeration of "Europe," a hypertrophy of pan-European democracy and bourgeoisness. It is thereby all the more unexpected that one encounters under this crust a distinctly heterogenous tradition of culture, running from the first immigrants through Benjamin Franklin and Emerson to the "self-made men" of Jack London: the tradition of the radical negation of philistinism and the way of life and affirmation of individual freedom. Where does the track of this tradition run? It is almost imperceptible, and "plasticity" only symbolizes it. It is in this tradition, and not in "capitalism," that American self-consciousness sees its spirit which had James as its professing prophet.

Such is the "Russian Sphinx." Despite its "non-historicity" in the "world-historical plan," Russia is a highly complex historical formation. It is not difficult to distinguish the most diverse layers in Russian everyday life - Varangian, Byzantine, Slavic, Tatar, Finnish, Polish, Muscovite, "Saint-Petersburgian" and others. And it is not difficult to ascribe these sedimentary formations to definite causes and actions. It is as if bridges lay themselves down to the Norman "armed merchants," to Byzantine Caesaropapism and the Nomocanon, to the Golden Horde and nomadic others, to the Jesuits and the Szlachta, and so on. But this everyday life does not explicitly exhaust Russian being. Tyutchev wrote: "In the form of a slave the King of Heaven traversed all of you, blessing all," including the Russian steppes and forests. The threads of a web-like subtlety stretch from Dostoevsky and Tolstoy, from Gogol and Samarin, from Father Ambrose and Confessor Seraphim somewhere back further, to the thickets of the Volga, to Nilus of Sora, to Venerable Sergius of Radonezh, and from there to Athos and onward to the glowing expanses of Thebaid. Through centuries and space, the unity of the creative element has been unmistakably felt. The points of its condensation almost never coincide with the centers of everyday life - they are not to be found in Saint Petersburg, in the old capital of Kiev, in Novgorod, nor even in "motherly" Moscow. The intensity of the Russian folk and Orthodox spirit is felt in secluded Russian monasteries such as those of Sergius, Barlaam of Khutyn, Cyril of Beloozero, in Sarov and Diveyevo. The focal points of cultural creativity have lain here since ancient times. To this very day, does the "invisible Kitezh," recognizable only to the faithful eye in the remote wilderness of the forest, on the banks of a spellbound lake, not draw toward itself through magical enchantment the dispersed streams of the national element? The tradition of culture is intangible and immaterial. Its forces are mystical, inter-individual interactions. Its threads intersect in the unknown recesses of the creative human spirit. Its seat is in the deep, intimate bowels of man. When we deconstruct the living currents of Russian cultural life into their components and mint them into sculpted forms, something always slips through our fingers. The intuitively undoubtable Russian "culture," the "Russian element," appears empty before rational analysis. Its outbursts seem to resemble breaks of "tradition," riddles, and deformities. Is such not Dostoevsky's "Russian Marquis de Sade," or Turgenev's sense that man "accepted" Tikhon of Zadonsk "into his heart long ago and with delight," in his own words? In terms of everyday life, such is the product of the terrible city of Peter. In culture, it is the offspring of Optina Pustyn.

Genuine creativity and authentic novelty are always "inexplicable." Mutational outbursts and the turns of hereditary pathways always remain beyond the limits of rational consciousness. But does this mean that they are "causeless," that they do not hail from the "past"? The world is "cosmic," not chaotic, and not for one mind alone. "Improvisations" have their own immanent necessity. Creativity, like the adaptability of everyday life, has its own traditions. But these cultural ties are not comprehended by reason, nor by discursive analysis, but by a sense of feeling which condenses ages into a single moment. Mystical intuition grasps all at once, "all that is, was, and will come in ages" in their subterranean, mysterious connection. Mystical sense feels and cognizes the "God-bearing people," "Holy Rus," the "Orthodox East," and the "godless West." The religiously-enlightened eye sees under the constructive continuity of everyday images the tragic mystery of historical life, it perceives the world as a ceaseless struggle of God's all against the hailstorm of the Antichrist, a struggle tending toward apocalyptic cataclysms, a single drama that plays out over centuries. This eye grasps both its own cultural-psychological continuity and that of its enemies, and it feels itself to be in a certain line and direction. The "past" is invisible, and it does not oppress the present and the future with the blind irresistibility of Fate. The free servants of ideals perform their sacred roles in this mystery, in graceful communion with one another.

The ideals and premonition of the future which reveal themselves in intimate contemplation are the true stimuli of cultural creativity and life - not in the form of an exhaustive program of action or an infallible *regula vitae*, but as an inspiring faith assisted by love. The center of gravity moves into the depths of the personality. The future becomes the cause of the present, as Zarathustra prophetically spoke: "Whoever discovered the land 'human being', also discovered the land 'human future.'" However many or few generations have lived before me, whether I stand in a "pure" or "hybrid" line - this makes no difference. The inner, "supra-historical" voice, not genealogical calculations, tells whither to go.

Here lies the deep or, one might say, intuitive-mystical focal point of the "non-historical" perception of the world. It is not the *vis a tergo* of "vital impulse," nor the innumerable hosts of previous generations, nor irresistible skills which drive "culture" and creativity ahead, but the freely chosen ideal that invitingly draws one out to the horizon. "This voice still sounds in silence without reproach: the end is near, the desired will come true soon."[128]

*\*\*\**

---

128 Quote of Vladimir Solovyov - Ed.

# ON TRUE AND FALSE NATIONALISM

*Nikolai Trubetzkoy*[129]

\*\*\*

Man's relationship to the culture of his people can vary quite widely. Among the Romano-Germanics, this relationship is determined by a special psychology which can be called egocentric. "A man with a marked egocentric psychology unconsciously considers himself the center of the universe, the pinnacle of creation, the best, most perfect of all beings. In comparing two other beings, that which is closer to him, more alike him, is better, and that which is more distant from him, worse. Therefore, any natural group of beings to which this person belongs is recognized by him to be the most perfect. His family, his estate, his tribe and his race are better than all other comparable groups."[130]

The Romano-Germanics, being thoroughly saturated with this kind of psychology, build their entire appraisal of all other world cultures precisely on this basis. Therefore, only two types of attitudes toward culture are possible for them: either the recognition that the highest and most perfect culture in the world is the culture of the people to which the given "evaluating" subject belongs (German, French, etc.), or the recognition that the height of excellence belongs not only to this particular variety, but also to the entirety of cultures

---

129 Trubetzkoy originally planned for this text to be part two of *Europe and Mankind*, but published it as chapter eight of *Exodus to the East* (1921).

130 Nikolai Trubetzkoy, *Europe and Mankind*.

most closely associated with it, created in collaboration with all the Romano-Germanic peoples. The first type is what is called narrow chauvinism in Europe (German, French, etc.), the second type could best be described as "Pan-Romano-Germanic chauvinism." However, the Romano-Germanics have always been so naively confident that they alone were human that they have deemed themselves to be "humanity," their culture "universal civilization," and their chauvinism "cosmopolitanism."

Those non-Romano-Germanic peoples who have adopted "European" culture usually adopt the Romano-Germanic evaluation of that culture along with it, taken in by false terminology such as "universal civilization" and "cosmopolitanism" which masks the narrow ethnographic content of the corresponding concepts. As a result, these peoples no longer base their assessment of culture on egocentrism, but rather on some particular kind of "eccentricity," or more precisely, on "Eurocentrism." We have elsewhere already discussed the disastrous consequences to which the Eurocentrism of "Europeanized" non-Romano-Germanics inevitably leads. To avoid these consequences, the Intelligentsia of the Europeanized, non-Romano-Germanic peoples must undergo a fundamental revolution in their consciousness and methods of assessing culture and come to a clear understanding that European civilization is not a universal culture, but rather only the culture of a specific ethnographic group, the Romano-Germanics, to whom alone it is obligatory. This revolution should fundamentally alter the attitude of Europeanized, non-Romano-Gemanic peoples toward all problems of culture, replacing the old, Eurocentric assessment with a new one built on an entirely different basis.

The duty of every non-Romano-Germanic people is, firstly, to overcome their own egocentrism, and secondly to protect themselves from the deception of "universal civilization" and the desire to become "real Europeans" at all costs. These duties can be formulated in two aphorisms: "know thyself" and "be thyself."

The struggle against one's own egocentrism is only possible with self-knowledge. True self-knowledge will show a person (or people) their actual place in the world, it will show them that they are not the center of the universe or the world. This same self-knowledge will bring them to understand the nature of people (or peoples) in general, and to ascertain that they, as a self-knowing subject, are not at the center or apex, nor is anyone else.

From the comprehension of one's own nature, a person or people will in the process of deepening self-knowledge eventually come to an understanding of the equivalence of all people and peoples. The conclusion of these insights is the affirmation of one's own identity, the desire to be oneself, for he who has not come to know himself cannot be and is incapable of being himself. Only by comprehending one's nature, one's essence with perfect clarity and fullness does it become possible to remain unique without self-contradiction, self-deception, or deceiving others. It is only in the establishment of a harmony and integrity of identity on the basis of clear and full understanding of one's nature that the highest earthly happiness is attainable. At the same time, this constitutes the very essence of morality, for genuine self-knowledge allows one to hear the voice of conscience with extraordinary clarity; a person who lives in such a way that he never comes into contradiction with himself and always remains authentic will undoubtedly also be moral. This is the highest spiritual beauty a person might attain, for self-deception and internal contradiction, being inevitable in the absence of true self-knowledge, always make a person spiritually ugly. In this very self-knowledge lies the highest wisdom available to man, both the practical and worldly and the theoretical, for all other knowledge is illusory and vain. Finally, only in having achieved an identity founded in self-knowledge can a person (or people) be certain that they are truly fulfilling their purpose on earth, truly becoming that which they were created to be. This is an end in itself, but also a means.

This is not a new thought - in fact, it is very old. It had already been expressed by Socrates some 23 centuries ago, and

**183**

even then it was not Socrates himself who came up with the phrase "know thyself," it was something he had read among the inscriptions of the temple at Delphi. Nonetheless, Socrates was the first to clearly formulate this idea, the first to realize that self-knowledge is a problem of both ethics and logic, as much a matter of right thinking as it is a matter of moral life. The maxim "know thyself" assigns each person a task that is exactly the same, yet essentially different. It is precisely this synthesis of the relative and subjective with the absolute and general that makes it a timeless and universal principle, equally acceptable for all people regardless of nationality or historical era. This principle remains valid to the present day, and moreover, for all peoples. It would be simple to prove that not a single religion exists today which rejects or excludes Socrates' maxim - in fact, some religions confirm and deepen it. It would be quite possible to show that Socrates' principle is congruent with most religious concepts.[131] However, this would lead us too far astray and distract us from the immediate goal of our present reasoning.

It is important to note that the results of obtaining self-knowledge can differ depending not only on differences between self-conscious individuals, but also in relation to the depth and forms of knowledge itself. The work of the Christian ascetic, which consists of overcoming the seduction of sin and striving to be the type of being God created man to be, is essentially self-knowledge produced under the guidance of grace and constant

---

131 In essence, "know thyself" as a rule of life is based on a certain philosophical optimism, on the recognition that the true nature of man (as well as the entire universe) is good, reasonable and beautiful, and that everything malign in life (evil, ugliness, nonsense and suffering) is a result of deviation from from one's nature, from a lack of consciousness of one's true essence. Therefore, the Socratic rule is unacceptable only for advocates of extreme philosophical pessimism. For example, a consistent Buddhist who recognizes all existence as fundamentally evil, meaningless, ugly and associated with suffering, should *a priori* reject Socrates' demand. For such a Buddhist, the only way out is suicide - not physical suicide (which is not advisable due to the doctrine of the transmigration of souls) but spiritual suicide, the destruction of one's spiritual individuality (*nāmarūpa*), i.e. "Nirvana," or "overcoming birth and death without a trace," according to Buddhist terminology. However, most Buddhists are far from being this consistent and limit themselves to the theoretical recognition of some of the basic principles of the Buddha. In practice, they are adherents of a morally-indifferent polytheism and, as such, can also accept the Socratic rule to a certain extent.

prayer. This leads the ascetic not only to moral perfection, but also to mystical insight into the general meaning of being and creation. Socrates' self-knowledge, devoid of specific metaphysical content, led to the harmony of the psychological personality, to wisdom in behavior, and even to a certain insight into earthly matters despite its complete agnosticism regarding metaphysical issues. For some, self-knowledge follows a course strongly predominated by logical reflection, while for others irrational intuition plays the decisive role. The forms of self-knowledge are extremely diverse, it is only important that their result is a clear and more or less complete picture of oneself, clear knowledge of one's nature and the specific gravity of each of its elements and manifestations in their mutual interrelation.

All that has been said so far relates not only to the individual, but also to collective self-knowledge. If we consider a given people as a psychological whole, as a collective personality, we must also recognize that some form of self-knowledge is both possible and obligatory for it. Self-knowledge is logically connected with the concept of personality: wherever there is a personality, there can and should also be self-knowledge. And if, in the sphere of a private human life, self-knowledge serves as an all-encompassing goal exhaustive of an individual's happiness and all of the morality, spiritual beauty and wisdom one has attained, then the same universal principle must hold for the collective personality of a people as well. The particularity of this collective personality lies in the fact that a people lives for centuries during which time it is constantly changing, and therefore, the self-knowledge attained in one era is no longer valid in the next; it will, however, still serve as the basis for beginning any new effort toward self-understanding.

"Know thyself" and "be thyself" are two aspects of one and the same position. Outwardly, true self-knowledge is expressed in the harmonious original life and activity of a given person. For a people, this takes the form of an original national culture. A people can be said to know itself if its spiritual nature or individual character finds its most complete and vivid expression in an original national culture and if this culture is completely harmonious, i.e. its individual parts do not contradict one another. The creation of such a culture is the true goal of every people, just as the goal of any individual belonging to a given people is to achieve a way of life in which their original spiritual nature is fully, brightly, and harmoniously embodied. Both of these tasks (the task of the people and the task of each individual within it) are intimately connected with each other, mutually complementing and conditioning one other.

In developing one's own individual self-knowledge, every person understands themself, among other things, as a representative of a people. The spiritual life of each person always contains elements of the national psyche, just as the spiritual appearance of any given individual representative of a people exhibits features of the national character in different ways depending on the specific individual in question, their connections with other individuals and more particular elements such as family and estate. In self-knowledge, all of these national features find expression in their connection with an individual character, wherein they are affirmed and refined. In knowing oneself, a person begins to "be themself," and thus becomes a vivid representative of their people. Their life, being a complete and harmonious expression of their conscious, distinctive individuality, inevitably embodies national features. If this person is engaged in creative cultural work, then their work, in bearing the imprint of their personality, will inevitably also express their national character, or at the very least not contradict it. But even if the person in question does not actively participate in cultural production, only passively assimilating its results or playing a more functionary role in the cultural life of their people, even in this case the very fact that their life and activities fully and vividly embody the national character (mainly in terms of tastes and predispositions) will surely contribute to emphasizing and strengthening the general national tone of the everyday life of their people. It is everyday life which inspires the creator of cultural values, giving them tasks and material

186

for creativity. Thus, individual self-knowledge contributes to the identity of a national culture, an identity which, as we have indicated, is a correlate of national self-knowledge.

At the same time, an original national culture also contributes to the individual self-knowledge of specific representatives of a given people. It facilitates their understanding and cognition of those features of their individual natures that serve as manifestations of the general national character. In true national culture all these features find vivid and salient embodiment which allows each individual to more easily find them in himself, to know them (through culture) in their true form and to give them a proper assessment in day-to-day life. Harmoniously self-sufficient national culture allows each member of this national whole to be and to remain themself, while at the same time being in constant communication with their fellow tribesmen. Under such conditions, a person can take part in the cultural life of his people quite sincerely, without pretending, before others or himself, to be something he has never been and will never be.

All of this should make clear that there is a tight, inner connection and constant interaction between the individual and national self-knowledge. The more members of a given people who "know themselves" and "become themselves," the more successful efforts to achieve national self-knowledge and create an original national culture will be, which is, in turn, the key to the success and intensity of individual self-knowledge. Only in the presence of such an interaction between individual and national self-knowledge is the correct evolution of national culture possible. Otherwise national culture may stop at some point while the national character, composed of distinctive individual characters, continues to change. In such a case, the entire meaning of the original national culture will be lost. The culture will no longer invoke a lively response in the psyche of those who instantiate it, will cease to be the embodiment of the national soul, and will turn into the traditional lies and hypocrisy which complicate rather than facilitate individual self-knowledge and individual identity.

If we admit that man's highest earthly ideal is complete and perfect self-knowledge, then we must also recognize that a culture is only genuine insofar as it contributes to this self-knowledge. In order to promote individual self-knowledge, a culture must embody those elements of psychology common to all or at least most of the individuals involved in this culture, i.e. the sum of the elements of the national psychology. Moreover, a culture should embody these elements vividly and prominently, for the more vividly they are embodied, the easier it is for each individual to recognize them in himself through the medium of culture. In other words, only a completely original national culture is genuine, and only this kind of culture is capable of meeting the ethical, aesthetic and even utilitarian requirements demanded of any given culture. If a person can only be recognized as truly wise, virtuous, beautiful and happy when they come to know themself and thus "become themself," then the same must also apply to the people as a whole. Applied to a people, "being oneself" means "having an original national culture." Demanding that culture grant "the greatest happiness to the greatest number" does not alter the matter. Indeed, true happiness does not lie in comfort, nor in the satisfaction of particular private needs, but in the balance, in the harmony of all elements of mental life (including "needs"). By itself, no culture can give such happiness to man, for happiness can only be found within man himself, and self-knowledge is the only path to achieve it. Culture can only help a person achieve happiness, it can only facilitate one's striving toward self-knowledge. And this is only possible if the culture in question is alike that which we identified earlier: completely and vividly original.

Thus, the cultures of all peoples should be different. Every people should vividly reveal its entire individuality in its national culture, but in such way that all of its elements harmonize with each other, expressing a unified national tone. The stronger the differences between the national psychologies of particular nations are, the stronger the differences should be between various national cultures.

Peoples which are close to one another in their national character will have similar cultures, but a universal culture, identical for all peoples, is impossible. Given the manifold diversity of national characters and mental types, such a "universal culture" would either be reduced to the satisfaction of purely material needs with total disregard for spiritual needs, or it would impose a way of life arising from the national character of a singular ethnographic type on all peoples. In both cases, this "universal" culture would not meet the requirements expected of any authentic culture. Such a culture cannot bring real happiness to anyone.

Therefore, the aspiration to establish a universal culture should be rejected. On the contrary, it is the aspiration of each people to create its own special national culture which finds complete moral justification, while all cultural cosmopolitanism and internationalism deserves decisive condemnation. However, not all nationalism is logically and morally justified. There are different types of nationalism, of which some are false and others true, and only true nationalism can be an unconditional positive principle of the behavior of a people.

From the preceding it is clear that only a nationalism which emanates from an original national culture or is directed toward such a culture can be recognized as truly, morally and logically justified. The thought of this culture should guide all the actions of the true nationalist: he must defend it and struggle for it. Everything that facilitates an original national culture he must support, and everything that interferes with it, he must eliminate.

However, if we apply these standards to the existing forms of nationalism, we will quickly come to the conclusion that the majority are not true, but false. More often than not, when we come across nationalists, they are those types for whom the originality of the national culture of their people is completely unimportant. They instead seek exclusively to ensure that their people receive state autonomy at all costs, that they are

**189**

recognized by the "big" nations and "great" powers of the world as full members of the "family of nation-states," and that they become exactly like these "big nations" in their own everyday lives. This type of nationalism is found among different peoples, but appears especially frequently among the "small," non-Romano-Germanic nations, where it takes on particularly ugly, almost caricatured forms. Self-knowledge does not play any role in such nationalism, given that its supporters do not even want to be "themselves," but on the contrary, want to be more like the "others," more like the "big nations," more like "the masters," despite the fact they are often neither big nor masterful themselves. When historical conditions arise wherein a given people falls under the power or economic dominance of another people that is completely alien in spirit, leaving it unable to create an original national culture without freeing itself from the political yoke or economic dominance of these foreigners, striving for emancipation and national independence is altogether thoroughly, logically and morally justified. However, one must always keep in mind that such an aspiration is justified only when it appears in the name of an original national culture, for national independence is meaningless as an end in itself. Meanwhile, among the nationalists in question, national independence and 'great-power' status becomes precisely such an end. Furthermore, original national culture is sacrificed for the sake of this end. In order to make their people more like "real Europeans," the nationalists of the type in question try to impose on them not only forms of Romano-German state, law and economic life which are often completely alien in spirit, but also Romano-German ideologies, art and material life. Europeanization, the desire to accurately reproduce the pan-Romano-Germanic model in all areas of life, ultimately leads to the complete loss of any national identity. The peoples led by such nationalists are quickly left with nothing original other than their belaboured "native language." And even this latter element is greatly distorted in the process of becoming an "official" language and adapting to new, alien concepts and forms of everyday life, absorbing an enormous amount of Romano-Germanic words, phrases and clumsy neologisms. In the end, the official "state" languages of many of the "small" states that adopt this type of nationalism end up being almost incomprehensible to the genuine masses of people who have not yet "succeeded" in denationalizing and depersonalizing to the level of "democracy in general."

It is clear that the kind of nationalism which strives only for resemblance to the existing "great powers" rather than for original national identity or national self-realization can by no means be recognized as true. This type of nationalism is based not on self-knowledge, but petty vanity, which is the antipode of true self-knowledge. The term "national self-determination" with which representatives of this type of nationalism like to operate (especially if they belong to one of the "small nations") can lead only to delusion. In fact, there is nothing "national" and no aspect of "self-determination" to be found amidst such attitudes, and it is therefore unsurprising that the ideology of "self-determination" is so often connected with socialism, which always contains elements of cosmopolitanism and internationalism.

Another kind of false nationalism is manifested in militant chauvinism. Here, the matter boils down to the desire to extend the language and culture of one's people to the greatest possible number of foreigners whose own national identities have already been eradicated. The falsity of this type of nationalism should be evident without much explanation. After all, the identity of a particular national culture is valuable only insofar as it harmonizes with the mentality of its creators and bearers. As soon as a culture is transferred to a people with an alien mental structure, the entire meaning of this identity disappears and the self-assessment of the cultural changes. The basic fallacy of aggressive chauvinism lies in ignoring the correlation of any given form of culture with a specific ethnic subject. Such chauvinism, based on vanity and the denial of the equivalence of peoples and cultures - in a word, on egocentric self-exaltation - is impossible to imagine in relation to true national self-knowledge, and therefore stands in opposition to true nationalism.

A special form of false nationalism should be recognized in that kind of cultural conservatism which artificially equates national identities with certain cultural values or forms of life as they existed in the past, not accepting changes to these values even after they have clearly ceased to satisfactorily embody the national psyche. In this case, just like aggressive chauvinism, the living connection between a culture and the psyche of those who instantiate it is ignored at any given moment and the culture is given an absolute value independent of its relationship to the people: "the culture is not for the people, the people are for the culture." This again abolishes the moral and logical meaning of identity as a correlate of continuous and unceasing national self-knowledge.

It is not difficult to see that all the types of false nationalism considered here have practical consequences which are disastrous for national culture: the first type leads to national depersonalization and the denationalization of culture; the second to a loss of purity among the bearers of this culture, and the third to stagnation, the harbinger of death.

It goes without saying that the individual types of false nationalism which we have examined are also capable of merging into various mixed types. All of them have one thing in common, which is that they are fundamentally not based on national self-knowledge in the above-defined sense of the word. However, even those forms of nationalism which are ostensibly derived from national self-knowledge and seek to substantiate an original national culture on this basis are not always true. The fact of the matter is that self-knowledge is often understood too narrowly and achieved incorrectly. True self-knowledge is often hindered by some label which a given people has stuck to itself for some reason or another and does not want to abandon. For example, the direction of the cultural work of the Romanians is to a large degree a result of the fact that they consider themselves to be a Romance language and people on the grounds that among the elements from which the Romanian nationality was created in the distant past, there was a small detachment of Roman soldiers. Similarly, modern Greek nationalism, being essentially a mixed form of false nationalism, exacerbates its falsity with a unilateral view of the Greeks' own lineage. Despite actually being a mixture of several ethnic groups which went through numerous stages of cultural evolution alongside other "Balkan" nations, the Greeks consider themselves to be exclusively descended from the ancient Greeks. Such aberrations depend solely on the fact that, in all these cases, self-knowledge is not produced organically and is not the actual source of this nationalism, but only an attempt to historically substantiate self-deterministic and chauvinistic tendencies.

Observing the various forms of false nationalism in turn underscores what true nationalism should be by contrast. Emerging from national self-knowledge, true nationalism is based on the recognition of the need for an original national culture, the creation of which it sees as its highest and only task, regarding all phenomena in the field of domestic and foreign policy and every historical moment in the life of a given people precisely from the point of view of this main task. Self-knowledge grants the true nationalist a kind of self-discipline which prevents him from forcibly imposing his original national culture on other peoples and from slavishly imitating those people which are alien in spirit but for some reason enjoy prestige in a certain anthropogeographic region. In his relations with other peoples, a true nationalist is devoid of any national vanity or ambition. Building his worldview on self-sufficient self-knowledge, he will always be fundamentally peaceful and tolerant of any foreign identity. In fact, he will feel alienated by artificial national isolation. Having comprehended the original psyche of his people with great clarity and completeness, he will grasp in all other peoples those features similar to his own with particular sensitivity. And if another people has managed to give one of these traits a successful embodiment in the

**193**

form of one or another cultural value, a true nationalist will not hesitate to borrow this value, adapting it to the common inventory of his original culture. Two peoples who are close in their national character and who live in communication with each other, if both are led by true nationalists, will certainly have cultures very similar to each other precisely as a result of the free exchange of cultural values acceptable to both sides. But this cultural unity is still fundamentally different from the artificial unity that comes as a result of one people's aspirations to subjugate its neighbors.

If, in the light of all these general considerations, we begin to consider the types of Russian nationalism which have existed thus far, we will be forced to admit that true nationalism has not existed in post-Petrine Russia. Most educated Russians have not wanted to be "themselves" at all, but instead "real Europeans"; and because Russia, despite its aspirations, could not become a real European state, many of us despised our "backward" homeland. Therefore, most of the Russian intelligentsia, until very recently, eschewed all nationalism. Others called themselves nationalists, but in reality they understood nationalism to mean the desire for great-power statehood, for international military and economic might and for Russia to attain a prominent international position. In order to accomplish these goals, they considered it necessary to bring Russian culture closer to the Western European model. Some Russian "nationalists" based their demand for "Russification" on the same slavish attitude toward Western models. This has mainly entailed encouraging conversion to Orthodoxy, enforcing the introduction of the Russian language and replacing foreign geographical names with more or less awkward Russian ones - all of this was done only because the Germans had done so, "and the Germans are a cultured people." Sometimes this desire to be nationalists "because the Germans are" took on deeper and more systematic forms: since the Germans justified their nationalist arrogance by emphasizing the Germanic race's merits in creating culture, our nationalists also tried to talk about some kind of original Russian culture of the 19th century, inflating to semi-cosmic dimensions the significance of any work by a Russian or Russian subject if it even slightly deviated from Western European standards, declaring such creations "a rich contribution of Russian genius to the treasury of world civilization." Pan-Slavism was created as a parallel pan-Germanism, and Russia was attributed the mission of uniting all the Slavic peoples "following the path of world progress" (i.e. exchanging their identity for a Romano-Germanic one) so that Slavdom (as a linguistic concept) could take a "befitting" or even "superior" place in the "family of civilized peoples." In recent times, this type of Westernizing Slavophilism has become fashionable in Russia even among circles where the word "nationalism" was previously considered indecent.

Similarly, the older form of Slavophilism cannot be considered a pure form of true nationalism. It is not difficult to identify it with all of the three types of false nationalism which we discussed earlier, with the third type prevailing at the beginning, followed later by the first and second. There has always been a tendency to build Russian nationalism on the model and likeness of Romano-Germanic nationalism. As a result of these characteristics, the old form of Slavophilism was bound to degenerate, despite the fact that its starting point was a sense of originality and the beginning of national self-knowing. Obviously, these elements were not clearly understood or framed.

Thus, true nationalism, based entirely on self-knowledge and demanding in its name the complete restructuring of Russian culture in the spirit of originality, has hitherto been the concern of only isolated individuals (for example, some of the "early" Slavophiles); it has yet to become a real social current. This current stands to be created in the future. This will require the complete revolution in the consciousness of the Russian intelligentsia which we discussed at the beginning of this article.

\*\*\*

# CONTINENT-OCEAN: RUSSIA AND THE WORLD MARKET

*Petr Savitsky*[132]

\*\*\*

In the study of economic realities, economic knowledge is concerned with, alongside "internal-economic" relations, i.e. the socio-economic structure of society, "external-economic" relations, first and foremost trade relations on the interregional and international levels. In the context of the latter relations, every country, and within a country, every region, district, or smaller geographic division, is examined independently of the dominant social structure of the economy as "units" of economic exchange, as indecomposable wholes in their contacts and ways of exchange with the "units" of the surrounding region and the whole world.

If we set out to determine the factors which condition the course of such exchanges, then our attention will be drawn to, among other things, the significance of whether goods are being moved and taken into the process of exchange by the ocean or on the continent. Transportation costs are of substantial significance to the formation of interregional and international exchange. It could even be said that if the problem of production (as the starting point of any exchange) is taken to be related in its dynamic nature to problems of the "internal-economic" structure of society, then transportation expenditures turn out

---

132 Text first published as the tenth chapter of *Exodus to the East* (1921).

to be nearly the most important determinant factor of the whole process of exchange, in any case being the least regulated by state power and, in this sense, as an economist of the classical school would say, "natural" or invariably in force. The state, both through its customs policy and by way of influencing the rates of railway tariffs and shipping freights, authoritatively intervenes in and directs the relations of interregional and international exchange. However, even with the most comprehensive regulation of tariffs and freight, the state can only partially eliminate the influence of transportation costs as an autonomous economic element. Moreover, state policy on customs, tariffs, and freight can change, while transportation costs, with the same technology, could remain the same. Therefore, insofar as technology has not been perfected to the point that transportation costs could approach zero, these consequences remain a defining element for the sphere of "external-economic" relations. All the while, maritime and overland freight transportation costs can differ substantially. The German railway tariff before the [First World] War was calculated to be "approximately 50 times higher than oceanic freight" for the same distance, "while even the rates of Russian American railways (which, let us add, were more often than not lower than the cost of production) exceeded sea transport by 7-10 times."[133] Proceeding from the difference in scale between sea and land transport costs, the following conclusion arises: those countries and regions which by virtue of their position can primarily use sea transport are to a much lesser degree dependent, over the course of processes of international and interregional exchange, on distance than are those countries whose economic life is primarily oriented toward continental transport. The former can, in the determination of the paths of exchange which they choose, disregard distance to a certain extent. The latter countries, however, have to handle transportation sparingly and attempt to reduce distance by any means. Because of this, it could be said that in the dominant principles of the sphere of international and interregional exchange the "oceanic" principle

---

133 Carl Ballod, *Grundriss der Statistik; enthaltend Bevölkerungs-, Wirtschafts-, Finanz- und Handels-Statistik* (Berlin, 1913), p. 115.

of the conglomeration of economically complementary states which are not dependent upon distance stands in contrast to the principle of using continental "neighborhoods." Of course, this opposition need not be taken literally, as the cost of oceanic transport is by no means zero. However, in the field of maritime transport, distance is of importance only in extreme cases or, conversely, in cases of close-distance transit. Distance plays a role when it comes to choosing between "long-distance" and "coastal" navigation, as sailing along the coasts and ports of a country where one and the same language, laws, and customs are dominant presents navigators and a vessel with significantly different, lesser demands than does "long-distance" navigation. But since the "long-distance" character of a voyage is presented as a given, the distance loses significance within certain limits.

The ocean is one. The continent is divided. For this reason, the world economy as a single whole is inevitably perceived as an "oceanic" economy, and the scope of oceanic exchange inevitably comes to supply every country and every region of the world economy. Meanwhile, certain countries and regions of the world find themselves in far from similar positions with respect to the ocean. Some are in all of their corners close to the shore of the ocean-sea. In order to join oceanic exchange, it is enough for these latter to, roughly speaking, load and unload their own products onto the ships visiting their ports. Others, however, are completely, to greater or lesser extents, distant from the sea. In order to enter into the general system of world exchange, these countries need to expend additional efforts on delivering the products to the coast and transporting within the continent the goods which they receive from the world market. A view of the situation of given countries from the standpoint of the question which interests us is offered by the so-called "equidistant zone maps" on which the points located at a given distance from the ocean-sea coast are connected by a line.[134] Several such lines are drawn, for instance, across points at a distance from the coast of 400, 800, 1200, 1600, 2000, and 2400 kilometers.

---

134 Such a "sea-lake" as the Caspian is not taken into account.

Examining such maps gives an idea of the different ways by which certain regions of the world are removed from the ocean. There are immense territories within which there are no points that are further from the sea than, say, 600 kilometers. This is the case, for example, of Western Europe in its boundary from the West to the Pulkovo Meridian. Australia has no localities further than 800-1000 kilometers from the ocean coast. The most "continental" points of the three landmasses of Africa, North America, and South America are located no more than 1600-1700 kilometers from the sea coast. Only in Asia are there places from which the distance to the ocean-sea coast is more than 2400 kilometers, as is the case of Ghulja and a significant part of the Russian Semirechye.

On the equidistance maps, the eternally ice-free coasts of the southern seas and, for example, the coasts of the Arctic Ocean near Cape Chelyuskin which are almost never free from ice, are treated as completely equal. In considering the economic question which concerns us, the corresponding correction should be made: the freezing-over of the sea, or the lack thereof, and the duration of such, determine the significance of this water basin to world trade. Given this correction, some regions of North America and Eastern Europe, as well as significant parts of Central and Northern Asia, would seem to be even more remote from the ocean. In England's turnover of foreign and domestic goods, the amount spent on continental transportation per unit of goods appears to be insignificant. But if the Semirechye were to enter into the system of world exchange, the costs of transporting goods from sea to sea would be considerable. Let us presume a uniform price for a single item on the world market. What would this assumption mean for the  costs for the Semirechye to move goods to and from ocean coasts? If all sellers on the world market would get the same price, then so would the producers of the Semirecyhe. Yet no one besides them would have to accept the costs of delivering a product to the world market. These expenses would be deducted from their revenue. Compared to the goods which they acquire on the world market, the cost price would be increased by the cost of transporting these goods from the Semirechye to the world market. In other words, the cost of moving goods from sea to sea would be a loss for Semirechye producers and consumers, one which is not borne by the producers and consumers whose economic activities take place not far from ocean-sea coasts. In our examination, we shall ignore for the time being the existence of inland waterways within continents whose respective natures individually perturb the cost of intracontinental transport, and we will set aside other individual geographic and economic factors which influence the cost of transport. Instead, we will consider the cost of transports on the continent and by sea respectively in direct proportion of distance. Let us imagine the "world market" to be similar to that of London, which is to say a point on the sea coast, on an island. We resort to this concretization of the notion of the world market in order to link participation in "global exchange" in all scenarios with the factor of having to overcome a certain ocean-sea space. Such a presumption seems to us to have empirical grounds. With this assumption, we can definitely say that the scale of the distance from the Semirechye to the coasts, which is unprecedented in the rest of the world, determines the Semirechye's particular "destitution" in the course of the Semirechye joining the system of global exchange. It will receive less for its goods than all other regions of the world, and the imports it needs cost more than for all others. In the field of industrial development, this region's competitiveness in relation to the world market is negligible, and it is conceivable that, even given favorable natural conditions for industrial development, the Semirechye would be doomed to industrial "non-being." With regard to agricultural development, forms of a belated, insecure, but wholly extensive culture find application.[135] Thus, the double destitution of both

---

135 In this case, applicability will arise for those forms of agricultural development which in arguments over land "differential" rent are depicted as the lot of a land plot placed in the least favorable conditions, and which in the Thünen model of the wholly continental "isolated state" positioned in concentric circles around its industrial center fall to the share of the far, most distant zone from the center.

producer and consumer cannot but - ceteris paribus - render the Semirechye a kind of "backwoods of the world economy."

We have cited the Semirechye as an example, although the reasoning applied to it could be valid for any region of the globe marked by a certain distance from the ocean-sea. To what regions and countries of the world does this prospect of being the "backwoods of the world economy" have real significance? If we take the conventional distance from coast at, for instance, 800 kilometers, and look at just which world regions lie at this and an even greater distance from the sea, then it turns out that these regions are:

1.  A small part of the interior Australian desert;

2.  Parts of inner Africa: part of the Southern Sahara and Sudan, the upper Nile, the Congo, and the Zambezi;

3.  Regions in the middle of the Amazon, the Matto grosso plated in Brazil, and the eastern (lowland) part of Bolivia and Paraguay.

Given the current system of economic technology, some of these regions are partially incapable of economic prosperity (desert 1) while those which are do not show signs of intensive economic development because they are economically "rubbed out" by those regions which, although economically similar to them, are closer to coastal zones. Moreover, all of these regions lie within the tropical zone, which in modern times has not yielded any examples of high, intense economic life. It is possible to predict that if any of these regions experience economic flourishing, this will likely be based on the intensive use of those sometimes excellent interior waterways which connect these regions with the ocean (especially the rivers of South America, e.g. the Amazon, which is partially accessible to sea vessels, its tributaries, and the Parana and Paraguay rivers) and thereby fully integrate these regions into the single global "oceanic" economy.

Of greater significance in modern times are the continental regions of North America, i.e. central Canada (Manitou Bay,

Saskatchewan, and Alberta), the northern part of the United States from the Missouri headwaters to the Great Lakes, and some of the middle states that form a triangle between the southwestern tip of Lake Erie, the city of Santa Fe in New Mexico, and Salt Lake City. These areas already partly enjoy strong economic life and, as far as we can judge, further development is within their reach. Despite the existence of inland waterways leading to the "ice-free" ocean (an exception being Canada's rivers), the "continentality" of these regions is now and should be in the future essential to the structure of exchange and overall economic life of North America. This can be said with even greater certainty of the relatively continental regions of Eastern Europe and Asia. Those separated by 800 or more kilometers from sea coast here are:

1. The central and western parts of the Chinese Empire;

2. Kashmir, Punjab, and the adjacent areas of India;

3. Northeastern Persia, all of Turkestan, and all the parts of Siberia and the Far East accessible to economic culture (excluding the Primorsky and Amur regions, east of Blagoveshchensk, all of the Ural and central Volga regions, with a decent portion of the central black soil lands, e.g., Tambov and Penzensk).

It should be noted that among these regions of Europe and Asia, a significant portion of China's "continental" provinces is represented by the Gobi desert and the infertile Tibetan plateau. It could be thought that the far-western parts of China ("outer" Mongolia, eastern Turkestan, and Ghulja) which are separated from the metropolis by the Gobi and Tibet are predestined to be economically adjoined to Russia. Northern India, meanwhile, is "pushed" toward the ocean by the hitherto impassable ranges of the Hindu Kush and the Himalayas which separate it from the rest of the circle of continental lands. The continental regions of China proper tend partly to the waterway of the Yangtze-Kiang, which brings vessels from the ocean into the depths of the Heavenly Empire to Hankou. Despite this, the continentality of China's vast expanses cannot but be reflected in its economic life. As a natural-economic given, as a kind of irremediable fact of nature, this life is to a significant extent weakened in its economic significance by the fact that China's long-stretching eastern territories look to the open and ice-free expanses of the Great Ocean. Vice versa, the continentality of those territories which we call the regions of the "Russian world," i.e. Russia proper, far-western and North Western China, as well as Persia, is greatly enhanced by the fact that the seas which these regions are drawn to, and which to access they have to cover hundreds and thousands of kilometers of continental space, are in all cases closed, "continental," "inland" seas and, in most cases, are ones which freeze over, at times for more than six months. The "isolation" of such a sea, since it does not pass into a "lake" (excluding the water basin from the number of oceanic-sea spaces) is, it would seem, a geographical feature of no significance to economics. This is because if the sea were connected to other parts of the world's water basins by straits or "necks," it would remain open to world economic exchange. But the geographical features of this region are "condensed" into economic reality when correlated with the fact of the political insecurity of freedom of trade, which provides for easy military blockage of access to a water basin. Such political and military circumstances are in essence real factors of Russian economic activity, insofar as we are speaking of such seas as the White, Black, and Baltic or the Japanese in the East.

It would even be comical to state that Russia has, in terms of the prospects of broad great-power expansion and with the exception of the coastline of remote Kamchatka, never made it and never had the chance to make it to the coasts of the "open" sea in the precise geographical sense of the word, i.e, the water basin participating in the hydrographic circulation of the World Ocean. Even the Arctic Ocean extending between Greenland, Iceland, and Scotland (the so-called Wyville Thomson Ridge) has been excluded from general oceanic circulation due to its shallow zone (of less than 600 meters) and it does not even operate like a coastal sea (like the "Chinese" seas or the Antilles) but has a closed, "continental" order. In the South, at the extreme boundary of conceivable Russian expansion, are the Mediterranean and the Persian Gulf, which are characteristically "continental" basins.[136] The "continentality" of such a basin as the one that stretches along the shores of Murmansk is an "abstraction" in an economic sense. But even on the path of such a geographically-derived "abstraction," it would be poignant to establish that, no matter how much Russia aspires in its open political-economic actions within the geographical world to reach the "open" sea, it will never see before itself the free World Ocean that splashes at the docks of New York or San Francisco, the coasts of Ireland or Brittany, and almost all of South America, Australia, and Africa.

However, of even greater economic significance is the freezing-over of the vast majority of those seas to which Russia-Eurasia does have access. Some fanatics of oceanic exchange who have considered the economic opportunities of Siberia have already dreamed of "modern technology creating in the shortest span of time... a Mediterranean out of the Kara Sea, in which the trade ships of all countries will meet."[137] With respect to the Kara Sea, the only thing one can do is refer to future technological miracles. For now, it is inaccessible to any ships for three-quarters of the year. Arkhangelsk is open for shipping for six months. The port of Saint Petersburg freezes over for four to five months, and even the ports on the lower Dnieper, the Azov Sea, and Astrakhan are closed to navigation for one, two, or three months. It bears understanding that the freezing-over of such seas is, in the general structure of world economic-geographic relations, a phenomenon that is in some way "exceptional."

---

136 The Persian Gulf is connected to other of the world's water spaces by a strait that is less than 100 kilometers wide and, moreover, is blocked by islands and shallows, like the whole Persian Gulf itself, of less than 200 meters deep, which on the scale of oceanic depths is completely negligible.

137 "Die Verteilung des Landbesitzes in Sibirien," in *Dr. A Petermanns geographische Mitteilungen*, Vol. 66 (Gotha: Justus Perthes, 1920), p. 254.

Besides Russia-Eurasia, this situation is familiar only to Northeastern Sweden and Canada. However, no matter how endowed Northeastern Sweden is with natural resources of iron ore, white coal, and lumber, it is but a small corner with no chance at playing a decisive role in the economic life of the world. Among the great economic wholes of the planet, the freezing-over of the sea is determined to be some kind of fate - needless to say, not a happy one - facing "Eurasia" and Canada. No matter how much the world listens to the discourses of Russian enthusiasts of "oceanic" and "Pontic" policy on "accessing the ice-free sea," these discourses should, from the perspective of world economic relations, be seen as oddities. Nine-tenths of humanity do not know any "frozen sea" whatsoever. Even in Canada which, as we have seen, is close to Russia in these terms, there is no talk of "accessing unfrozen sea," because it "organically" wields such access on both its Atlantic (e.g. Halifax) and Pacific coasts.

Examining the situation of certain regions of the world in relation to the ocean-sea inevitably leads us to the conclusion that the most "destitute" countries of the world, in the sense of their deprivation of participation in oceanic exchange, is that economic-geographical sphere which we designate as Russia-Eurasia. We would even say that the combination of the regions' exceptional remoteness from seacoast, the freezing-over of its seas, and its "closedness" (which raises the risk of political-military suppression of exchange) puts Russia-Eurasia in a situation with no parallel anywhere else in the world and generates a number of problems which are unheard of beyond its borders. Next after Russia-Eurasia comes China and North America. But if we set aside the Gobi desert, Tibet and those regions west of it, then the economic-geographic significance of China's "continentality" is lessened (as noted above) not only by the comparative insignificance of its most remote regions from the sea (no further than 1600 kilometers), but also by the fact that the seas to which these regions are drawn do not freeze over and are not closed. The same circumstances moderate "continentality" in the southern half of North America, but not in Canada and the northern parts of the United States bordering it. The closedness of those basins to which these regions gravitate - the Hudson Bay and the Gulf of St. Lawrence - are, in the context of the New World and given its lower level political and military tension, perhaps insignificant to the calculations of economic practice. In our opinion, the freezing-over of these basins renders central Canada and the adjacent part of the United States the most "continental" world-sphere following Russia-Eurasia, despite the fact that these regions are separated from the Hudson Bay by no more than 1000-1200 kilometers. Russia-Eurasia on the one hand and Canada and the adjacent United States on the other are not only the most "continental" countries in the world, but, taken together, are also the coldest, in the very least out of all regions of economic significance today. More precisely, they are countries with the lowest average annual temperature.

Here unfolds the connection between "continentality" and the character of climate and, moreover, the certain parallelism, even if only formally logical, between the data of climatology and the economic data with which we are dealing in these lines. As is well known, the main distinction in climatology is that between continental and sea climates (*Das Land- and Seeklima*) and proceeds from the fact that land and water are characterized by different properties "in relation to insolation and heat radiation, i.e. the two main factors which determine the temperature of air." "The specific thermal capacity of water is greater than any other known body. If we take equal weight, then the heat capacity of a unit of the Earth's solid surface is expressed as 0.2, but if we take equal volumes, then the thermal capacity of water is 0.6." Does this juxtaposition not have analogue in the sphere of international and interregional economic exchange's contrast between the "oceanic" principle, expressed in the independence of economically-complementary countries from distance, and the principle of continental neighborhoods? Just as climatological contrast is derived from the specific thermal capacity of water and land, so does economic contrast rest on the difference in the costs of transportation by ocean and land respectively.

For those countries which are distinguished among the regions of the world by their "continentality," the prospect of being a "backwoods of the world economy" is, provided their intensive participation in world oceanic exchange, a foundational reality. In isolation from the world, economic primitiveness is associated with the system of "natural economy." In joining the "world economy," the power of economic-geographical "destitution" is inescapable. The whole "oceanic" world fully expects continental countries to bear the burden of this destitution without complaint, and thereby the countries of the "oceanic" circle can receive additional products and additional markets for their own sales. But is it not possible that the "continental" regions could, avoiding the isolation of the primitive natural economy, at least in part eliminate the unfavorable consequences of being "continental"? The way to this elimination lies in terminating the complete domination of the oceanic "world" economy within the continental world, in the establishment of economic complementarity between spatially contiguous regions of the continental world, and in their development through mutual ties. If a continental country receives minimal revenue minus the cost of transportation for a particular product on the world market, then would it not be more profitable to sell this good not by sending it to the "world market" but to somewhere "close," somewhere "in the neighborhood"? If the cost of buying a product on the world market is higher than it it would be for anyone else due to the additional transportation costs, then is it not possible for the good to be purchased from somewhere from which transportation would be cheaper and at a price which, given the difference in transport costs, would be a gain? Both the seller and the buyer in the intra-continental world would be incentivized to mutual exchange. This exchange will take place given that a good produced in a "continental" area has demand in neighboring continental countries and insofar as this product needed by a continental region is produced within neighboring continental areas. Given the presence of this condition, the intra-continental buyer would profit from purchasing within the continental world, insofar as the cost of transportation from the inner-continental place of production would be cheaper than delivery from the world market. This is so in the case of a continental seller putting up their goods at their site of production at the full price of the world market, but the latter would calculate a discount, since in the case of exporting a good to the world market they would receive the full market price but only enjoy the part which remains after the deduction of the cost of transporting the product from the inner-continental site to the world market. The seller has reason to enter into a transaction with an inner-continental buyer in all cases of the latter's agreement to leave in his hands at least some part of the sum which would have to be allocated for transporting the good to the world market. In all of these scenarios, the seller will earn more than what he would on the world market.

Let us denote the cost of transporting a unit of goods from an inner-continental place of production to an inner-continental place of consumption by "z" and the cost of transporting this unit from its continental site of production to the world market as "x+a," wherein "x" denotes the cost of laneway transportation to the nearest point of oceanic-sea coast and "a" stands for the cost of sea transport from this point to the "world market." The cost of importing this unit from the world market to an inner-continental center of consumption can be represented as "b+y," "b" being the cost of sea freight from the world market to the nearest continental port-center and "y" being the cost of land transport from this port into the continent. With these variables, we can say that inner-continental attraction will remain in force, i.e. there will be reason for the continental producer and consumer to exchange with one another without the mediation of the world market, insofar as $z < x+a+b+y$, which is to say, as long as the cost of intra-continental transportation will be less than the cost of exporting a product from an inner-continental center to the world market plus the cost of delivering this product from the world market to the inner-continental point of consumption. The greater the difference is: $(x+a+b+y)= z$, the more economically effective the intracontinental ties will be. This difference can, in one or another combination, be shared for mutual benefit by the continental seller and consumer. In what proportion they will divide such among themselves depends on the specific conditions of inner continental supply and demand. By dividing this difference, the intracontinental seller and buyer can at least in part eliminate the consequences of that economic-geographical "destitution" which irritates their economic activities. The smaller the "$x$" and, therefore, the larger this difference, the less, all other things being equal, it will affect the level of intracontinental sales and purchase prices of economic-geographical "deprivation."

As mentioned above, in order for such a "division" to be carried out, there must be corresponding production and consumption within the continental world. It thus becomes clear in what sense the economic development of continental countries is conditioned by their mutual ties. The effects of intracontinental exchange between inner-continental regions can only be favorable when the economic state of these regions provides the space for such exchange: for any continental region to rise out of the position of the natural economy, it is necessary for there to be interests within this continental world not only in its own economic development, but also interest from the surrounding continental countries, interests which are concerned precisely with the intracontinental region under such a long latitude and longitude and not just any other country of the world. Countries which lie on ocean shores and have already developed can, thanks to the typically oceanic capacity to ignore distances, seek economic "complement" across the whole space of the globe, and their demands can be satisfied by any country in the world regardless of what part of the world it is located in, as long as it produces the necessary products cheaply enough. The interests of inner-continental regions which have achieved a certain degree of success lie in developing not just any regions of the world economy, but definite ones, namely, neighboring regions, through exchange with whom - and only with whom - can the specific disadvantages of "continentality" be overcome.

The demand for international and interregional exchange affecting the sphere of the "oceanic" economy is, of course, no coincidence, as it is on this exchange, as an expression of the "international division of labor," that the economic development of modernity rests. What is in a certain sense coincidental is the combination of one or another region of the "oceanic" sphere satisfying mutual demands through exchange. Currently, a combination of various "complementary" countries is being implemented: for instance, frozen meat is currently transported to England mainly from New Zealand, but after some time, the combination of other regions will be equally successful, as frozen meat will come to England not from New Zealand but, say, from Argentina. Within the continental world, not only is the demand for international and interregional exchange not coincidental (as it is here a factor of economic success), neither is the combination of certain economically-complementary regions and districts, as certain countries of the inner-continental spheres are tightly bound together by certain ties of economic reciprocity as long as the costs of overland transportation are high - there is nowhere else from which to obtain products cheaply if not from a neighboring country. It would be bad for the Ural mountain mining district if it had to get meat for a length of time not from the Ufa and Perm provinces or West Siberia, but from New Zealand or Argentina.

There is no need to think that the principle of intra-continental economic attraction only affects the life of particularly "continental" regions. Even in such oceanic countries as England or Japan the above-mentioned conditions apply within definite limits: for example, it is more profitable for cities to feed on the products of rural districts than it is to import them from abroad. Continental attraction acquires its greatest significance wherever:

1. The sphere of contiguous continental regions has the greatest spatial extent;

2. These regions are of the greatest diversity of economic nature.

The factors of the first type expand the spatial zone within which intracontinental attraction is effective, while the second factor multiplies the number of economic goods and products which are relevant.

Here it is necessary to note that the inner-continental sphere bears the quality of attracting to specifically intra-continental exchange not only those regions which are far from the ocean-sea, but also those coastal areas lying between them and the sea. These coastal areas lie on the path of inner-continental products to the world market. Therefore, insofar as such coastal lands are consumers, it is beneficial for them to buy the products which they find in the countries of their Hinterland, and precisely in the latter. Thanks to their proximity, they can use the difference (determined, according to our assumption, by the cost of transportation) between the price of the world market and the price of the continental "briar patch" to obtain goods for cheaper than if they were to import them from the world market. Inasmuch as they are producers, they can expect to sell their goods to inner-continental buyers as much as they are in demand. Even in selling a product at the place of production at the full price of the world market (a scenario which in a different situation would be inconceivable) they can deliver such to inner-continental buyers at a price cheaper than the cost of a product bought from the world market. The more vast the Hinterland, the more economically diverse are its constituent areas, and hence the more definitive the ties between coastal areas and the Hinterland. The greater the number of products which a coastal country can find in inner-continental areas, the greater the number of products it can sell to them.

It is enough to establish these most simple provisions for us to understand how grandiose and established such political-economic entities as China, North America, or Russia are in their economic spheres. Taking only the eastern parts of China, we can see that, following in continental continuity, the regions accessible only to the most "northern" crops and the regions with average annual temperatures below zero (zones in Manchuria along the Middle Amur) are those provinces where all the agricultural cultures characteristic of the temperate zone are (central and southern Manchuria), followed by the lands of cotton and rice which are warmer and subtropical, which are then followed finally by the topical lands of China's southern border. These regions are interspersed with districts possessing the most rich industrial resources, primarily iron and coal, where the most powerful mining and metallurgic industries already partially exist (and in the future may develop) - so powerful that according to current views and natural data, only North American industry is capable of competing with them. By virtue of its natural conditions, China is generally quite similar to the eastern (i.e. the most productive and important) zone of North America, which has its climatological basis in the fact that both of these geographical spheres are located on the eastern side of their continents. But in North America, the harsh (but at the same time favorable for human development) regions of wheat culture (the black soil lands of Minnesota, Manitoba, Saskatchewan, and Alberta) are stronger and even more tightly close to both the climatically temperate regions of the middle states and New England and the cotton districts of the South and the owners of tropical resources, such as in Florida and Texas. Finally, as for Russia, it is true that the range of climatic diversity of its agricultural regions is not as complete as those of China or North America. If China encompasses agricultural regions with average annual temperatures of -2° Celsius up to +21.7° (Canton) and higher, and if North America (encompassing the United States and Canada) has a range stretching from the harshest climatic conditions in which a human can possibly live to that of southern Florida with an average annual temperature of +25°, then in Russia, the climatic range starting with the

213

coolest climates breaks off at an average annual temperature of +16° (in the Batumi region), and no possible expansion of Russia in the short-term can significantly change this. Northern Persia (whose warmest place is the Caspian coast) and Afghan Turkestan would supplement the Russian world regions with annual average temperatures of +17° and +18°. Only access to the Persian Gulf could give Russia areas that approach, in average annual temperature, tropical levels (Bushir + 23.1 ° C), but even that would have much lower winter month temperatures than in the actual tropics (January in Bushir + 13.0 ° C).

Yet, regardless of this noted climatic "defect," Russia still encompasses an astounding richness and diversity of temperately-cold belt zones (including the forested and agricultural non-black earth lands of the North, the black lands of the "center," the South, and the East), plus temperately-warm regions (the North Caucasus and Crimea) as well as partly subtropical ones (Transcaucasia and Turkestan). Within these regions one encounters districts which are predetermined by nature to be exclusively engaged in forestry (such as the Taiga), richly gifted for agriculture (the black soil lands), or predestined for "pure livestock breeding" (the Caspian area and the Kyrgyz steppes). This sphere is also interspersed with regions possessing resources for the development of industry (first and foremost the Donets basin, the Urals, Altai, the Semirechye, and then the Belomorsk-Ladozhsky district for "white coal"). Based on what we know so far, we would think that these resources, especially iron and coal, cannot in their totality match the resources of China and North America, but they are fully on par with the great industrial countries of the West, such as England and Germany, in their European borders, and they surpass everything, according to our knowledge, in the rest of the world, i.e. all of Western Europe besides England and Germany, and all of Africa, Australia, South America, and South Asia.

To what conclusion are we led by observing such diversity in the economic nature of the regions constituting China, North America, and Russia if we were to compare these two with the above-indicated positions of these geographical worlds relative to the ocean, as well as the arising inner-continental economic "attraction" within these continental spheres? Does this diversity mean that these spheres can, in the process of their economic development, approach a state of "economic self-sufficiency"? Such an assumption is absurd, insofar as "self-sufficiency" is thought of as something absolute, as a kind of "Great Wall of China." It is altogether likely that in the near future even China will not be in the position or have the capacity to erect such an economic "wall."

However, in rejecting the utopian idea of "self-sufficiency," one cannot shut their eyes to the essentially distinct position which is currently occupied and will inevitably be kept in the future by different political-economic entities of the world economy in relation to the "world market." For some of them, connection with the world market accomplishes the most basic processes of economic exchange, processes of "equalizing" extracting and processing industries, the "industry" of agriculture, as well as processes of economic "adding" to both the industrial and agricultural regions of the temperate zone from those agricultural countries of the warm zone (e.g. the import of cotton, rice, tea, coffee, spices, etc.). Such an order of phenomena reigns in those political-economic entities whose customs and geographical borders cover a relatively narrow range of land and whose border regions are relatively homogeneous in economic nature - for example, those which are clearly predestined in their totality for the predominance of industry, which necessitates the import of agricultural products inasmuch as there are agricultural regions lying within one and the same climatic zone. Such are the main industrial countries of Western Europe, i.e. England and Germany. As countries which are effectively and potentially by and large "industrial," they turn to the world market in need of food products as well as raw materials from both the moderate and warm zones. The situation stands differently wherever various countries are joined into a customs and spatial whole, including those which are essentially industrial and those substantially agricultural, those of the moderate zone and those of the warm zone. Here the processes of "equalizing" industry and agriculture and the complementarity of countries of different climatic zones can take place within a geographical sphere without the medium of the "world market" to a much greater extent than in those political-economic entities of the first type. Instead of mirroring the course of those fundamental processes of industrial-agricultural and inter-climate exchange, as has been and is the case of the foreign trade of Germany and England, the foreign trade items of such economic-geographical spheres acquire the character of being individual adjustments to the phenomena of complementarity and mutual balancing between the major branches of economic life in these spheres. These adjustments become less significant and fewer in quantity the more that the countries of the inner-continental world achieve economic success corresponding to the givens of their economic yields, and in correlation to the obstacles posed to this sphere by the natural-geographical conditions which hinder them from joining the world economy, rendering them more "destitute" and more "continental" with regard to the possibility of oceanic exchange.

These two conditions push the structure of conceivable relations between modern Russia and the "world economy" in two opposite directions. It would be mad to preach in a depleted and devastated country the principles of economic "self-sufficiency" - what intracontinental attractions can there be when there is nothing to "attract"? However, it would be wrong to think that the state of intensive import of foreign goods, and above all the products paid, at best, by the export of raw materials which will come after Russia reopens for international exchange, is a normal and lasting condition... Of all the great entities of the world economy, Russia is the most "destitute" in terms of the possibilities of oceanic exchange. Having discovered in recent centuries, and in particular in recent years, the great potential of its political and cultural might, and having discovered the great intensity of its quest, Russia is not satisfied, of course, with the role of "backyard of the world economy" dictated by this deprivation. In its economic striving, Russia will inevitably come to intensify its agriculture within its cold and temperately-warm regions, to expand the use of adjacent subtropical regions (which are in most cases irrigated), and to partially reconstruct and partially create anew a powerful, satisfactory internal demand for industry wherever there are natural grounds for it, i.e., first and foremost, in some of the southern and eastern European and Asian provinces, and then in its center and in the Northwest. The logistical "destitution" of Russia's enormous range of regions, related as such is to its ostentatious "continentality," prompts it not to rely on the world market, but to bring to life centers for the production of many hitherto imported products within its borders. The establishment of such centers in turn will expand the foundation and increase the effectiveness of intracontinental attraction. One can be sure that with the intensive use of its continental neighborhoods, the geographical world of Russia-Eurasia really presents a model of some kind of economic "self-sufficiency" - not literally, of course, but in the sense of enclosing within this world's borders the main phenomena of mutual-balancing and mutual-equalizing the most important geographico-economic elements of modern economy. Among the political-economic units of the world, Russia-Eurasia will reveal itself to be a sphere of self-sufficiency *par excellence* in its combination of regions defined not by the whim of political fates, the likes of which we see in the current "colonial," "oceanic" empires, but by virtue of what is, in the absence of any technological shift, the necessary, irremovable mutual-attraction of countries toward one another between the "oceanic" force and "destitution." Such mutual-attraction is defined by the objective geographical-technological factor. State policy aiming for the establishment of "self-sufficiency" can only add to and strengthen the influence of this factor.

From the point of view of these provisions and categories, it is necessary to evaluate the long-time prevailing policy in

Russia to seek "access to the ice-free sea." One cannot, of course, deny the grounds justifying the aspiration of the Hinterland to possess a sea coast. But this aspiration has not moved our theoreticians of oceanic-Pontic policy alone. Insofar as the Russian Hinterland's access to the coast more often than not does not entail access to the "non-freezing," much less "open" sea, this access has been sought at least away from the main circle of the lands of the Russian world, and found it on the Kwantung peninsula: but the Dalniy erected here was truly superfluous. Those who ordered its construction did not understand that the quest for an "outlet to the sea," as a path for the realization of the bulk of industrial-agricultural and inter-climatic exchange, was not in front of them but behind them, that is to say, to be found not in the ocean-sea, but in the continent-ocean. What the ocean gives in economic terms by connecting, for instance, England with Canada as a country of wheat, with Australia as a country of wool, and India as a region of cotton and rice, is in the Russian world provided by the continental coupling of the Russian industrial regions (Moscow, Donetsk, the Urals, and the potential of the Altai and Semirechye), the Russian black-earth provinces (wheat), the Russian pastoral steppes (wool), and the "Russian subtropics," i.e. Transcaucasia, Persia, Russian Turkestan, and the potential of even Afghan, Chinese, and Ghulja Turkestan (cotton and rice). With regard to the real and conceivable economic self-affirmation of these regions and the mutual economic ties and "self-sufficiency" which such would generate, accessing the ocean through Dalian was in truth an outlet into the void.

The tragic poverty and misery of the contemporary Russian economy should not be forgotten for a minute. Beyond the sorrows of the moment, in the prospects of the future as the result of success and creativity, the Russian economy will always to a certain extent remain incomplete, not only in the sense that it cannot within its own womb satisfy, for instance, its demand for specifically tropical products, but in many other senses. Therefore, to a certain extent, the sea, as a connection with the "world market," is necessary and will remain necessary for Russia. but it is necessary to understand the essentially limited role that falls to the "oceanic," "sea" principle in building the Russian economy. A real guarantee should be sought assuring that the enemy fleet would not be allowed to pass through the straits and would not come to smash the Black Sea coast. It would be useful to acquire access to the Persian Gulf, at least from the point of view of the possibility of organizing the cheapest and most convenient means for importing tropical products to Russia through such an "outlet." But it must be remembered that in the case of Russia's economic formation, both this and other tasks remain to a certain extent fundamentally secondary. Whatever outlet to the Mediterranean Sea or the Indian Ocean Russia might find, the sea will not carry its foam to the Simbirsk "Precipice." Simbirsk, along with the boundless range of other regions and places of Russia-Eurasia, will still have to orient itself not toward this newfound outlet to the "warm sea," but to the continentality inherent to it. It is not in copying the "oceanic" policy of others, which is in many respects inapplicable for Russia, but in the consciousness of "continentality" and adaptation to it, that Russia's economic future lies.

\*\*\*

# EURASIANISM

*Petr Savitsky*[138]

\*\*\*

## I.

The Eurasianists are representatives of a new beginning in thinking and life; they are a group of figures actively working to radically transform hitherto predominant worldviews and life-systems, and to do so on the basis of a new approach to the root questions that define life, an approach which has arisen out of everything that has been endured over the past decade. At the same time, the Eurasianists have proposed a new geographical and historical understanding of Russia, as well as that whole world which they call Russian or "Eurasian."

The Eurasianists' name is of geographical provenance. The point is that they, the Eurasianists, have, where hitherto geography has counted two continents, "Europe" and "Asia," discerned a third, middle continent on the mainland of the Old World, that of "Eurasia," from which they derive their name.

In the opinion of the Eurasianists, the notion of "Europe" as a totality of Western and Eastern Europe is, in a purely geographical sense, inane and farcical. In the West, in terms of geographical outlines, one finds the richest development of coasts, the thinning of the continent into a peninsula, an island; whereas in the East there is a solid, continental mass whose only disconnect is to be found toward the sea coasts. Orographically,

---

138 Article first published in the journal *Evraziiskii vremennik* [*The Eurasian Annals*] No. 4 (1925).

**221**

the West is constituted by a most complex arrangement of mountains, hills, and lowlands; whereas the East is home to the enormous plains whose outskirts alone are edged by mountains. Climatically, the West is of a seaside climate with a relatively small difference between winter and summer. In the East, this difference is sharply pronounced with hot summers, harsh winters, and so on and so forth. It could be rightfully said that the Eastern European, or as the Eurasianists call it, the "White Sea-Caucasian" plain is in its geographical nature much closer to the West-Siberian and Turkestan plains lying to the East than it is to Western Europe. These three plains, together with the elevations separating them from one another (the Ural Mountains and the so-called "Aralo-Irtysh" watershed) and bordering them from the East, South-East, and South (the mountains of the Russian Far East, Eastern Siberia, Central Asia, Persia, the Caucasus, Asia Minor), represent a special world, one which is united in and of itself and geographically distinct from the countries lying both to the West, East, and South of it. If you apply the name "Europe" to the first and the name "Asia" to the second, then the world just named, as the middling and mediating world, will bear the name "Eurasia."

The necessity of distinguishing on the mainland mass of the Old World not two, as hitherto done, but three continents, is not a mere "discovery" by the Eurasianists. Rather, this discernment also arose out of views previously expressed by geographers, especially Russians (for example, Prof. V.I. Lamansky in his work of 1892). The Eurasianists sharpened this formula and once again gave to this "visible" continent the name that was once attached to the whole landmass of the Old World, to both old "Europe" and "Asia" in their totality.

Russia occupies the main space of the land of Eurasia. The conclusion that Russia's lands are not split by two continents, but rather together constitute a certain third, independent continent, is not only of geographical significance. Insofar as we also ascribe to the notions of "Europe" and "Asia" some kind of culturo-historical content, and as we think of "European" and "Asian" or "Asiatic" cultural circles as something concrete, the designation of "Eurasia" also acquires the meaning of a compressed culturo-historical character.[139] This designation indicates that Russia's cultural being, in its internally comparable proportions, has come to include elements from the most diverse variety of cultures. The alternating influences of the South, the East, and the West, have consistently prevailed in the world of Russian culture. The South manifested itself in these processes mainly in the paradigm of Byzantine culture, whose influence on Russia was long and fundamental. The special intensity of this influence can be seen in the era from approximately the 10th to the 13th centuries AD. The East, in turn, acted mainly in the form of "steppic" civilization, which is conventionally considered to be characteristically "Asian" ("Asiatic" in the above sense). The example of Mongol-Tatar statehood (Genghis Khan and his successors), which managed to master and govern an enormous portion of the Old World for a definite historical period, undoubtedly played a positive role in the creation of Great Russian statehood. The lifestyle of the steppes of the East also exerted broad influence on Russia. This influence was particularly strong from the 13th to the 15th centuries. Starting with the end of the latter century, the influence of

139 In Russian and some Romano-Germanic languages, two adjectives for "Asia" have been created: "Asian" and "Asiatic." The first, in its historical meaning, referred primarily to the Roman province encompassing the Western part of Asia Minor, and then to the diocese, whenceforth the mainland continent of the Old World acquired this name. "Asia," "Asian," and "Asians" were employed in the original, narrower sense in *Acts of the Apostles* 19:20. The adjective "Asiatic" concerns the whole continent. The root of the words "Eurasia," "Eurasian," and "Eurasians" is the first, more ancient designation, yet not because "Asianness" was constructed exclusively for the Roman province and diocese, but rather because the Eurasianists appeal to a much wider historical and geographical world. Due to a number of misconceptions, the word "Asiatic" has on the tongue of Europeans acquired an odious connotation. This odious seal, which testifies only to ignorance, can be removed by way of appealing to the more ancient name, as is accomplished in the designation of "Eurasianism." In this term, "Asian" refers to the cultural circle not only of Asia Minor, but of "Greater" Asia. In particular, the Eurasianists highly appreciate the cultures that inhabited Asia in the apostolic and subsequent centuries, i.e., Hellenic and Byzantine culture, and the Eurasianists by all means seek paradigms for modern spiritual and cultural creativity in some branches of this culture.

European culture prospered and reached its height by the 18th century. Among the categories which, while not always precise, nevertheless highlight the real essence of the division of the Old World's cultures into "European" and "Asiatic-Asian," Russian culture belongs to neither one nor the other. Russian culture combines elements of both and converges them toward a certain unity. Therefore, from the point of view of specifying distinctions between cultures, the qualification that Russian culture is "Eurasian" expresses the essence of the phenomenon more than any other. Of all the cultures of the past, two of the greatest and most versatile cultures known to us were genuinely "Eurasian": (1) Hellenistic culture, which combined elements of the Hellenic "West" and ancient "East," and its continuation, (2) Byzantine culture in the broader Eastern Mediterranean cultural world of late antiquity and the Middle Ages (these prosperous realms both lie exactly South of the main historical core of the Russian regions). The historical connection between Russian and Byzantine culture is highly noteworthy. The third great "Eurasian" culture was to a certain extent born out of the historical succession of the two preceding ones.

The "Eurasian," Russian cultural environment, in terms of the geographical, spatial terms of its existence, received its grounds from and, as it were, strengthened the skeleton of historical culture from another "Eurasian culture." With the subsequent, successive superposition of Asiatic-Asian (the influence of the East) and European (the influence of the West) layers on Russian soil, this quality of Russian culture was strengthened and affirmed.

By defining Russian culture as "Eurasian," the Eurasianists act as the conscious bearers of Russian cultural identity. On this matter, they boast even more precedents and predecessors than implied in purely geographical definitions. All those thinkers of a Slavophile orientation, including Gogol and Dostoevsky (as philosophers and authors), ought to be recognized as such. In the chain of ideas, the Eurasianists are the heirs to the powerful tradition of Russian philosophical and historiosophical thinking. This tradition most immediately traces back to the '30s' and '40s of the 19th century, when the Slavophiles began their activities.[140] In a broader sense, a number of works of Old Russian literature, the oldest of which date back to the 15th and 16th centuries, should be counted as part of this tradition as well.

When the fall of Tsargrad [Constantinople] in 1453 sharpened Russians' consciousness of their role as the defenders of Orthodoxy and heirs to Byzantine cultural succession, Russia gave birth to ideas which, in a certain sense, can be considered the precedents for the later Slavophile and Eurasianist ideas. Such "pioneers" of Eurasianism as Gogol and Dostoevsky, as well as other Slavophiles and related thinkers like Khomykov, Leontiev, and others, surpass the contemporary "Eurasianists" in terms of the sheer scale of their historical figures. But this does not annul the condition that they and the Eurasianists share the same thoughts on a number of questions, and that the Eurasianists' formulation of these thoughts has been more accurate than their predecessors. Insofar as the Slavophiles relied on "Slavdom" as the element that defines the culturo-historical uniqueness of Russia, they took up positions which are difficult to defend. Without a doubt, there is a culturo-historical and, above all, linguistic connection between Slavic

---

140 From the point of view of historiosophical concepts, Eurasianism as a matter of course lies in the same sphere as the Slavophiles. However, the problem of the relationship between these currents cannot be reduced to that of a simple succession. The prospects opening up before Eurasianism are conditioned, on the one hand, by the scale of the ongoing catastrophe and, on the other, by the emergence and manifestation of completely new culturo-historical and social factors which, naturally, did not play a role in the construction of the Slavophile worldview. Moreover, much of what the Slavophiles considered to be foundational and indisputable has since become obsolete over the past several decades or has been exposed to be essentially inconsistent. In some sense, Slavophilia was a provincial and "domestic" current. Now, in connection with the real opportunities opening up before Russia to become the center of a new European-Asiatic (Eurasian) culture of the greatest historical significance, any conceptualization and realization of a holistic, creatively conservative worldview (as Eurasianism considers itself to be) must determine its appropriate, unparalleled paradigms and scales.

peoples. But as an element of cultural uniqueness, the notion of Slavdom, in its empirical content as it has developed up to the present time, has little to offer.

The creative revelation of the cultural identity of the Bulgarians and Serbo-Croat-Slovenians belongs to the future. In a cultural sense, the Poles and Czechs belong to the Western "European" world and represent one of the latter's cultural regions. Russia's historical uniqueness clearly cannot be defined as exclusively, or even predominantly, belonging to the "Slavic" world. Intuiting this, the Slavophiles appealed to Byzantium. But while emphasizing the importance of Russia's ties with Byzantium, Slavophilia did not and could not offer a formula that fully and proportionately expresses the character of the Russian culturo-historical tradition and which captures the "oneness of nature" of Russia and its Byzantine cultural continuity. "Eurasianism" expresses both to a certain extent. The formula "Eurasianism" takes into account the impossibility of explaining and defining the past, present, and future cultural uniqueness of Russia in terms of any preferential appeal to the notion of "Slavdom." It also points to the source of this uniqueness in Russian culture's combination of "European" and "Asiatic-Asian" elements. Since this formula affirms the presence of the latter in Russian culture, it establishes the connection between Russian culture and the broader creative world of "Asiatic-Asian" cultures in their historic role, and this connection is exhibited as one of the strong sides of Russian culture, and it compares Russia with Byzantium, which in this very sense also wielded a "Eurasian" culture.[141]

---

141 This determination can claim substantial historical accuracy. The essence of Byzantine culture was determined by a combination of the most diverse elements. Currents of religious, artistic, and other impulses which flowed from the East - from Palestine, Syria, Armenia, Persia, and Asia Minor, as well as some parts of Africa - mixed with perceptions of the Western state and legal tradition (as in the existence and development of Roman law in Byzantium). Moreover, the contact with steppe cultures that was so definitive to the formation of Russian culture did not fail to leave its traces in Byzantium as well. Much in Byzantine fashions and mores can be traced back to being borrowed from the steppe "barbarians" who in successive waves closed in on the borders of the empire.

## II.

Such, in brief, is the place of the Eurasianists as conscious expounders of Russia's culturo-historical uniqueness. But the Eurasianists' doctrine is not limited to this recognition. Rather, with this recognition they substantiate a common concept of culture and derive from this concept concrete conclusions for interpreting what is happening in the present. We shall first present this concept, and then move on to conclusions concerning the present time. In both cases, the Eurasianists feel themselves to be the successors of the ideological cause of the above-named Russian thinkers (the Slavophiles and adjacent thinkers).

Independently of the views expressed in Germany (by Spengler), but approximately simultaneously with the appearance of the latter, the Eurasianists put forth the thesis of denying the "absoluteness" of modern "European" (i.e., in common terminology, Western European) culture, of denying the claim that the latter's qualities constitute the "perfection" of the whole hitherto process of the cultural evolution of the world. Until altogether recently, the affirmation of such "absoluteness" and such a quality of "European" culture was firmly insisted upon, and today persists in the brains of "Europeans." Moreover, this assertion has been blindly accepted in the form of a faith by the higher circles of "Europeanizing" societies and peoples, particularly by the greater part of the Russian intelligentsia. The Eurasianists have challenged this situation with the recognition that many of the achievements and structures of "European" consciousness, especially those of an ideological and moral nature, are relative. The Eurasianists have noted how the European has time and again called "savage" and "backwards" everything which can by no means be objectively seen as standing below their own achievements, and everything which is simply not similar to the European's own manner of seeing and acting. Even if it were possible to objectively show the superiority of the latest science and technology in some fields over all the other achievements of this type accomplished over the course of observable world history, it is still essentially impossible to offer any such proof when it comes to matters of ideology and morality. In light of the internal sense of morality and freedom of philosophical conviction which, for the "Eurasian" concept, are the only criteria for evaluating the ideological and moral fields, the much younger and more modern Western European turns out to not only not be superior but, on the contrary, inferior in comparison with the corresponding achievements of various "ancient," "savage," and "backwards" peoples.[142] The Eurasian concept signifies a decisive rejection of culturo-historical "Eurocentrism," and this rejection stems not from some emotional worries, but from certain scientific and philosophical preconditions. One of the latter is the rejection of the universalist perception of culture which reigns among modern "European" notions. This universalist view encourages Europeans to indiscriminately qualify certain peoples as "cultured" and others as "un-cultured." It bears recognition that in the cultural evolution of the world we encounter "cultural environments" and "cultures," some of which have achieved a great deal, others less so. Yet, determining precisely what a given cultural environment has achieved is only possible upon distinguishing between branches of culture.

A cultural environment which is low in some sectors of culture might time and again prove to be higher in others. There can be no doubt that the ancient inhabitants of Easter Island in the Great [Pacific] Ocean "lagged behind" the modern English in very many branches of empirical knowledge and technology, but this did not prevent their culture from manifesting a measure of originality and creativity against which the sculpturing of modern England can lay no claims. Similarly, Muscovite Rus of the 16th-17th centuries was behind Western Europe in many industries, but this did not hinder it from creating a "self-initiating" epoch of artistic

---

142 The same situation applies to the field of art, and in particular to some branches of fine art (artistic architecture, sculpting, painting), where the inadequacy of the latest "European" creations is especially evident in comparison with that achieved in more ancient epochs and by other peoples.

creativity or from developing its own unique and remarkable types of "towered" and "patterned" churches which cannot but force one to admit that, in terms of artistic creation, Muscovite Rus stood above the majority of Western European countries of its time. The same is the case in other eras of the existence of this "cultural environment." Muscovite Rus of the 16th-17th centuries gave birth, as previously said, to a "self-initiating" era of church building, but its developments in iconography marked a clear decline in comparison to the achievements of Novgorod and Suzdal in the 14th and 15th centuries. We have cited such examples from the sphere of fine arts as the most obvious. But also in the case of knowledge of an external nature, if we distinguish between the fields of "theoretical knowledge" and "living vision," then it would turn out that the "cultural environment" of modern Europe, while attaining success in the field of "theoretical knowledge" has, in comparison with many other cultures, seen decline in the field of "living vision." The "savage" or "black man" perceives a number of natural phenomena more subtly and precisely than the most learned modern "naturalist." Examples of this could be multiplied to infinity; let us say further that the whole sum of "facts of culture" is but one continuous example of the fact that only upon examining culture with a view to deconstructing and differentiating between fields can we arrive at any complete knowledge of its evolution and character. This examination can be accomplished with three basic concepts: "cultural environment," the "eras" of the latter's existence, and "cultural fields." Any analysis is duly confined to a certain "cultural environment" and a certain "era." Where we draw the borders of these depends on the point of view and purpose of study. The character and degree of division of "culture" into "fields" depends on these factors. It is important to emphasize the fundamental necessity of such division, as it eliminates the uncritical examination of a culture as an undifferentiated totality. A differentiated consideration of culture shows that there are no indiscriminate "cultured" and "uncultured" peoples, and that the most diverse peoples whom "Europeans" call "savages" by all means wield "culture" in their customs, traditions, and knowledge, and in some fields and from some points of view they stand high.

## III.

The Eurasianists are close to those thinkers who deny the existence of any universal "progress" which is, at any rate, determined by the above-presented concept of "culture." If the evolutionary line moves differently in different fields, this means that there is not and cannot be any common upward movement, any gradual, steady, common "perfection," insofar as one or another cultural environment, or a whole number of cultural environments, while "improving" from one or another point of view, might often be declining in another. This postulate is applicable to the "European" cultural environment in particular: its scientific and technological "perfection" has been bought, from the point of view of the Eurasianists, at the price of ideological and most of all religious impoverishment. This dual nature of its achievements is clearly expressed in its approach to the economy. For many long centuries in the history of the Old World, there existed a certain common relationship between the ideological-moral-religious element on the one hand and the economic on the other. More precisely, there existed a certain ideological subordination of the economy, and it is precisely this permeation of the whole approach to economic matters by the religio-moral element that allowed historians of economic doctrines (for example, the old 19th century German-Hungarian historian Kautz, whose works retain a certain significance to this day) to unite into one group on the grounds of their approaches to economic matters such diversely ranging landmarks as the literature of China, the Iranian laws of the Vendidad, Mosaic law, and the works of Plato, Xenophon, Aristotle, and Western medieval theologians. The economic philosophy of these milestones is, in a definite sense, a philosophy of "subordinated economy." These doctrines emphasize, as something necessary and due, the link between the satisfaction of our economic needs and the common elements of morality and religion. The economic philosophy of the European "new age" is the opposite of this view. Albeit not always in direct words (but often enough in the foundations of its worldview) the new European economic philosophy asserts the circle of economic phenomena to be something self-sufficient, a value in itself which encompasses and manifestly exhausts all the ends of human existence. It would be a sign of spiritual blindness to deny the enormity of those purely cognitive achievements and successes in understanding and envisioning the economic phenomena which the new political-economy has realized and amassed. But in acting as an empirical science, and being to a certain and large extent no more than such, the new political-economy, in a number of its postulates, imposes itself upon minds and eras as a metaphysics. Similarly to how the economic ideas of ancient legislators, philosophers, and theologians were associated with certain metaphysical views, so are the economic ideas of modern economists tied to such values. If the metaphysics of the former was the philosophy of "subordinated economics," then the metaphysics of the latter is the philosophy of "militant economism." The latter is, in a certain sense, an ideological price which the new Europe has paid for the quantitatively enormous economic rise that it has experienced in the modern age, especially over the past century. There is something instructive to be found in this picture: at the end of the Middle Ages and in the early modern centuries, the ancient wisdom of the primordial moral covenant which restrained man's selfish instincts with words of exhortations and denunciations - in a word, the philosophy of "subordinated economics" - collapsed under the pressure of the new ideas of modern times which presumptuously asserted the theories and practices of "militant economism."[143] Historical materialism is the most complete and acute expression of the latter.

---

143 Militant economism, as an element in the spirit of the human being, has existed and exists everywhere. Yet it is significant that it is in the new Europe that this principle has been elevated to be an ideological principle.

Thus, the link between the philosophy of "subordinated economics" on the one hand, and "militant economism" on the other, is in terms of a certain approach to matters of religion observable in empirical ideological reality. If the philosophy of "subordinated economics" is and has always been an appendage to one or another theistic worldview, then historical materialism is ideologically tied to atheism. Hence the atheistic essence concealed within historical materialism which, like the wolf of a fairy tale, conceals itself from time to time with the mask of the sheep's clothing - that of empirical science. In Russia, the atheistic worldview has accomplished an historic triumph, as state power is in the hands of atheists and has become an instrument of atheistic preaching. Without going into the question of the "historical responsibility" for what is happening in Russia, but while also not wishing to annul anyone's accountability, the Eurasianists understand that the essence of that which has been received and subsequently introduced into life by Russia - by virtue of the receptivity and excitement of its spiritual being - is, at its source, in its spiritual origin, not the Russian essence. The Communist sabbat has dawned in Russia as a perfection of more than two centuries of "Europeanization." Recognizing that the spiritual essence of the Communism of the ruling state in Russia is, in a special way, the reflected ideological essence of European modernity (the "new age"), is a postulation which is empirically grounded to a high degree. Here one should also consider the origins of Russian atheism in the ideas of the European "Enlightenment," the introduction of socialist ideas into Russia from the West, the link between Russian Communist "methods" and the ideas of the French Syndicalists, as well as the significance and "cult" of Marx in Communist Russia. In seeing the ideological essence of the European "new age" in such a way, taken to its logical conclusion, the Russians who have not accepted Communism and, at the same time, have not lost their abilities to think consistently, understand that they cannot return to the foundations of modern "European" ideology.

From the experience of the Communist revolution, a certain truth follows for the consciousness of the Eurasians, both old and new: healthy social housing can only be built on an inseparable connection between man and God, man and religion. Non-religious housing and a non-religious state must be rejected. This rejection harbors no preconceived claims regarding specific constitutional-legal forms. Such a form, in the Eurasianists' view, could exist harmlessly under certain conditions, such as in the "separation of Church and state." But in essence, it is yet highly significant that what is perhaps the first government in world history to be consistently atheist and which has turned the profession of atheism into the official confession of the Communist government, has turned out to be, as in the prophetic words of the most profound Russian philosopher of the late 19th century, Leontiev, "organized torment" - that is to it say it has become a system of shocking and destroying the "common blessing" or "common good" (supposedly in whose name the Communist authorities have installed themselves), of such abuse of the human personality that all images fade and all words are powerless in describing the terrible, unprecedented, blasphemous atrociousness of this reality. We shall repeat: the circumstance that the domination of the first consistently atheistic government has turned out to be the domination of all that is beast-like is not a coincidence. Historical materialism and its complementing atheism unveil and unleash all those primordial, creatural instincts, including those primordially economic ones which, in the final analysis, amount to extortion. The main determining force of social being under the conditions of the ideological reign of materialism and atheism is hate, and its worthy fruit is the torment of all which, sooner or later, cannot but lead to the final fruit: the torment of the tormentors.

Russia has carried out the triumph of historical materialism and atheism, but the laws which have manifested themselves over the course of its revolution far from concern Russia alone. The cult of primordial economic interest and    animalistic primordiality has, by virtue of abundant germination, sprouted in the consciousness of peoples beyond Russia. Yet this cult cannot form the basis for long and prosperous community outside of Russia. The destructive forces that have accumulated under these conditions will sooner or later exhaust the forces of social creation. This problem must be beheld in all its depth and breadth. The pressure of materialist and atheist views must be opposed with an ideological essence whose content must be precious and voluminous. There can be no hesitation.

With hitherto unprecedented directness and uncompromising determination, and on the broadest possible front - everywhere - it is necessary to initiate and lead a struggle against all that is to even the slightest degree related to materialism and atheism. This evil must be traced back to its roots: it is necessary to literally eradicate it. It would be superficial and impotent to attempt to combat only the most acute manifestations of historical materialism, atheism and Communism. The problem is posed much deeper and more substantially. We must declare war on "militant economism" wherever it manifests itself. In the name of a religious worldview, we must gather forces to fight with passionate feeling, clear thoughts, and full understanding against the specific spirit of the new Europe.

Insofar as the latter has reached its historical and ideological limits at which it finds itself presently, it can be said with great certainty that at some point in the future one of the two following scenarios will happen: either the cultural environment of the new Europe will perish and dissipate like smoke in torturous, tragic shock, or the "critical epoch," as the Simonists term it, which began in Western Europe with the end of the Middle Ages will come to its end and be replaced by an "organic epoch," an "epoch of faith."

Ancient wisdom cannot be flouted with impunity beyond well known limits for sake of the fact that it is truth. It is not on the basis of erecting a higher principle out of primordial, selfish human instincts as taught by the philosophy of "militant economism," but on the basis of curbing and restraining these instincts with an enlightened religious pulse that the highest measure of the "common good" possible on earth can be achieved.

A society which succumbs to an exceptional concern with its earthly goods will sooner or later be deprived of them - such is the terrible lesson that is translucent in the experience of the Russian Revolution. The Eurasianists have attempted to fully and entirely understand and consciously grasp this experience, to derive all the lessons that stem from it, and to be fearless on this matter, unlike those who, reeling in turmoil and timidity from the bestial image of Communism, cannot abandon that which constitutes the basis or root of Communism - those who, holding the plow, look backwards; those who try to pour new wine into old furs; and those who, upon seeing the new truth of the abomination of Communism, are incapable of renouncing the old filth of "militant economism" in any and all of its forms. Personal faith is insufficient. A faithful person must be part of the greater spiritual community.

The Eurasianists are Orthodox. The Orthodox Church is that light that illuminates the path ahead of them. The Eurasianists call upon their countrymen to strive toward Her, toward Her Gifts, and toward Her Grace. The Eurasianists are not disconcerted by the terrible distemper that has been instigated by the atheists and theomachists that are rising in the Russian Orthodox Church. The Eurasianists believe that there is enough spiritual strength, and that struggle leads to enlightenment. The Orthodox Church is the realization of higher freedom. Its primordial element is that of conciliation, unlike that of the element of power which prevails in the breakaway Roman Church. It seems to the Eurasianists that in harsh worldly affairs, one cannot do without harsh authority, but in spiritual and Church affairs, only graceful freedom and conciliation compose the essence of good leaders. "Europe," meanwhile, in some of its parts, is destroying the effectiveness of government and introducing tyrannical power into Church affairs.

The Orthodox Church has for many centuries only shone upon those peoples who have remained faithful to Her; she has shed light through the truths of her creed and the feats of her ascetics. Perhaps new periods are now coming: the modern Orthodox Church, continuing the succession of the ancient Eastern Church, has received from her, as a central principle of its being, complete impartiality toward forms of economic life (as opposed to the methods of the Western Church, which for many centuries struggled against charging borrowed interest[144]) and toward the achievements of human thought. Perhaps it is for this reason that none other than the Orthodox Church has been called upon, to the greatest extent and as part of the new religious epoch, to cover the achievements of the latest economic technology and science, to cleanse them of the ideological superstructures of "militant economism," materialism, and atheism, just as in the times of Constantine, Theodosius, and Justinian, the Ancient Eastern Church succeeded in encompassing, in a genuine and inspired "era of faith," an altogether complex and developed economic life alongside significant freedom in theological-philosophical thinking.

In modern economic technology and empirical science, regardless of their hitherto development, there is nothing that would exclude the possibility of their existence and prosperity in the bosom of a new era of faith. The combination of modern technology and science with the ideology of "militant economism" and atheism is by no means necessary and inevitable. From a religious point of view, economic technology is, regardless of the limits of its abilities, a means to realize the Covenant bestowed by the Creator upon the creation of the human race: "They may rule over the fish in the sea and the birds in the sky, over the

144 The Eastern Church, in rejecting the proposal of a ban on borrowed interest at the Council of Nicaea in 325, thereby recognized authoritative interference into economic life to be unbefitting of the Church. The Eastern Church stood on this position in all subsequent centuries and continues to stand on it today. The practice of the Western Church has been different: the ban on the charging interest on loans was maintained for a millennium and still in the 18th century Turgot was forced to reckon with such as a reality of life.

livestock and all the wild animals, and over all the creatures that move along the ground" (Genesis 1:26). Empirical science is, from a religious point of view, the revelation of a picture of the Divine world that, as knowledge progresses, more perfectly, fully, and evermore clearly reveals the wisdom of the Creator.

## IV.

Eurasianism is not only a system of historiosophical or theoretical assessments. It strives to combine thought and deed and to ultimately lead to the affirmation of a certain methodology of action alongside this system of theoretical views. The main problem which stands before Eurasianism in this regard is the problem of synthesizing a religious view of life and the world with the greatest empirically founded practicality. The posing of this problem is substantiated by the whole character of Eurasianism. The Eurasianists are essentially and at once advocates of religious principles as well as consistent empiricists. Their ideology is born out of facts. In their characterization of the Russian world as "Eurasian," it is as if their bodies are adjoined to each expanse of their native land, to each section of this world's history.

Understanding facts is insufficient. Facts need to be governed in the plastic process of history. As people who perceive and feel the world religiously arrive at this task, they find themselves faced with the problem of evil in all of its nakedly glaring and mystically shocking reality. The Eurasianists feel the reality of evil in the world to the utmost extent - in themselves, in others, and in private and social life. They are the least utopian of all. In their consciousness of the harm of sin and the empirical imperfection of human nature arising out of such, they in no way agree to build their calculations on the premise of the "goodness" of human nature. Insofar as this is the case, the task of acting "in the world" arises as a tragic task, for "the world lies in evil." The tragedy of this task is inescapable: the one thing toward which the Eurasianists strive is to be in harmony in their thoughts and deeds at the very height of this tragedy. Firm philosophical conviction and, we would say, the very nature of the Russian historical and national character in which the Eurasianists participate, exclude the possibility of sentimentally approaching this task. Consciousness of the sinfulness of this world does not exclude, but, on the contrary, demands courage in empirical decisions. No ends justify the means. Sin always remains sin. But while acting "in the world," sin must not be feared. There are situations in which one must take burden upon himself, for idle "holiness" would be an even greater sin.

In the practical sphere, for the Eurasianists, the problem of "right" versus "left" political and social solutions has been annulled. This subdivision is irresistibly important to those who, in their ultimate ends, cling solely to the limited realities of human existence and have lost their minds amidst the notions and facts of political and economic application. Whoever relates to these questions in this manner has no other values beyond concrete political and social resolutions of "left" or "right"; and for every such resolution, every such person is supposed to stand steadily and "with frenzy," for beyond such resolutions and himself, like of the spiritual heights, nothing remains. If once the accepted political and economic direction turns out to be inconsistent with the requirements of life and impractical, then a consistent person will still hold on to it, because this direction is already implicit. This is not the attitude to the practical decisions of the Eurasianist. For the Eurasianists, religious reliance is essential, and it is acquired beyond the sphere of political and economic empiricism. Insofar as decisions in the latter sphere allow for religious appraisals, a "right" or "left" decision may be good in different situations, just as one or the other may be bad in others.

The religious point of view is indifferent to any large quantity of applied decisions. In understanding the importance of political and economic applications while at the same time not presupposing supreme values for them, the Eurasianists can bring applications to religiously-indifferent spheres with

an open-mindedness and freedom that is inaccessible to people
of other worldviews. In all practical decisions, the demands
of life are, beyond any prejudice, the guiding principle of the
Eurasianist. Hence in some decisions the Eurasianist may be
more radical than the most radical, while in other cases more
conservative than the conservatives. Historical perception
is organically inherent to the Eurasianist, and the sense of
continuing historical tradition is an integral part of their
worldview. But this feeling is not regenerated into a template.
The Eurasianist is bound to no templates whatsoever - only the
sheer essence of the matter, with a full understanding of the
historical nature of the phenomena, shines through to them
from the depths of each problem.

The present Russian reality more than any other demands
precisely such an approach - "to the essence." The Eurasianists'
approach to the spiritual element of the revolution has been
expressed previously, but in its material-empirical guise, in
the ratio of political power between separate groups which
it has created, and in the new distribution of property, the
revolution should in large part be seen as an unavoidable
"geological" fact. A sense of reality and an elementary state
instinct compels this recognition. Of all the effective groups of
the "non-revolutionary" spirit, the Eurasianists can, perhaps,
go the farthest along the path of a radical and comprehensive
recognition of this fact. Facts of political influence and
the distribution of property, which in this case the matter
concerns, are not of primary, self-evident importance to the
Eurasianists, but are only secondary values. This eases the task
of recognizing fact for the Eurasianists. But the fact in many
cases is the product of abomination and crime. In this lies
the severity of the problem. But since abomination and crime
have been allowed by the Will of God to become an objective
historical fact, it must be considered that the recognition of
this fact does not contradict the Will of God. Some measure
of direct factual worship lies in the empirical necessities of
eras that have to find a way out of the revolution. In religious

terms, this necessity of fact-worship can be equated to temptation through which one must pass: to render unto Caesar what is Caesar's (that is, to take into account all the empirical political-economic demands of the era), without surrendering and harming God. From the point of view of the Eurasianists, the task at hand is to redeem and transform this abomination and crime with the establishment of a new religious era that will shine its radiant light upon all that is sinful, dark, and terrible. This is possible not in the order of the dialectical disclosure of history, which mechanically and "in the Marxist style" turns all "evil" into "good," but in the process of the internal accumulation of moral force, in the face of which even the necessity of fact-worship would pose no overwhelming temptation.

\*\*\*

# PAN-EURASIAN NATIONALISM

## Nikolai Trubetzkoy[145]

***

If hitherto the main factor consolidating the Russian Empire into a single whole was the fact that the entire territory of this state belonged to a single Russian master, the Russian people headed by their Russian Tsar, then this factor has now been destroyed. The question arises: what other factor can now solder together all of the parts of this territory into a single, integral state? The revolution put forth the realization of a famous social ideal as such a unifying factor. The USSR is not simply a group of separate republics, but a group of socialist republics striving to realize one and the same ideal of social system. It is precisely this common ideal that unites all of the republics together.

The commonality of the social ideal and, therefore, of the direction in which the state will of all the separate parts of the present USSR is striving, is, of course, a powerful unifying factor. Even if the character of this ideal will change with time, the same principle of binding participation in the common ideal of social justice and the common will to reach this ideal will continue to lie at the heart of the statehood of all the peoples and regions currently unified in the USSR. But the question is whether this one factor for unifying different peoples into one state is sufficient. In fact, that the Uzbek

---

145 Article first published in the journal *Evraziiskaia khronika* [*The Eurasian Chronicle*] No. 9 (Paris: 1927).

Republic and Belarusian Republic are both guided in their domestic policy by the aspiration to achieve one and the same social ideal by no means implies that both these republics will necessarily unite under the canopy of one state. What's more, it does not follow that these two republics will not quarrel or fight amongst themselves. It is clear that a common social ideal alone is insufficient, and that nationalist-separatist aspirations in individual parts of the USSR must be opposed with something else.

In the contemporary USSR, the antidote against nationalism and separatism is class hatred and the consciousness of the proletariat's solidarity in the face of constantly impending danger. In each of the peoples comprising the USSR, only proletarians are recognized as full citizens and the Soviet Union itself is essentially composed not so much of peoples as the proletarians of these peoples. By seizing power and exercising its dictatorship, the proletariat of the USSR's different peoples feels itself simultaneously threatened by its internal enemies (insofar as socialism has not been established, the existence of capitalists and even a bourgeoisie within the USSR in the 'transition' period must be admitted) as well as foreign enemies (in the face of the rest of the world left at the mercy of the rule of international capitalism and imperialism). In order to successfully defend the power it has seized against the machinations of its enemies, the proletarians of all the peoples of the USSR must unite in a single state.

Thanks to this view of the meaning of the existence of the USSR, the Soviet government is able to fight separatism: the separatists seek to destroy the state unity of the USSR, but this unity is necessary for the proletariat to defend the power it has seized, therefore, separatists are the enemies of the proletariat. The fight against nationalism is thus possible and necessary for the same reason, as it can easily be interpreted as a form of covert separatism. In addition, according to Marxist doctrine, the proletariat is void of nationalist instincts, as such are attributes of the bourgeoisie and the fruit of the bourgeois

**244**

system. The struggle against nationalism is realized by the very fact of shifting the center of the people's attention from the sphere of national emotions to the sphere of social emotions. The consciousness of national unity, being the precondition of any form of nationalism, is undermined by the aggravation of class hatred, and the majority of national traditions are tarnished by their relationship to the bourgeois order, aristocratic culture, or "religious prejudices." Moreover, the ambitions of each people are to a certain degree flattered within their own borders, as their languages are recognized, administrative and other positions are supposed to be filled with people of the given local environment, and the region itself is often named after the people inhabiting it.

Thus, it can be said that the factor linking all the parts of the contemporary USSR into a single integral state is the official recognition of a single master of the entire state territory. Only before, the Tsar of the Russian people was recognized as such a master, while now such is considered to be the proletariat of all the peoples of the USSR led by the Communist Party.

The disadvantages of the above-described contemporary resolution of the issue are obvious. Not to mention the fact that the division into proletariat and bourgeoisie is, in relation to many peoples of the USSR, either entirely impracticable or completely irrelevant and artificial. It is particularly worth emphasizing that the resolution of this question in itself bears an indication of its temporality. In fact, the state unity of the peoples and countries in which the proletariat has seized power is feasible only from the standpoint of the current stage of the proletariat's struggle against its enemies. The proletariat itself as an oppressed class, according to Marxism, is a temporary phenomenon subject to be overcome. The same is said of the class struggle. Thus, state unity in the above-described solution does not rest on any fundamentally permanent basis, but on a fundamentally temporary, transitory foundation. This gives rise to an absurd situation and a whole number of entirely unhealthy phenomena. In order to justify its existence, the central

**245**

government must artificially inflate the danger threatening the proletariat, and itself create the objects of class hatred in the form of a new bourgeoisie against which the proletariat must be incited, etc. In a word, it comes to supporting the idea in the consciousness of the proletariat that its position as the unified master of the state is extremely fragile.

The purpose of this article is not to criticize the communist conception of the state as such. We are examining the idea of the dictatorship of the proletarian in only one aspect, namely, as the factor unifying all the peoples of the USSR into an integral state opposed to nationalist-separatist tendencies. It should be recognized that even though this aspect of the idea of the dictatorship of the proletariat is still effective, it cannot become a lasting, enduring solution to the issue. The nationalism of the separate peoples of the USSR is evolving as these peoples increasingly come to grips with their new position! The development of education and literature in different national languages and the filling of administrative and other posts first and foremost by locals deepens the national differences between individual regions and creates among native intellectuals a jealous fear of competition with "alien elements" and a desire to more firmly strengthen their positions. At the same time, class partitions within each individual people of the USSR are fading just as class contradictions are gradually withering away. All of this creates the most favorable conditions for the development of nationalism with a separatist slant among each of the peoples of the USSR. The idea of the dictatorship of the proletariat is impotent against this. The proletariat, having come to power, turns out to wield sometimes even strong doses of nationalist instincts which, according to the doctrine of Communism, should be absent among the real, contemporary proletariat. And such a proletariat ascending to power turns out to care far less for the interests of the global proletariat than the doctrine of Communism suggests.

Thus, the idea of the dictatorship of the proletariat, the consciousness of the proletariat's solidarity, and the incitement of class hatred shall ultimately turn out to be ineffective means against the development of nationalist and separatist aspirations among the peoples of the USSR.

The current resolution of the state unification of parts of the former Russian Empire is a logical consequence of the Marxist teaching on the class nature of the state and Marxism's typical neglect for the national substrate of statehood. It should be recognized that, for the supporters of this doctrine, there is no other way than replacing the idea of the rule of one people with the idea of the dictatorship of one class, i.e., substituting the class substrate for the national substrate of statehood, and this substitution itself implies everything that follows. In any case, the Communists are thus more right and consistent than those democrats who, rejecting the national substrate of Russian statehood, preach broad regional autonomy or a federation without class dictatorship, failing to understand that the existence of a unified state is impossible under such circumstances.

For the individual parts of the former Russian Empire to continue to exist as parts of a single state, the existence of a single substrate of statehood is necessary. This substrate can be national (ethnic) or class-based. The class substrate, as we've seen above, is capable of uniting individual parts of the former Russian Empire only temporarily. A durable and permanent union is therefore possible only in the presence of an ethnic (national) substrate. Such was the Russian people up until the revolution. But now, as indicated above, it is already impossible to return to the situation in which the Russian people was the sole owner of all the state territory. It is also clear that no other people living on this territory can fulfill the role of the sole proprietor of all of the state's territory.

Consequently, the national substrate of the state which was formerly called the Russian Empire but now the USSR can only be the totality of peoples inhabiting the state, considered as a special, multinational nation and as such, one wielding its own nationalism.

We call this nation Eurasian, its territory Eurasia, and its nationalism Eurasianism. Applied to Eurasia, this means that the nationalism of each people of Eurasia (the modern USSR) must be combined with a pan-Eurasian nationalism, i.e., Eurasianism...

Every citizen of the Eurasian state should be aware not only of the fact that he belongs to such a people (or such a variety of a people), but also that this people itself belongs to the Eurasian nation. The national pride of the citizen should find satisfaction in both the former and latter consciousness. Accordingly, a nationalism should be built out of every one of these peoples. A pan-Eurasian nationalism should present itself as an extension of the nationalism of each of the peoples of Eurasia, a kind of merging of all of these individual nationalisms together.

Between the peoples of Eurasia, some kind of fraternal relations have always existed and easily formed which suggest the existence of subconscious attractions and sympathies (the opposite cases, i.e., cases of subconscious repulsion and antipathy between two peoples in Eurasia, are very rare). Of course, there is not enough of some of these subconscious feelings. What is necessary is making the brotherhood of the peoples of Eurasia a fact of consciousness and, moreover, a vital fact. What is necessary is for each people of Eurasia to recognize itself above all as a member of this brotherhood and occupying a certain place in it. What is needed is for the consciousness of belonging to the Eurasian brotherhood to become stronger and brighter for each of these peoples than the consciousness of belonging to any other group of peoples. After all, some individual features can include an individual people of Eurasia in another, not purely Eurasian group of peoples. For example, by virtue of language, the Russians are included in the group of Slavic peoples, and the Tatars, Chuvash, Cheremis, and others can be included in the group of so-called "Turanian" peoples, just as the Tatars, Bashkirs, Sarts, and others are included in the group of Muslim peoples on religious grounds.

These ties must be less binding and vivid for all these peoples than those unifying these peoples in the Eurasian family. Neither Pan-Slavism for the Russians nor Pan-Turanism for the Eurasian Turanian peoples nor Pan-Islamism for Eurasian Muslims should be in the foreground, but Eurasianism. All these "pan-isms" strengthening the centrifugal forces of these individual nations' nationalisms emphasize the one-sided connection of this people with some other peoples according to only one characteristic, and are therefore incapable of creating a real and lively multinational nation and character out of these peoples.

In the Eurasian brotherhood, peoples are connected with one another not by one or another unilateral number of characteristics, but by the community of their historical fates. Eurasia is a geographical, economic, and historical whole. The fates of the Eurasian peoples are intertwined, firmly tied into a massive knot that is impossible to untangle to the extent that one people can refuse this unity only by artificial violence against nature, which can only lead to suffering.

Nothing similar can be said of those groups of peoples that lie at the basis of the concepts of Pan-Slavism, Pan-Turanism, or Pan-Islamism. Not one of these groups' peoples are united to such a degree by historical fate. None of these "pan-isms" are as pragmatically valuable as pan-Eurasian nationalism. This nationalism is not only pragmatically valuable, but even directly, vitally necessary. After all, we have already seen that only the awakening of the consciousness of the multinational Eurasian nation's unity is capable of giving Russia-Eurasia that ethnic substrate of statehood without which it will sooner or later begin to disintegrate to the great misfortune and suffering of all its parts.

In order for a pan-Eurasian nationalism to successfully fulfill its role as a factor unifying the Eurasian state, it is therefore necessary to re-cultivate the consciousness of the peoples of Eurasia. Of course, it can be said that life itself is handling this re-cultivation. The very fact that all the Eurasian peoples (like no other people in the world) have for a few years already experienced and outgrown the Communist regime – this fact alone creates a thousand new psychological and cultural-historical ties between these peoples and forces them to clearly and truly feel the commonality of their historical destinies. But this, of course, is not enough. It is imperative that those individual peoples who have now clearly and vividly realized the unity of the multinational Eurasian nation preach this conviction in each of the Eurasian nations in which they work. Here awaits an uncharted land of work for philosophers, publicists, poets, writers, artists, musicians, and scholars of the most diverse specializations. It is necessary to reconsider a number of sciences from the standpoint of the unity of the multinational Eurasian nation and construct new scientific systems to replace the old, dilapidated ones. In particular, this necessitates constructing a new history of the peoples of Eurasia, including that of the Russian people...

In all of this work re-cultivating the national self-consciousness from the standpoint of the symphonic (choral) unity of the multinational nation of Eurasia, it might be the Russian people that will have to strain its hand more than any other Eurasian people. Firstly, the Russian people need more than others to deal with the old attitudes and points of view that situate the Russian national identity outside of the real context of the Eurasian world and divorce the past of the Russian people from the common perspective of the history of Eurasia. Secondly, the Russian people, which until the revolution was the sole sovereign of all of the territory of Russia-Eurasia, and is now the first (in number and significance) among the Eurasian peoples, naturally needs to set an example for the others.

At the present moment, the Eurasianists' work on re-educating this national self-consciousness is taking place in extremely difficult conditions. Such work, of course, cannot be openly carried out on the territory of the USSR. The emigration is predominated by people who are cognitively incapable of recognizing the objective shifts and results of the revolution. For such people, Russia continues to exist as a set of territorial units conquered by the Russian people and belonging to the Russian people alone by full and indivisible right. Therefore, these people cannot understand the issue of creating a pan-Eurasian nationalism and affirming the unity of the multinational Eurasian nation. For them, the Eurasianists are traitors because they replace the concept of "Russia" with that of "Eurasia." They do not understand that it is not Eurasianism, but life itself that has produced this "replacement." They do not understand that their Russian nationalism in modern conditions is simply Great Russian separatism, and that the purely 'Russian' Russia which they want to "revive" is possible only given the separation of all the "outskirts" within the boundaries of ethnographical Great Russia. Other trends in the emigration attack Eurasianism from the opposite side, demanding that any kind of national identity be abandoned, and suggest that Russia can be built only on the basis of European democracy without putting forth any unified national or unified class-based substrate for Russian statehood. Being representatives of the abstract Westernizing sentiments of the Russian intelligentsia's old generations, these people do not want to understand that for a state to exist, what is needed first and foremost is for this state's citizens to be conscious of organically belonging to this whole, to this organic unity, be it either ethnic or class-based. In modern conditions, only two solutions are possible: either the dictatorship of the proletariat, or consciousness of the unity and originality of the multinational Eurasian nation and pan-Eurasian nationalism.

\*\*\*

# THE GEOGRAPHICAL AND GEOPOLITICAL FOUNDATIONS OF EURASIANISM

## Petr Savitsky[146]

***

There are significantly more grounds for calling Russia the "middle state" (*Zhongguo* in Chinese) rather than China. The more time that passes, the more these grounds will make themselves evident. For Russia, Europe is nothing more than a peninsula of the Old Continent that lies to the West of its borders. On this continent, Russia itself occupies the main space, its torso. The total area of European states, taken together, is close to five million kilometers squared. The area of Russia within the borders of the contemporary USSR is significantly larger than 20 million kilometers squared (especially if one includes the space of the Mongolian and Tuva national republics of former "Outer Mongolia" and the "Uryankhay land" which at the current moment are parts of the Soviet Union).

With rare exception, the Russian people of the late 19th and early 20th centuries forgot about the spaces beyond the Urals (one of those who remembered them was the genius Russian chemist Dmitri Mendeleev). Now, another time has come. The whole "Ural-Kuznetsk combine," with its blast furnaces, coal mines, and new cities with hundreds of thousands of inhabitants

---

146 Article authored in Prague, Czechoslovakia in late 1933 - early 1934, first published in the journal *Orient und Occident* No. 17 (Leipzig: 1934).

each is being built behind the Urals. The Turkestan-Siberian Railway ("Turksib") is being laid. Nowhere else is the expansion of Russian culture so wide and spontaneous as in another region beyond the Urals, in the so-called "Central Asian republics" (Turkmenistan, Tajikistan, Uzbekistan, and Kyrgyzstan). The entire "torso" of Russian lands, the "shot from Negoreloe to Suchan station," is coming to life.

The Eurasianists have their share of merit in this turn of events. At the same time, the nature of the Russian world is being lucidly revealed as the central world of the Old Continent. There were moments when it seemed that between the periphery of Western Europe to which the Russian lands up to the Urals belong (the "European Russia" of the old geographers) and Asia (China, India, Iran), there was only void. The Eurasianist arrangement of the Russian present is filling this void with the pulse of animate life. Since the end of the 19th century, a direct path from Europe to China and Japan has been laid through Russia - the Great Siberian Railway. Geography points out with absolute certainty that there is no other way to run roads from Europe (at least from its northern part) to Persia, India, and Indochina. Even today, such opportunities have not yet been fully realized. The Trans-Persian railway, cutting through Persia from the direction of the Northwest toward the Southeast and connected with the same route network as British India and Europe (through the Caucasus, Crimea, and Ukraine), was close to fruition on the eve of the World War. At present, the project has lost all grounding due to political circumstances. There are no connections between the railways of Russian Turkestan (the "Central Asian Republics") and India, and Russian railway networks are not oriented toward transit between Europe and India. But sooner or later, this movement will become a fact, whether in the form of railway paths, automobile lines, or air traffic. For the latter, the shortest distances are, let us say, of especially large importance for Russia. The greater the weight that will be procured by air traffic with its propensity and desire to fly in straight lines, the clearer the role of Russia-Eurasia as the "middle world" will become. The establishment of transpolar lines can still further enhance this role. In the Far North, Russia is a neighbor of America over a vast expanse. With the opening of a route through the pole, or rather over the pole, Russia will become the connecting link between Asia and North America.

Successive articles will discuss the Eurasianists' aspiration to offer a spiritual synthesis of Eastern and Western elements. Here, however, it is important to point out the correspondences of this aspiration which are found in the field of geopolitics. Russia-Eurasia is the center of the Old World. If one eliminates this center, then all of the other parts of the Old World, this whole system of continental margins (Europe, Western Asia, Iran, India, Indochina, China, and Japan) becomes a mere "scattered temple." This world which lies to the East of Europe's borders and to the North of "classical" Asia is the link that binds together the unity of all of these pieces. This is obvious in the present, and it will only become clearer in the future.

The linking and unifying role of this "middle world" has made itself felt throughout history. For several millennia, political dominance in the Eurasian world belonged to nomads. Occupying the space stretching from Europe to China, while simultaneously reaching toward Western Asia, Iran, and India, the nomads served as intermediaries between the disparate worlds of settled cultures in their original states. Let us recall that historical interaction between Iran and China was never so close as in the era of Mongol rule (from the 13th to 14th centuries). And thirteen to fourteen centuries earlier, only through the nomadic Eurasian world did the paths of the Hellenic and Chinese cultures cross, as is shown by the latest excavations in Mongolia. It is an inalterable fact that the Russian world has been called to play a unifying role within the confines of the Old World. Only to the extent that Russia-Eurasia fulfills this vocation can it turn into an organic whole combining all of the diverse cultures of the Old Continent and remove the confrontation between East and West. This fact is not yet sufficiently recognized in our time, but the

**255**

correlations expressed by it lie in the very nature of things. The tasks of unification first and foremost boil down to tasks of cultural creativity. A new and independent historical force, Russian culture, has emerged at the center of the Old World to fulfill a unifying and conciliatory role. Russian culture can fulfill this task only by cooperating with the cultures of all the surrounding peoples. In this regard, the cultures of the East are just as important for Russia-Eurasia as the cultures of the West. The particularity of Russian culture and geopolitics lies precisely in such a simultaneous and even-footed approach to both East and West. For Russia, there are two equal fronts - Western and South-Eastern. The Russian field of view can and should become one which first and foremost covers the entire Old World to an equal and full extent.

Let us return, however, to phenomena of a purely geographical nature. In comparison to the Russian "torso," Europe and Asia both represent the outskirts of the Old World. Moreover, from a Russian-Eurasian point of view, Europe is, as has been said, everything that lies to the West of the Russian border, while Asia is everything that lies to the South and Southeast of it. Russia itself is neither Asia nor Europe. Such is the fundamental geopolitical thesis of the Eurasianists. In this view, there is no "European" or "Asiatic" Russia, but merely parts of Russia which lie to the West or East of the Urals, just as there are parts of it lying to the West and East of the Yenisei River, and so on. The Eurasianists continue: Russia is neither Asia nor Europe, but instead represents its own special geographical world. How does this world differ from Europe and Asia? The Western, Southern, and South-Eastern outskirts of the continent differ to a significant extent in their coasts and topographical diversity. This cannot be said of the main "torso" which constitutes Russia-Eurasia. This torso consists first and foremost of three plains (the White Sea Plain, the West Siberian Plain, and the Turkestan Plain), and the regions lying to the east of them (including the low, mountainous countries to the east of the Yenisei river). The zonal composition of the Western and Southern outskirts of the continent are marked by "mosaic-fractional" and far from simple contours. Forested areas, in their natural state, are replaced here in a bizarre sequence by, on the one hand, steppe and desert regions, and on the other by tundra areas in the high mountains. This "mosaic" is contrasted on the central plains of the Old World by relatively simple, "flagged" distribution of zones. With the latter designation we point to the fact that, when applied to a map, this distribution resembles the contours of the horizontal stripes of a flag. Going from South to North, deserts, steppes, forests, and tundra follow each other successively. Each of these zones forms a continuous latitudinal band. The broad latitudinal division of the Russian world is further emphasized by the latitudinal stretch of mountain ranges framing the plains from the South: the Crimean ridge, the Caucasus, the Kopet Dag, the Parapamiz, the Hindu Kush, the main mountain ranges of the Tien Shan, the ranges in the North of Tibet, and the Ying Shan in the area of the Great Wall of China. The latter of these ranges lies on the same line bordering the southern, elevated plain occupied by the Gobi desert. This is linked to the Turkestan plain via the Dzhungarian gates.

In the zonal structure of the Old World's mainland, one can also note features of a peculiar East-West symmetry which render the character of phenomena in its eastern outskirts analogous to those in its western edges and which differ from the character of phenomena in the middle part of the continent. Both the eastern and western margins of the continent (the Far East and Europe) are located at latitudes between 35 and 60 degrees North which are naturally covered by forested regions. Here the boreal forests directly touch and gradually transition into the forests of southern flora. Nothing of the sort can be observed in the middle world, where forests of southern flora exist only in the regions of its mountainous peripheries (Crimea, the Caucasus, and Turkestan) and never meet forests of northern flora or boreal ones, being separated from such by a continuum of steppe-desert strips. The middle world of the

257

Old World can thus be identified as the region of the steppe and desert band stretching in a continuous line from the Carpathians to the Khingan taken together with its mountain frame (in the South) and those regions lying to the North of it (forest and tundra zones). It is this world that the Eurasianists call Eurasia in the exact sense of this word (Eurasia sensu stricto). This must be distinguished from the old "Eurasia" of Alexander von Humboldt which encompassed the whole of the Old Continent (*Eurasia sensu latiore*).

The Western border of Eurasia runs along the Black Sea-Baltic bridge, i.e. the region where the continent narrows between the Baltic and Black Seas. Along this bridge and in general in the direction from Northwest to Southeast run a number of indicative botanical-geographical borders such as, for example, the Eastern borders of yew, beech, and ivy. Starting on the shores of the Baltic Sea, each of these tree types then extends all the way to the Black Sea. West of these borders, i.e. where the aforementioned species still grow, the stretch of the forest zone is continuous along the entire length from North to South. To the East begins the division into the forest zone in the North and the steppe zone in the South. This boundary can be considered the Western border of Eurasia. Eurasia's border with Asia in the Far East runs along the longitudes at which the continuous strip of steppes dips in its nearing the Pacific Ocean, i.e., at the longitude of the Khingan.

The Eurasian world is a world of "both periodic and symmetric zone systems." The boundaries of the main Eurasian zones conform with significant accuracy to the spanning of certain climatic boundaries. For example, the Southern border of the tundra matches the line joining the point of average annual relative humidity of 79.5% at 1 P.M. (The relative humidity in the afternoon is of particularly great importance for the life of vegetation and soils). The Southern border of the forest zone lies along the line connecting points with the same relative humidity of 67.5%. The Southern border of the steppe (with its tip into the desert) is matched by the uniform relative humidity at 1 P.M. of 55.5%. In the desert, it is always lower than this value. Attention should be drawn here to the equality of intervals covering the forest and steppe zones. These coincidences and this rhythmic distribution of intervals can be established in accordance with different indices (see our book *The Geographical Particularities of Russia - Part 1*, Prague: 1927). This gives grounds to speak of a "periodic table of the zone systems of Russia-Eurasia." Russia-Eurasia is a symmetric system, not in the sense of the East-West symmetry which we discussed in the preceding, but in a South-North symmetry. The treeless tundra of the North is matched by the treeless steppes of the South. Moreover, the calcium content and percentage of humus in soil from the middle parts of the black soil zone symmetrically decrease when moving in the directions of North and South. This symmetric distribution of phenomena can also be noted in terms of soil colors, which reaches its greatest intensity in the very same middle portions of the horizontal zone. Moving both Northward and Southward, the soil color weakens (passing through shades of brown to whitish ones). In terms of sand and rock substrates, there is also a symmetrical divergence from the border between the forest and steppe zones: between the steppe islands to the North and the "islands" of forests in the South. Russian science defines this phenomenon as "extrazonal." The steppe sectors in the forest zone can be characterized as a "southward-bearing" phenomenon, while the forest islands in the steppes are essentially a "northward-bearing" phenomenon. The southward-bearing formations of the forest zone match the northward-bearing formations of the steppes.

Nowhere else in the Old World is such a gradual transition in zonal systems, with both its "frequency" and simultaneous "symmetry," displayed so clearly as on the plains of Russia-Eurasia.

The Russian world thus possesses an exceedingly clear geographic structure. The Urals do not play the defining and divisive role in this structure which they have been attributed (and still are) by geographical "clichés." By virtue of their orographic and geological specificities, the Urals not only do not divide but, on the contrary, rather closely tie together "pre-Ural" and "post-Ural" Russia, thereby once again demonstrating that, taken together, both geographically constitute the "single undivided continent of Eurasia." The tundra, as a horizontal zone, lies both to the West and to the East of the Urals just as forest extends beyond one side and the other. The same is the case regarding the steppes and desert (the latter borders the southern continuation of the Ural-Mugodzhary from both the East and West). We can observe no significant changes in geographical environment signified by the "border" of the Urals. More substantial is the geographical border of the "Intermarium," i.e. the space between the Black and Baltic Seas on the one hand, and the Baltic Sea and the coast of Northern Norway on the other.

This distinctive, lucid, and at the same time simple geographical structure of Russia-Eurasia is tied to a number of important geopolitical circumstances. The nature of the Eurasian world is minimally favorable to any sort of "separatisms," be they political, cultural, or economic. The specific "mosaic-fractional" structure of Europe and Asia facilitates the appearance of small, confined, and isolated worlds offering the material preconditions for the existence of small states, cultural modes specific to a city or province, and economic regions possessing large economic diversity within a narrow space. But Eurasia is quite another case. The wide-cut sphere of "flag-like" zonal distribution is not conducive to anything of this sort. Endless plains habituate horizontal breadth and the spread of geopolitical combinations. Within the steppes, moving across land along the forests and numerous bodies of water, such as rivers and lakes, man found himself in constant migration, continuously changing his place of inhabitance. Ethnic and cultural elements are drawn into intensive interaction, cross-fertilizing, and mixing. In Europe and Asia, it sometimes happened that one could live only by the interests of his own "belfry."

But in Eurasia, if this happened at all, then in an historical sense this lasted only an extremely brief period of time. In Northern Eurasia there are hundreds of thousands of kilometers of forests among which there is not a single hectare of arable land. How can the inhabitants of this space survive without contact with the more Southern regions? In the South, on no less vastly spread steppes suitable for livestock and partly for agriculture, there is not a single tree across many thousands of kilometers. How can the population of these regions live without economic interaction with the North? The nature of Eurasia prompts people to the necessity of political, cultural, and economic association to a significantly greater extent than is observed in Europe and Asia. It is thus no wonder that what was in many respects a "unified" way of life, such as that of the nomads, existed across the whole space of the Eurasian steppes from Hungary to Manchuria, and throughout history from the Scythians to the modern Mongols. It is similarly no wonder that such great attempts at political unification were born on the expanses of Eurasia, such as those of the Scythians, Huns, and Mongols (in the 13th-14th centuries), and others. These attempts included not only the steppes and desert, but also the northern forest zone and the southernmost "mountain hem" of Eurasia. It is no coincidence that the spirit of a sort of "brotherhood of peoples" is blowing over Eurasia, having its roots in the centuries-old contact and cultural mergers of peoples of the most diverse races, ranging from Germanic peoples (the Crimean Goths) and Slavs to the Tungus-Manchurians with links via the Finnish, Turkic, and Mongolian peoples. This "brotherhood of peoples" is reflected in the fact that there is no opposition between "higher" and "lower" races, but rather a mutual attraction, much stronger than any repulsion, which easily awakens a "will for a common cause." The history of Eurasia from its first chapters to its latest is solid proof of this. These traditions were embraced by Russia in her foundational, historic cause. In the 19th and 20th centuries, they were at times clouded by deliberate "Westernism," which demanded that Russians feel themselves to be "Europeans" (which they in fact weren't) and treat the other Eurasian peoples as "Asians" or an "inferior race." Such an interpretation led Russia to nothing other than disaster (such as Russia's Far Eastern adventure at the beginning of the 20th century). It should be hoped that this concept has been completely overcome by now in the Russian consciousness and that the remnants of Russian "Europeanism" still hiding in emigration are void of any historical significance. Only by overcoming deliberate "Westernism" can the path be opened to real brotherhood between the Eurasian peoples - the Slavic, the Finnic, the Turkic, Mongolian, and others.

Eurasia has previously played a unifying role in the Old World. Contemporary Russia, absorbing this tradition, must resolutely and irrevocably abandon the old methods of unification belonging to an outlived and overcome era, such as those of violence and war. In the modern period, the cause is one of cultural creativity, inspiration, insight, and cooperation. This is what the Eurasianists say. Despite all the modern means of communication, the peoples of Europe and Asia are still, to a large extent, sitting in their own quarters, living by the interests of their own belfries. Eurasian "place-development" propels this common cause by virtue of its fundamental qualities. The Eurasian peoples have been appointed to draw other peoples of the world along these paths by example. And then the relations of ethnographic kinship by which a number of Eurasian peoples are connected with various non-Eurasian nations, such as the Indo-European ties of the Russians, the Near-Asian and Iranian relations of the Eurasian Turks, and those points of contact that exist between the Eurasian Mongols and the peoples of East Asia, will become useful for the ecumenical cause. All of these relations can be beneficial to the construction of a new, organic culture for the "Old" World, which is (we believe) still young, carrying in its womb a grand future.

\*\*\*

CPSIA information can be obtained
at www.ICGtesting.com
Printed in the USA
LVHW082257050322
712719LV00020B/168